Public Services and Market Mechanisms

Competition, Contracting and the New Public Management

Kieron Walsh

MACMILLAN

1097262 5

First published 1995 by
MACMILLAN PRESS LTD
Houndmills, Basingstoke, Hampshire RG21 2XS
and London
Companies and representatives
throughout the world

ISBN 0–333–58806–1 hardcover
ISBN 0–333–58807–X paperback

A catalogue record for this book is available
from the British Library.

10   9   8   7   6   5   4   3   2   1
04   03   02   01   00   99   98   97   96   95

Copy-edited and typeset by Povey–Edmondson
Okehampton and Rochdale, England

Printed in Malaysia

Series Standing Order   (Public Policy and Politics)

If you would like to receive future titles in this series as they are
published, you can make use of our standing order facility. To place a
standing order please contact your bookseller or, in case of difficulty,
write to us at the address below with your name and address and the
name of the series. Please state with which title you wish to begin your
standing order. (If you live outside the United Kingdom we may not
have the rights for your area, in which case we will forward your order
to the publisher concerned.)

Customer Service Department, Macmillan Distribution Ltd,
Houndmills, Basingstoke, Hampshire, RG21 2XS, England

Public Policy and Politics

Series Editors: Colin Fudge and Robin Hambleton

PUBLISHED

FORTHCOMING

Public Policy and Politics

Series Editors: Colin Fudge and Robin Hambleton

Public policy-making in Western democracies is confronted by new pressures. Central values relating to the role of the state, the role of markets and the role of citizenship are now all contested and the consensus built up around the Keynesian welfare state is under challenge. New social movements are entering the political arena: electronic technologies are transforming the nature of employment: changes in demographic structure are creating heightened demands for public services; unforeseen social and health problems are emerging; and, most disturbing, social and economic inequalities are increasing in many countries.

How governments – at international, national and local levels – respond to this developing agenda is the central focus of the *Public Policy and Politics series*. Aimed at a student, professional, practitioner and academic readership, it aims to provide up-to-date, comprehensive and authoritative analysis of public policy-making in practice.

The series is international and interdisciplinary in scope, and bridges theory and practice by relating the substance of policy to the politics of the policy-making process.

Contents

List of Tables and Figures

Tables

Figures

Acknowledgements

I would like to thank all those who have helped by commenting on drafts of this book, particularly Robin Hambleton, Steven Kennedy, and especially Gerry Stoker. The book draws on work done under Economic and Social Research Council grants (YE1 32500 D1 and L110251007).

KIERON WALSH

Introduction

Throughout the world there is a search for a new approach to public sector management, for the 'reinvention' of government (Osborne and Gaebler, 1992). In the United States the management of the federal government and of health and education is central to the political success of the presidency. In the previously communist regimes of Eastern Europe and the Soviet Union the organisation of basic services, health, housing and water, along with the privatisation of public enterprises, presents huge problems. In less-developed countries economic difficulties and external pressure are leading to a re-examination of the role of the state in the economy. In Australia and New Zealand there has been a programme of micro-economic reform, which is intended to change the basis upon which public services operate. European countries, to varying degrees, are introducing new approaches to the management of the public sector. In Britain, perhaps most of all, there is a revolution in progress in the way that government manages itself.

A major feature of the 'new public management' (Hood, 1991) is the introduction of market mechanisms to the running of public service organisations: the marketisation of the public service. The earliest form of marketisation was the introduction of competitive tendering for public service (Ascher, 1987). Since the late 1980s there has been a rapid expansion of the use of competitive tendering but other approaches, such as internal markets, have also been developed. The focus of this book is the emerging process of marketisation.

The most radical change in the management of public services has involved outright privatisation, particularly in the United Kingdom and Japan, and increasingly in Eastern Europe and the Soviet Union (Clarke and Pitelis, 1993). Other countries have pursued a less ideological line, and the extent of privatisation has, in most cases, been limited. Even where it has been extensive, privatisation should be seen as a change of the nature of government involvement, rather than its total withdrawal, with regulation replacing direct ownership and control. As Foster (1992) says:

While some privatized enterprises can be let loose upon a free market to be subject to its disciplines, the old public utilities, when privatized, need be no more under market disciplines as private monopolies than they were as public monopolies. To remedy this in Britain, ministerial control has been replaced by regulation (p. 3).

More generally governments' regulatory role in relation to the private sector has been expanding, as has that of supranational bodies such as the European Union.

As outright privatisation runs up against the immediate limits of practicality and public acceptability, reform within the public service is becoming the more important issue. Arguments can be made for radical privatisation of services and functions that have come to be seen as quintessentially public. Saunders (1993), for example, argues that the wholesale privatisation of the consumption of public services such as education and health, by moving 'away from provision in kind and towards income support and subsidy' (p. 65), would enhance citizenship.

The privatized society which is slowly emerging out of the ruins of the collectivist welfare system holds out the prospect not of social and moral disintegration, but of new and active forms of citizenship based on individual competence and the development of genuinely collective forms of association and sociability springing up from below (p. 88).

The Adam Smith Institute in the UK has made a similar case, while from the left there are arguments for provision of welfare through associations (Hirst, 1993) or for similar forms of privatisation, as proposed by Roger Douglas, the former New Zealand Finance Minister (*The Observer*, 13.3.94).

So far this radical agenda has made little headway; what governments have been willing to do has been to engage in transformation of the way that they are managed. This has generally involved two main strands: the introduction of managerial techniques from the private sector, and the development of market mechanisms within the public services.

The new public management

The first strand of the new public management is managerialism, defined by Pollitt (1990, pp. 2–3) as involving:

● continuous increases in efficiency
● the use of 'ever-more-sophisticated' technologies
● a labour force disciplined to productivity
● clear implementation of the professional management role
● managers being given the right to manage

This approach to the management of the public services has a long history, and has been the subject of continual debate. F. W. Taylor, the pioneer of scientific management, had, it might be remembered, an influence on government services in the United States before the First World War (Nesbitt, 1976, p. 284). Throughout its history the public sector has intermittently rediscovered the need for a focus on productivity, performance and control. In the 1980s we witnessed no more than the continuation and enhancement of a managerialist process that had long existed. Indeed, in the British civil service in particular, many of the developments of the 1980s can be seen as little more than the implementation of approaches that had been proposed in the 1960s and before, for example by the Fulton Commission. In that sense the 'new managerialism' is no more than another wave of a tide that had long been flowing, however slowly.

The increasing acceptance of the Taylorist agenda has been described as Fordist, to be compared with a post-Fordist phase of development in public service management that became increasingly strong from the late 1980s (Stoker, 1989). The post-Fordist approach is:

. . . to fragment the organization and leave each constituent part or unit to deal with the detailed problems of resource allocation, methods of work, organisation charts and so on . . . At the centre, top management would be left with strategic tasks only . . . (Harrison *et al.*, 1992, p. 15).

The aim of managerialism is to gain more effective control of work practices.

The second strand of the new management is based upon indirect control rather than direct authority. The strategic centre attains its objectives through creating processes of management that involve appropriate incentives and value commitments. The emphasis is not so much upon managers' right to manage, as the need for managers to be appropriately motivated and believe the right things. The reduction of trade union power in the 1990s has made the cry for managerial control less affecting. The characteristics of the second strand of the new management are:

- continual improvements in quality
- emphasis upon devolution and delegation
- appropriate information systems
- emphasis upon contracts and markets
- measuring performance
- increased emphasis on audit and inspection

The two strands of the new public service management are quite distinct. The first, Taylorist, strand, is based on the adoption of industrial production engineering techniques within the public sector. It is not a rejection of bureaucracy but its fulfilment. The second is based on the primacy of market-based coordination. This approach to management involves the creation of a core-periphery model of organisation, intended to enhance flexibility. At the core are the central strategists, while at the periphery are those who deliver services, frequently with a less permanently established position than they had in the traditional bureaucracy. This model is being pursued by a range of mechanisms from 'outsourcing' to the creation of internal markets.

Meyer and Rowan (1977) have argued that the process of institutionalisation in the public sector partly depends upon the need to adopt what is seen as best practice in the private sector. The difficulty of demonstrating the performance levels of intangible public services leads to the adoption of ideas in good currency in order to gain legitimacy. There is a process of mimesis (Di Maggio and Powell, 1983) that is particularly strong in the public service, since one organisation cannot afford to be left behind in the chase for legitimacy, which often brings funding with it. Pollert (1988) argues that:

. . . the public sector is now turning to the 'flexible firm' framework as legitimation for restructuring on commercial lines, precisely because the model is seen as the 'leading edge' practice in the private sector . . . (p. 308).

The language of 'enabling' (Ridley, 1988) has now become established within the public sector, so that, even if one wishes to argue against the new orthodoxy, one must start from its ideological presuppositions. The failure of traditional approaches is taken as axiomatic, even if on limited evidence.

The user of public services has an explicit place within the new management as customer or consumer. The Citizen's Charter in the UK conceives the citizen as an amalgam of separate consumer positions giving rise to a Parent's Charter, a Patient's Charter, a Passenger's Charter, a Victim's Charter and so forth. Individual citizens have rights, and must be allowed the maximum choice in the services that they use, and that choice, bolstered by systems of complaint and redress, will act as the spur to maintaining and improving public service quality and efficiency. The need for collective choice at the political level is then significantly reduced, and politicians play a strategic role. The management of public services is the central issue in public sector reform.

The development of the new market-oriented public service management allows ministers to argue that democracy is essentially concerned with providing efficient service. The exercise of choice in the marketplace for public service is seen as more effective than the use of the vote. William Waldegrave (1993), the minister responsible for the implementation of the Citizen's Charter, argues that:

. . . there is no guarantee – indeed there may not even be a sporting chance – that by periodically expressing his or her democratic decision at the ballot box the citizen (by the use of that sovereign power) will necessarily obtain on a continuous basis efficient, properly accountable, responsive public services. You don't have to go far back in history to see that.

The key point in this argument is not whether those who run our public services are elected, but whether they are producer-responsive or consumer responsive. Services are not necessarily made responsive to the public simply by giving citizens a democratic voice, and a distant one at that, in their make-up. They *can* be made responsive by giving the public choices, or by instituting mechanisms which build in publicly approved standards and redress when they are not attained (p. 13).

In this system, accountability operates at two levels – the strategic level for which politicians are responsible, and the operational one which is the sphere of the managers. The test of the legitimacy of the public service is the acceptability of the services it produces for the citizen.

The development of the welfare state involved the integration of the political and the managerial level of public services, particularly through the role played by professionalism; the new public management involves their radical separation. The ability of people to participate in the control of their own lives is seen as resulting from the return, as far as possible, of public services to the private sphere. Citizenship relates less to participation in the public realm than to consumption in the private realm. The radical privatisation of the public service through individual choice is more possible in Britain than many other countries because of the limited explicit development of the concept of citizenship in this country, and because of the fragmented structure of public institutions. This privatisation of citizenship can be contrasted with a view of citizenship as participation in the public realm.

Some would see the equation of citizenship with consumption as limiting. Hansen (1993), discussing the work of Hannah Arendt, says:

To deprive humans of the possibility of acting and speaking together in a common world is to imprison them in the subjectivity of their singular experience, which does not cease to be singular if the same experience is multiplied innumerable times.

By contrast Harrison (1991, p. 12) argues that:

It might be feasible, for instance, to argue that privatised forms of social provision (and access to 'choices' in markets) amount to an alternative form of 'modern citizenship' which has been expanding and securing certain types of household welfare in Britain recently.

This is a fundamental debate, which affects the very basis of liberal democracy. It has commonly been argued that the creation of the welfare state was necessary to the full development of citizenship. The critics on the New Right argue that, on the contrary, the welfare state has prevented the development of effective citizenship:

> The paradox of social cohesion, then, is that the more governments try to sustain it through the extension of 'citizenship rights' (broadly defined) the weaker it becomes (Saunders, 1993, p. 85).

The way that the citizenship can be created, on this view, is to make citizens into consumers/customers with choice, rather than subjects of the public bureaucracy. Introducing market processes within public service organisations is a central part of this process.

From state to market

A variety of market mechanisms have been proposed and adopted for the reform of state bureaucracy, apart from outright privatisation. The first is the introduction of pricing and charging for public services, in order to create market pressures on politicians and officials. More services are charged for, and charges have been brought closer to those that might apply in a free market. There have been attempts to give the users of public services the ability to act as customers with choices through the use of vouchers. There has been extensive development of pricing and charging within public service organisations, involving a move from 'hierarchies' to 'hierarchies with markets'. There is a process of internal privatisation.

The second and most fundamental mechanism for changing public service management, is the development of contract. The simplest form of the use of contract is the buying in of services from private providers. The public organisation may be allowed to compete with potential private providers in a market-testing programme or work may simply be externalised. Contract has become, along with the concept of customer, a fundamental metaphor for the changes that are being made in the public service. It is as likely to be used to characterise relationships within the organisation as those with private providers. Authority relations are being redefined as contracts.

Contract is allied with performance measurement to produce an individual focus on the public sector worker, making the employment contract more like that for purchase on the market. The public service is becoming a 'nexus of contracts', rather than a bureaucratic hierarchy.

The use of prices and contracts is being extended in the UK through the development of internal markets, most explicitly in the National Health Service, but, increasingly, in other public services. Purchaser and provider are separated, and relate to each other through quasi-contracts, with prices and charges operating to ensure the match of supply and demand. Internal purchasers are increasingly free to buy where they want, a development encouraged by the Audit Commission (1994), which puts downward pressure on service costs and creates incentives to increase productivity and efficiency. Purchasers, acting as surrogates for ultimate users, are forced to be more explicit about the rationing decisions that they make.

Large public service organisations, organised along bureaucratic lines, are being broken down into smaller independent units, with autonomy to operate relatively freely. Schools, colleges and hospitals have been allowed independence from overseeing authorities. Autonomy has been increased within organisations through the creation of internal agencies operating at 'arm's length'. These independent, or internally autonomous agencies operate according to quasi-market principles, relating to each other through contracting and the purchase of services. They are monitored and controlled through performance measurement and targets. The public service is becoming a more or less integrated network of organisations that relate through contract and price rather than authority.

The market that is developing for public services is managed. There is close regulation of the way that it operates, and control of the pattern of change. In the British National Health Service, for example, the government has been unwilling to allow the unbridled operation of the market to lead to wholesale hospital closure. What is emerging is a new form of organisation that is neither market nor hierarchy, but which lies rather uncomfortably between the two.

Efficiency and organisation

The argument for the introduction of market processes is that it increases both efficiency and accountability. Efficiency is argued to follow from the clearer statement of what is to be provided, and the pressure that results from consumer choice. The argument for the greater efficiency of the market compared to traditional bureaucracy is often simply asserted, with little attempt at justification. In practice the evidence for the greater efficiency of the new pattern of public service management is limited. The evidence on effectiveness and the quality of service is even more debatable. The lack of clear evidence is no more than might be expected, given the complex nature of public services, and the early stage of development, but it makes the introduction of the market a matter of faith as much as technique.

The 'new public management' has a considerable impact on patterns of organisation within the public service. Organisations are becoming more differentiated, through the separation of purchaser and provider and the creation of more operational autonomy for those delivering services, such as schools and hospitals. Existing patterns of management involving traditional Weberian approaches to organisation are giving way to decentralised forms. New patterns of integration, appropriate to a more differentiated structure, are needed to replace authority and planning. Networks are developing in contrast to unified, authority-based organisation. Planning is giving way to more general strategic management and coordination through market processes and adjustment. Power is shifting from professionals to managers. The basic assumptions that have guided the organisation of the welfare state are being challenged.

The basis of organisation is changing from hierarchical authority to contracts and markets. To some extent this change parallels developments in the industrial sector, where there is a growing use of contracts and alliances alongside competition (Lorange and Roos, 1992; Sako, 1993). Internalisation is giving way to complex links between organisations, taking a variety of forms from franchises to joint ventures, and from contracting to co-production. These changes are not easily established and depend upon the development of an appropriate underlying culture and set of values. Much emphasis is laid upon trust, which is not easily or quickly developed.

Markets for public services are at an early stage of development, and are characterised by high levels of monopoly and monopsony. In most cases they are, at best, quasi-markets (Le Grand and Bartlett, 1993), operating within organisations and with surrogates, such as health authorities or social services departments, acting for final recipients of services. There are clear examples of highly developed markets, for example in some parts of the British National Health Service (Appleby *et al.*, 1994), or in simple services such as building cleaning and refuse collection. There is a highly developed market for residential care for elderly people. Elsewhere, for example in education, markets can only be claimed to exist in a very limited sense. It might be possible to establish more effective markets in some cases by the use of vouchers, and in others by reducing regulation, but both of these approaches have been little developed. The development of markets in which the ultimate 'customer' chooses, and from which they can exit, is slow and faltering.

A central feature of the new management of the public service is the separation of politics and management. Politicians, it is argued, should play a strategic role, deciding broad policies and setting targets for managers, rather than being involved in day-to-day operational issues (Audit Commission, 1990b). This approach is maintained to be the route to overcoming the public choice problems identified by Niskanen and others, whereby both politicians and managers have an incentive to pad budgets and there is little to prevent them from doing so. A combination of internal markets, performance measures and inspection is seen as overcoming the incentives of self-interest. The voice of the 'customer' will be heard through complaints processes.

It is over issues of accountability that the new public management raises the most basic questions. Market-based approaches are seen as overcoming the dominance of the producer that has, it is argued, characterised the development of the welfare state. Producers will be put under market pressures and will be unable to put their own interests ahead of the public. As John Major has argued, the Citizen's Charter, the manifesto for the new management:

> . . . sees public services through the eyes of those who use them. For too long the provider has dominated: now it is the turn of the user . . . The principles of the Citizen's Charter, simple but tough,

are increasingly accepted. They give the citizen published standards and results; competition as a spur to quality improvement; responsiveness; and value for money to get the best possible service within the resources that the nation can afford. They give more power to the citizen and more freedom to choose. And where choice is limited in some of the key public services like schools, social services, probation and the police, the Charter is bringing in independent inspection with a strong lay element to ensure that the citizen's voice is heard (Prime Minister and Chancellor of the Duchy of Lancaster, 1992).

The move is from professional and political to market-based accountability.

Outline of the book

The purpose of this book is to analyse the nature and implications of the use of market mechanisms in the management of the public service. The central focus is upon the key market-like changes that have been introduced: charging, contracting, internal markets and the creation of autonomous units. Other elements, quality systems, performance measurement, inspection and others, will be examined but only to a limited degree. They are seen as secondary to the main development of a market-based management system for the public service. It is the success or failure of market principles that will decide the effectiveness of the new public service.

The book is in three parts. The first part examines the background to the development of a market-based approach to public service management. In chapter 1, I examine the basic argument for state action as a corrective to market failure. This traditional justification of public, collective, action has recently been criticised by liberal theorists, putting forward a parallel theory of government failure. The second part of chapter 1 considers this argument. In chapter 2, I analyse the theoretical issues that are involved in the development of market-based institutions for public service management. The chapter will draw upon recent developments in economics, law and organisation. In economics, I shall examine the implications of theoretical developments based upon transaction costs, principal-agent, and property rights theory. In law I shall examine developments in the theory of relational contracts. In organisation theory I shall discuss network-based management. This chapter will draw out key issues involved in the analysis of public service markets, such as information availability, trust, quality and risk.

In the third chapter I seek to develop an explanation of the pattern of development in public service management. It cannot simply be asserted that the new public management is the result of the New Right gaining political power. In many cases the introduction of the new public management has been undertaken by regimes of the Left, for example in Australia and New Zealand. I shall argue that change depends upon a variety of factors, and the way that they interact in different countries. The United Kingdom is important as an exemplar, in that it has developed the new market-based management further than most other countries.

The second part of the book is taken up by an examination of the components of the new market-based management. Chapter 4 presents evidence about charging and the use of prices in the public service. I also examine the slowly developing movement for introduction of vouchers. Contracts and competition are examined in chapter 5, and the use of internal markets in chapter 7. Finally I consider the devolution of control within public organisations, for example through the creation of trusts in the British National Health Service.

The final section of the book examines the implications of the new public markets. First I consider financial impacts, the effect on quality of service and the impact on users. These aspects of the new management are much debated, but the evidence is partial: large claims are being made with limited foundation. The final substantive chapter is concerned with the organisational and accountability effects of markets. This debate is fundamental to the issue of the effectiveness of markets. It is central to the question of whether or not we need a public realm of any size or not, which is considered in the final, concluding, chapter.

The core chapters of the book concentrate on the experience of the United Kingdom. This reflects the fact that the British government has taken the marketisation of the public service further than any other country. The case of the United Kingdom is placed in international context throughout the book, with particular attention paid to countries like New Zealand which has pursued even more radical policies in certain areas, and a broader comparative account is provided in the more general chapters.

PART I
THE STATE AND THE MARKET

1 The Traditional Model of Public Service Provision

The debate on the role of government in the 1980s and 1990s has not simply been about how its activities can be limited and controlled but also about the institutional character of the state. It is argued that the state must not only be smaller, but also different; it must become market-oriented, fired by the spirit of entrepreneurship (Osborne and Gaebler, 1992). The British welfare state, as it developed in the post-war years, was organised according to principles of hierarchy, planning, direct control, self-sufficiency, centralisation and professionalism (Stewart and Walsh, 1992). Premfors' (1991) description of the Swedish model captures the nature of the welfare state as now exists in the UK:

> The big problems of Swedish society, as perceived by the adherents of the model, were seen to require big solutions. Big solutions meant nationwide and uniform social programmes, planned and administered in a centralised fashion by big, hierarchically organised government agencies, and financed out of all-purpose tax funds. In some services, local governments would be appropriate producers and distributors, but only following a radical programme of amalgamation and centralisation.

It is this model that the new market-based public service management is intended to replace.

Public choice theorists, such as Buchanan and others (Buchanan and Tullock, 1962; Mueller, 1979), argue that the state is subject to failures just as is the market. The argument that is considered in this chapter is that, even if we accept the need for collective action at a political level to deal with problems of market failure, the state is not efficient in what it does, and that mechanisms must be found to make it so. I shall first lay out the positive arguments for the state as compensating for market failure, and describe the particular institutional and organisational character of government that emerged in the post-war period, namely large scale, hierarchically organised bureaucracy. I shall then consider the arguments of those who focus upon government failure, and the alternative approaches that have been proposed to cope with that failure. The position of the New Right is that even if state activity is necessary it need not be bureaucratic, but can itself follow market principles.

Public service provision

A basic argument for government production of goods and services is that, in certain circumstances, the market fails and that planning, collective decisions and public provision will be more effective in forwarding certain social purposes than processes of individual exchange. Even those who argue that the state should play a minimal role will generally accept that there are some matters over which government intervention is necessary, for example national defence or the maintenance of law and order. Only the most anarchic of libertarians equate freedom with a free-for-all (Friedman, 1973), and even such theorists as Nozick (1974) accept some minimal level of state action.

At the very least it is necessary for the state to create the institutional framework and legal structure which make social life and market activity possible. Most thinkers would see a need for the state to go beyond this minimum level of activity, and to intervene either in the production or the distribution process. In the case of distribution the action of the state is concerned with righting what are taken to be failings in the way that the market distributes resources. The moral basis of this activity lies in considerations of equity, fairness and justice. In the case of production the justification for state action is based in the argument that the market, left to itself, will fail to produce the optimum range and quantity of outputs. In both cases there is argued to be a need for political authority and planning to replace price and exchange as the bases for determining what should be produced and how it should be distributed.

A further argument for public service provision is that there are certain activities that are of such moral significance that they should not be provided by the market, even if they could be, because they will be tainted by the association with financial exchange and profit. The argument for direct provision of public services can be made in value terms as well as in terms of economic efficiency or distributional equity. In this sense the state is seen not simply as a mechanism for distribution or as a producer of last resort, but as having its own purposes in expressing and effecting the collective good. This case is often made for social services, education or health, for which the market may be seen as introducing pressures that will destroy the public service ethic. Walzer (1983) has argued that different social goods must be distributed according to different principles, and that the market is not an acceptable mechanism, for example, in the production and distribution of education or health care. It is clearly possible for such services to be provided by the market, as indeed, in part, they are, and those of a traditional liberal inclination never tire of arguing that extending market provision would increase efficiency. At the same time it can be argued that some things should not be open to trade in the market and to exchange, if only because of the fundamental nature or rights of human beings. On this argument certain services should be provided by the state because to subject them to exchange in the market would destroy efficiency enhancing social values and incentives. Titmuss (1969) makes a persuasive, though disputed (Institute of Economic Affairs, 1973), argument for the value of altruistic processes, not only in themselves but because of their greater efficiency, for example in the production of blood for transfusion. Altruism can be seen as a public good that the market, left to itself, will under-produce, requiring government action (Hahn, 1991).

The state must not only provide services but must also act to preserve the community through protective, regulatory and enforcement services..It is difficult to envisage any complex society operating without police officers, or a criminal justice and penal system, and, on a more mundane level, food and health regulation or trading standards. The public sector is utilising the state's legitimate control of the use of force when it carries out these functions. The argument against the introduction of the market into such services is that the state should not delegate its powers of enforcement because accountability would be weakened and corruption would follow. Private sector providers of protective, regulatory and enforcement services would be open to influence and capture by special interest groups, and by those they are meant to control. This argument has been made against the privatisation of prisons and other custodial services, and the privatisation of inspection and audit services (Donahue, 1989). It is also argued that private profit should not be made where there is an element of human suffering involved. Ryan and Ward (1989) discussing the possibility of the privatisation of prisons, argue that 'it is unacceptable to engage for profit in the deliberate infliction of suffering'. The issue is not only whether services could be provided by the private sector, but whether it is legitimate for the state to delegate certain activities.

The various roles of the state, acting as producer of goods and services including protective services, and as distributor and redistributer of resources, came together in the growth of the welfare state, which was based on the argument that, if people were fully to be citizens, then it was necessary that they should share in the basic goods of society such as education and health. Justice and fairness demanded that all should be able to play their part in society, which depended upon full access to those resources that were fundamental to community membership. As Marshall (1963) argued, full citizenship required social as well as political and civil rights. There have increasingly been arguments that the appropriate measures of economic and social deprivation are relative and not absolute, and that what is required to be a full member of society depends upon what other people have (Townsend, 1979). Redistribution, as a continuing process, will therefore be necessary as well as the establishment of basic level of provision. The need for the distribution of certain basic goods to be controlled by the state in order to ensure equity and fairness has tended to go along with the state actually producing many services, such as health, housing and education because the market is seen as an inappropriate or inadequate mechanism.

Market failure

Public goods

There are five particular sets of circumstances in which, it is argued, markets will fail to produce the optimum mix of goods and services and there will be a need for government intervention. First, the private market will not provide adequately for public goods, that is goods which are inherently available to all and for which one person's use does not preclude their availability to another. It will be in the interests of individuals to understate their needs or wants for such goods and to free-ride on the demand of others, but the more people do this, the less demand there will be and the market, left to itself, will underproduce or even totally fail. Everyone will end up worse off than they would have been if they had stated their true preferences. The state, acting on behalf of all, can, at least in theory, determine the true level of need or demand and produce the welfare-maximising level of output of public goods. Collective decision making will be superior in rationality to the results of the actions of independent individuals.

In practice it is difficult to justify the action of the state solely on the grounds that it produces public goods, because it is difficult to discover such goods in a pure form. Indeed, it has been argued that there is no such thing as a public good in an objective sense, and that it is a purely cultural construct (Malkin and Wildavsky, 1991). There are obvious and important examples, such as clean air, that are close to the concept of the pure public good, but it is more common to find goods that have public aspects but are also partly private goods. The more complex society becomes, and the more the actions of one person are intricately bound up with those of another, the more likely it is that any good will have public good characteristics, because of interaction effects. Certainly it can be argued that housing, education, health and other services, which clearly benefit specific individuals, many also be seen as having public good characteristics. They provide joint social benefits or disbenefits as secondary effects, for example through their impacts upon national economic success. At the very least, public services may be seen as creating legitimacy for the social system or preventing unrest, which are public goods.

It would be difficult to justify the whole of government activity on the basis of the production of public goods, especially if they are only secondary effects of what are essentially private goods. Clearly a great deal of what the state does, at least in direct terms, is concerned primarily with the provision of benefits to individuals. Nor, as we shall see, is there any necessary reason why public goods can only be produced by public sector organisations. Ostrom (1990) has recently argued that, given appropriate conditions, notably the ability to communicate, to enter into agreements, to arrange for monitoring, and to enforce contracts, individuals and communities will be perfectly capable of developing cooperative social solutions to common problems independently of the state. The state may not be the only institutional alternative to the free market even for the provision of public goods.

Increasing returns to scale

Markets are argued to fail, secondly, when there are increasing returns to scale, that is where there are continually decreasing unit costs as the scale of production increases. Increasing returns to scale are particularly likely when large capital investment is necessary for the full development of a service, as is the case for water, gas or electricity. In these conditions monopolies will tend to emerge which can hold down production and set prices above costs, and so increase profits but reduce the total public welfare. There will also be reduced incentives for innovation and change, and therefore a lack of dynamic efficiency, because of the lack of competition. The response in many countries has been to take such industries into public ownership, and to set levels of output and prices that will maximise the public good. The alternative to public ownership and control is regulation of the private sector monopoly. Either way there is seen to be a need for strong public control and planning of the industry if the common good is to be taken into account (Foster, 1992).

In Britain and other countries many public utilities have been returned to the private sector in the 1980s and subjected to various forms of regulation. The problems of regulation are that it may be difficult to obtain the information that is necessary to judge the activities of privatised utilities; that regulators may become the prisoners of those they regulate; and that the regulatory regime may serve as a block on technical progress. Regulation may create the worst of both worlds, neither defending the public interest effectively, nor generating the benefits of the private sector market. Kalt has argued that:

> Regulations adopted to address a specific and fairly well-defined problem create unintended economic distortions. These resulting problems are addressed with further stop-gap regulations. The

cycle repeats itself: at each stage there are economic winners and losers as regulation alters prices, costs, contracts, supplies, and demands. Affected parties that are well-organised and well-endowed financially are coalesced and inevitably influence the growing patchwork of regulation. The end result is a system that, in its overall design, accords with no one's conception of sound economic policy for the country but has well-entrenched special interest residing in each of its component parts (Kalt, 1983, quoted by Eggertsson, 1990, p. 146).

It is possible to make such criticisms of almost any rule system, and it is difficult to see how regulation can be avoided if the state is not itself to be a major provider of monopoly services. Deregulation may produce short term benefits but long term costs. It is not enough to argue that a solution is not perfect if the alternatives are worse. The precise pattern of regulation will be crucial. It has been argued, for example, that highly legalistic approaches with extensive involvement of the courts are ineffective, in comparison with systems that give the regulator substantial discretion (Foster, 1992, 406 ff).

Externalities

The third form of market failure results from externalities, which arise when the production decisions of an organisation give rise to costs or benefits which are not taken into account by the producer or consumer. When there are costs to society that are not taken into account, negative externalities, then firms will produce more than is socially desirable. So, for example, if a production process involves pollution for which the producer does not pay, then social costs will be understated, leading to over-production and over-consumption. The benefits of the product will be concentrated on the consumers and producers, while the population more generally will suffer the undesirable consequences. Equally when there are benefits that are not taken into account, positive externalities, then there is likely to be under-production and under-consumption, as, for example, may be the case with mass transportation systems if the benefits of reduced congestion are not fully considered.

Action by government can ensure that all the costs and benefits that are involved in the production of goods and services are taken into account, rather than simply those accruing to individual users and producers. The state, by virtue of its wider boundaries, can internalise what, to smaller units, would be externalities. It can be argued that government action will not be necessary to deal with problems of externality if a system can be established by which gainers compensate losers. This can be argued to be possible if property rights are appropriately distributed, and the transaction costs of making agreements for compensation are not excessive. It is difficult to see how such a system could be established in practice. The extent to which externalities are created and managed within any social system depends upon the institutional framework, which itself depends upon government action. Even if it were possible to establish a system of compensation it would be necessary for the government to enforce it (see the discussions in Pitelis, 1993; Hodgson, 1988).

Merit goods

The fourth argument for government provision in traditional economic theory is that relating to merit goods, namely goods which it is beneficial for society that all partake adequately in, but which individuals are likely, left to themselves, to underuse. Merit goods can be seen as a special case of public goods. Education and health are examples of merit goods, to which private markets may restrict access. Government action can produce and distribute merit goods in a way that ensures that all have appropriate levels of access to them. There are also demerit goods, for example drugs or alcohol, to which there is a case for limiting access. The need for the government to provide merit goods may arise because people lack information that will enable them to make effective consumer decisions, because of consumer irrationality, or because consumers do not want to make decisions and consequently consumer sovereignty is not attainable. Government needs to act to provide merit goods because individuals are not necessarily the best judges of what is in their own or the public interest.

Information asymmetries

Government action can, finally, be justified on the basis of information asymmetries between the producers and the users of particular goods and services. Where professionals, for example, make judgements about how much of a particular service individuals need, and the individuals cannot themselves assess whether or not that judgement is acceptable, then professionals may be tempted to overprovide. Alternatively, where individuals are unaware of their true need, then there may be too little demand and therefore underprovision. Significant problems also arise if the users of goods and services are unable to judge the quality of what is provided without excessive cost. The difficulty of assessing quality may lead to the assumption on the part of users that all providers are of average or low quality, thereby reducing the incentives of providers to invest in order to improve services or to make the effort to provide high quality services (Akerlof, 1970; Dingwall and Fenn, 1987). Information asymmetry is more likely to arise the more complex are goods or services. In these circumstances the government can act to even out the information imbalances in the market, by reducing the incentive for the producer to oversupply or the user to under-demand. Universal insurance systems, for example, may break the link between the cost of provision and the provider's reward. The government becomes the honest broker in the otherwise unequal and non-cooperative relationship between the producer and the user.

Each of these arguments for government action is based upon the premise that there will be allocative inefficiency because the market fails to create appropriate incentives either for producers or consumers or both. Patterns of revealed preference will not reflect real needs and underlying demands. The market leads to the production of a socially inefficient set of outputs, that is to a pattern of welfare that is not optimal. The government, it is argued, can take account of factors for which market processes do not allow, and produce the optimum pattern, quantity, and distribution of outputs. It is acting to complete the market, and setting the basic conditions necessary if the market is to produce morally acceptable results.

These various economic arguments for state action say nothing about *how* the state should actually ensure that market failures are overcome. In particular they do not necessarily imply that the government should actually be a producer of goods and services, or that it should organise itself in any particular way if it does produce services. Different countries have adopted very different models, involving different combinations of planning, regulation and markets. There is an obvious choice between regulatory and subsidy-based approaches and direct government production. There are also a multitude of ways in which regulation, subsidy or provision can be organised. There is nothing in any of these arguments that implies that the government need necessarily employ any staff or own any productive resources at all. The essential role of the government is to ensure rational collective decisions. Arguments from values are more likely to justify direct public production of goods and services, but still allow various patterns of internal organisation and management of the state. The changes in public sector management in the 1980s and 1990s have been characterised in large part by the government attempting to reduce its responsibility for the direct provision of service and to move towards what has come to be called an 'enabling' role. Market-based systems of management are proposed to replace traditional bureaucracy. In order to understand the alternatives that are being propounded by those who argue for the enabling state it is first necessary to outline the organisational character of government.

The organisation of government services

Public service organisations tend to have common characteristics. The first two relate to the vertical and horizontal division of labour. The vertical division of labour is based upon a hierarchical distribution of authority and responsibility, with those at the top having the right to make decisions that are binding on those below, and, in theory, being responsible for all actions taken by the organisation. At the top of the organisation there is a distinction to be made between the politicians and the senior bureaucrats. In the pure Weberian concept of bureaucracy the employed officials are there only to put into effect, in a disinterested fashion, the decisions of their political masters. The bureaucrat is concerned with the rational implementation of ends that are decided by others. It is equally possible to argue that the bureaucrats will have their own interests that are not the same as those of the institutional sponsors, as public choice theorists have maintained. Alternatively, it can be maintained that politicians and senior bureaucrats have common interests different from more junior members of the organisation. There are often close links between senior bureaucrats and politicians, so much so that they are seen by some as forming a joint elite (Stoker and Wilson, 1986). Whatever the character of the relationships at the top of the organisation, it is there that power and authority are concentrated in the characteristic state organisation.

The horizontal division of labour is reflected in the degree to which work is specialised, that is broken down into small units involving relatively narrow skills. The larger the organisation the more possible is specialisation, and, as public service organisations have grown in size, the degree of specialisation has increased. Production engineering techniques have increasingly been applied in the public service. In the late 1960s and the 1970s, in particular, there was a strong movement to adopt the work study and organisation and methods techniques that had long been used by the private sector. The new technology that began to have a major impact on the public service in the 1980s has contributed to greater specialisation and to the deskilling of certain types of activity, notably clerical work (Crompton and Jones, 1984).

In the pattern of public sector bureaucracy that developed in the post-war period both the horizontal and vertical divisions of labour were high. There was extensive differentiation. The result was organisations with extended hierarchies, in which the level of autonomy at lower levels was limited. Formal discretionary decision-making was reduced to a minimum through extensive use of rules and procedures, though, as Lipsky (1980) shows, informal discretion was still extensive. The actual pattern of operation may have diverged from that intended, but essentially control lay with the centre, and local discretion was exercised on a de facto basis rather than through formal authority.

The third characteristic of public service bureaucracies has been their self-sufficiency, that is the assumption that, if they had a function to perform, then they should employ the necessary staff. This did not mean that state organisations had to be capable of producing everything that they needed. However big the bureaucracy it will need to obtain certain goods and services from outside. Nevertheless, public service bureaucracies have typically employed those who produce the services for which they are responsible rather than buying them in from outside agencies. The result has been public bureaucracies that are very wide in the scope of their activities, producing direct services, but also indirect support services such as printing and transport. The wider the range of activities performed by the organisation the greater will be the complexity of coordination. The mode of coordination within the bureaucracy has been planning and authority, and, as the number of activities performed has grown, ensuring coordination has become more difficult.

Fourthly, public service bureaucracies are relatively large organisations. The scale of public service bureaucracies is enhanced by their self-sufficiency, but there has also been a belief in the value of large size because of supposed economies of scale. Size and self-sufficiency reinforced one another, because self-sufficient organisations grew large and because large organisations were more plausibly able to make the case for internal production. Large size also reinforced the need for the horizontal division of labour and an increasing hierarchy of authority. The result was highly complex organisations.

Public service organisations have tended to be organised along professional lines. Public service professionals, such as teachers and doctors, have largely been self-regulating, and have been able to influence the policy within which they work. They have been part of the policy networks that determined the nature of the services that government provided (Rhodes and Marsh, 1992). The interaction of hierarchy and profession created two further phenomena that have characterised the public service bureaucracies of the welfare state. First, the hierarchical division of authority created a career ladder. Large organisations had career structures and reward systems that would attract professionals. Second, there has been high mobility between organisations as individuals follow the hierarchical spiral from one organisation to another in pursuit of career advance. Mobility spread professional values and contributed to uniformity of approach. The high level of professionalism in public organisations has been accompanied by a strong producer control and acceptance of professional values and orthodoxies.

The arguments for bureaucracy at a theoretical level are clear. It operates without discrimination or favouritism, treating similar cases in a like fashion and unlike cases differently. It aims for uniformity of treatment. It is characterised by formal rationality and efficiency, being able to cope with large numbers of tasks. Formality and routinisation ensure that the organisation operates in a way that is independent of its members, so that there is a clear organisational memory, and the comings and goings of individual organisational members do not result in operational failure. It is difficult to envisage the modern world without bureaucracy. As Burnheim (1988) says:

> Abolishing bureaucracy would destroy in both public and private organisations significant economies of scale, the concentration of resources needed for important projects and the accumulation of information necessary to understand the impact of policy over a variety of sectors and over significant periods of time (p. 52).

It is not surprising, nor wholly to be regretted, that the institutional character of the welfare state becomes increasingly bureaucratised as the level of the demands upon it grow.

The failure of the state

The positive economic arguments for the state providing services through large bureaucratic organisations can be countered by arguments that there will inevitably be state failure. These arguments derive from a number of strands of economic thinking, and from claims about the nature of organisational functioning and public policy-making. The less general argument is that the particular institutional framework that has emerged to implement state activity and policy operates ineffectively, and that it is inevitably wasteful. The more fundamental argument is that of Hayek, who maintains that systems of planned production, whether of public services or manufactured goods, create information demands that cannot, in practice, be satisfied. The problem of the availability of knowledge is most obvious in command economies; as Nove (1983) says of the Soviet Union:

> The whole experience of the centrally planned economies indicates . . . that without a price and market mechanism the centre is deprived of vital information about what is most urgently needed, and that the micro detail would in most cases have to be decided at lower levels, closer to the suppliers and their customers (p.105).

The general argument against state provision of services is that operating on bureaucratic and rational planning principles is too demanding of knowledge, information and the ability to make informed decisions to be effective. State bureaucracy will be slow to respond.

This broad argument suggests that the state will only be able to operate effectively if it manages to mimic the operation of the market. In the market, at least in theory, the system of prices and the exchange process allow individuals to make effective choices, which determine levels of production. There needs to be some method of pricing that provides information on the value of the goods and services which the state produces. A system of shadow prices will be needed. Without an appropriate system of valuation it is difficult to see how anyone would know whether the activities of the government were producing anything that the market could not produce more effectively. Various proposals, from charging for services, to vouchers or tax credits, have been proposed to enable market mechanisms to operate within the state. This argument leads to the paradoxical conclusion that state activity may be seen to be needed, but that, if it is to be effective, then it needs to incorporate market principles. This is indeed the thrust of present policies that are intended to reform the management of public services, and the basis of the approach of those who argue that, while total privatisation is not possible, there is a need to reform the operation of the state.

Public choice

The simplest accusation against the public sector is that it is wasteful in the way that it uses resources because politicians and public officials have no incentive to control costs. Chapman (1979), a former civil servant who is one of the leading exponents of this view, argues:

> I am writing about waste in the old-fashioned sense – the waste involved in having ten men where five are enough, in using fuel to heat empty buildings, and in spending money to keep land idle and useless. It is waste that stems from inefficiency and mismanagement (p. 13).

Public choice theorists have gone further, arguing that the public sector will be subject to inherent failures, even if it is technically efficient. Buchanan (1986) maintains that political, collective decisions will inevitably involve their own externalities:

> . . . any attempts to modify an existing market situation, admitted to be characterised by serious externalities, will produce solutions that embody externalities which are different, but precisely analogous, to those previously existing (p. 172).

The world of public choice is essentially a rational world, with everybody pursuing their own best interests in the most efficient way possible, even when the result is social inefficiency. Patterns of motivation that determine outcomes will not be changed by the existence of government as opposed to market mechanisms of production and distribution. Self-interest will dominate.

There are three basic sources of failure in government organisations identified by public choice theorists. First, it cannot be assumed that politicians will demand the pattern of public sector outputs that reflects the best interests of society as a whole. They will have their own interests to pursue and they will be subject to conflicting demands and pressures from special interests. Second, the bureaucracy will not necessarily carry out the wishes of the politicians, even if the latter do express the public good, since it is likely to not be in the bureaucrats' interests to do so. Third, it is unlikely that bureaucrats will act efficiently in producing whatever it is decided should be produced, since it may be in their interests to be inefficient. These criticisms of politicians and bureaucracy lead to the conclusion that the public service will be characterised both by allocative inefficiency, the production of the wrong mix of services, and by X-inefficiency (Leibenstein, 1966; 1987), that is the production of less than it is possible to produce with the given inputs.

The pressures on politicians and their pursuit of their own interests will lead to allocative inefficiency, that is the production of a non-optimum set of outputs. The ability of bureaucrats to evade political controls will have the same effect. Public services will be wasteful because it is in the interests of public servants not to work harder than they have to and because they are able to act without effective supervision. It is also argued that government will not be dynamically efficient in developing improved technology and work methods, and therefore improving productivity, because it does not face competition. The public sector will be less innovative than the private and will take an ever greater proportion of national resources, because individuals do not reap the reward of technical advance, and so lack the incentive to improve methods. Productivity necessarily lags in the public service (Baumol, 1967).

The best known critical analysis of the efficiency of the public sector is that of Niskanen (1971), who argues that bureaucrats will tend to expand the production of public services beyond the socially optimum level. Niskanen's argument is based upon the classical economic assumption that bureaucrats are rational, self-interested, utility maximisers. They will attempt to maximise the bureau's budget because their own rewards, in terms of status, power, but most particularly income, will be directly related to the size of the budget. Politicians will not be able to prevent the bureaucrats pursuing budget-maximising behaviour, because they are more fragmented, and lack the detailed knowledge that is available to the bureaucrat. The bureau can use its monopoly of information to play political sponsors off, one against the other. Making certain basic assumptions, Niskanen is able to show that bureaucrats will tend to produce up to twice as much of a given output as is socially optimal. Niskanen's essential argument is that bureaucracy leads to allocative inefficiency, but there are also grounds for expecting X-inefficiency, because of the lack of incentives, since pay is not related to output, and because of the inability of the politicians effectively to monitor performance.

There have been many extensions, variations and criticisms of the Niskanen thesis within the public choice tradition. Breton and Wintrobe (1982) argue that the superior information that is available to the bureaucrat will not always be an advantage. The politician may find it easier to cut the bureau budget if the consequences are little known or ill-understood. It will be relatively easy for one level of government, or one set of bureaucrats, to cut the funds available to another. Knowledge cannot be equated with power, for ignorance on one side may make it easier to act against the other. Orzechowski (1977) argues that bureaucrats will tend to use inefficient combinations of labour and capital, with too much labour tending to dominate. De Alessi (1969) argues, by contrast, that capital intensity will be favoured because it will have the effect of driving up spending more quickly in the short run, leading to technical inefficiency. Peacock (1983) emphasises the bureaucrat's taste for taking leisure on the job and therefore producing less than is possible with the given inputs. Rowley and Elgin (1988) argue that public officials will have little incentive to keep costs down since they will not personally benefit from any savings.

There is little empirical evidence to support the arguments of the public choice theorists (Lewin, 1991; Self, 1993). Much is dependent upon the initial assumptions. Dunleavy (1991) has used public-choice style arguments to show that the self-interest of the bureaucrat could be expected to lead to different patterns of action depending upon the form of the bureau that is involved. For example, bureaus that are themselves responsible for the delivery of services will behave differently from those that are concerned with the transfer of income, or those bureaus that control the spending of others, such as the Treasury. Bureaucrats are less likely to be concerned about budget cuts if those budgets are being transferred elsewhere, and the core administrative budget remains untouched. Even if one makes the assumption that bureaucrats are self-interested, and will attempt to develop a pattern of spending that is in their interests, it is not immediately apparent what the result will be, because there is not a monotonic relationship between the bureaucrats' utility and the size of the total bureau budget. Despite the limitations, public choice theories have been influential in the reorganisation of government services.

Public choice and politicians

Critics of government argue that politicians will tend to produce decisions that are in their own personal political interests, but that reduce total social welfare. Log-rolling, the linking together of unrelated interests as a result of vote trading, produces benefits for minorities while reducing overall welfare. Politicians are argued to pursue policies that involve the production of highly visible outputs at the expense of the more beneficial but less obvious projects. Prestige projects, such as Concorde or the space race, typically of high capital intensity and technical sophistication, are pursued irrespective of their costs and the value of the result. The attempt to control costs gives little positive political satisfaction and does not advance political careers. At a more basic level politicians can be argued to favour spending patterns that will benefit them personally, for example through voting themselves healthy pay rises or travelling at the public expense.

Public choice theorists argue that politicians have a short term perspective, or, as the economists put it, to have a high time-discount rate. Their concern is to win the next election and this, it is felt, is more easily done by promising immediate rather than long term gains. The search for votes is, more generally, argued to reduce the choice available to the voter because political party platforms will tend to converge on the median voter's views, offering little choice within the political marketplace. The democratic agenda becomes constricted as politicians pursue their own interests and attempt to ensure that they retain power.

Mancur Olson (1982) has argued that the political agenda will be related to the pattern of interest group organisation in any country. It will always be difficult to form interest groups because the personal effort involved is likely to be great compared to the benefit that will flow to any individual. Over time interest groups will gradually be established, and political systems that exhibit long-term stability will have more such groups than those that have been subject to disruption by war or other events. Interest groups will tend to focus on questions of distribution rather than production, because the returns to pressing for redistribution in favour of a particular group will always be greater than those to action to increase the total social product. Interest groups are more likely to be concerned with how the cake is cut than trying to make it bigger. Investment in influence will be more rewarding than increasing production. The more stable the political system the more likely it is that the rate of economic growth will be slowed as the political agenda focuses on distribution rather than production. The result of long-term political stability is political sclerosis and economic stagnation as the influence of interest groups increases. Britain has been argued to be a key exemplar of this effect, because of its long history of political and social stability, though it may be argued that its comparative performance is more the result of the catching up process, with Britain suffering the penalty of the early start.

Information, control and entrepreneurialism

A further failing that is attributed to large-scale government bureaucracies is that they do not produce what they say they will, or what those in political control intend them to produce. The weak version of this argument is that within a large organisation, there will always be a degree of control and information loss between the various levels of the hierarchy. Whatever the motivations of those who work for the state there will always be failures of communication and misinterpretation. Large organisations also make necessary the delegation of control and responsibility, and delegation will always involve some degree of discretionary decision-making by those at the lower levels of the organisation. Policies as implemented are always likely to differ from what was intended. The larger the organisation the more likely it is that the outcome will vary from the intention because of the number of links that there must be between those who make policy and those who put it into effect. Hood (1976) has argued that there are inevitable limits to implementation, because the requirements for perfect administration are analogous to those for the perfect market, and are equally unlikely to obtain in practice. There must, for example, be adequate time for decisions to be put into effect and perfect communications and coordination. In practice administration and organisation are always imperfect; there are inherent processes of organisational failure just as there is market failure.

The information and control failings of large organisations are likely to apply as much in the private as in the public sector, but the critics of government would argue that it has characteristics which make it more likely that there will be failures to implement what was planned. The nature of politics is such as to encourage imprecision in policies. It does not do to be too clear about what one is planning to do, because that will mean that failure can easily be identified and blame apportioned. Failure accurately to implement policy is much more likely if the policy itself is not clear. Second, it is difficult to know whether there has been effective implementation because there is no simple measure of performance. For the private sector company there is the ultimate measure of financial performance and profitability. The public sector, despite much searching, has signally failed to find an acceptable set of performance indicators. It may be that the search is futile because whether or not a policy is successful, at least in the short term, will itself be a matter of political construction (Stewart and Walsh, 1994). Third, the private sector can argue that there will be external measures that will tell the organisation whether or not it is being successful, for example the price of shares on the stock market, and the various standard performance ratios. Measures of public sector performance tend to be internal to the organisation, and to be more claims to virtue and legitimacy than reflections of reality (Meyer and Rowan, 1977; Brunsson and Olsen, 1993).

Political scientists and policy analysts have also emphasised the importance of limitations on information. The major theory of public service budgeting in the 1970s and 1980s was incrementalism, according to which budgets change only at the margin (Wildavsky, 1964). Base budgets were not open to attack because of the nature of political institutions, entrenched bureaucracies, the lack of information, and the time that would be needed for comprehensive analysis. Bureaucrats and politicians were seen to use various mechanisms, such as shroud waving, to defend their budgets against attack. There was a failure to reassess budgets and to reallocate resources in line with changing needs and priorities. Decision-making was argued to be a disjointed activity in which different individuals and groups adjusted to each other, partisan mutual adjustment, as Lindblom (1959) calls it, rather than a linear rational process. Once established, a particular pattern of expenditure tended to become institutionalised and persist from one year to the next with little debate. Over time, spending patterns tended to become detached from patterns of need. The budget, in incremental theory, is seen essentially as a reflection of previous decisions and of past political victories.

Public service organisations can, finally, be argued to be likely to be technically inefficient because there is no entrepreneur. An entrepreneur is someone who organises people and material resources to produce an output. The entrepreneur must discover valuable outputs, bring together the necessary factors of production, and develop and enforce appropriate contracts. The entrepreneur risks resources, but also reaps the rewards when the income is greater than the costs incurred, acting as the claimant for any residual of income over expenditure. In the public sector, because there is no residual claimant to surplus, there is little incentive to look for new products or new and more productive patterns of organisation. The result is likely to be X-inefficiency and dynamic inefficiency. More generally Dunsire *et al.* (1988) emphasise the importance of organisational characteristics. They present an analytical model within which performance is predicted to vary with the degree of control, the extent of monopoly, and the number of organisational objectives. Public sector organisations are more likely to have multiple objectives, limited control, and monopoly characteristics, and so suffer efficiency problems.

The theory of government failure

The various explanations of the failure of state provision have been brought together in an emerging theory of government failure, developed most explicitly in the work of Wolf (1988). The theory is somewhat less formally developed than the theories of market failure, but is of the same form, arguing that the inherent characteristics of demand and supply for government services will lead to inefficiency. Wolf argues that the demand for public sector output has become more pressing over time. There are five reasons for this growth in demand: increased awareness of market shortcomings; political organisation and enfranchisement; the structure of political rewards; the high time discount of political actors; and the decoupling of burdens and benefits. Each of these conditions, he maintains, will tend to lead to the over-supply of publicly produced goods.

Wolf then argues that the supply characteristics of the public sector are distinctive. There is difficulty in defining and measuring output, both in principle and in practice, and there are particular problems in the evaluation of quality. Second, the supply of public sector goods is in the hands of a monopoly which has the backing of law, so that the market is not contestable. Third, the production technology is uncertain, in that the relation between inputs and outputs cannot easily be specified. Much of the public sector is concerned with the production of services for which there are inherent problems in the definition and control of production technologies. Finally, Wolf argues that there is no 'bottom-line' in the public sector and that there is no mechanism for the termination of unsuccessful public policies.

Wolf maintains that these characteristics of the supply and demand for goods and services in the public sector will lead to systematic non-market failures. First, the mechanisms that bring the supply and demand of public services into equilibrium are weak, because it is 'essentially a political process characterised by lags, bottlenecks, coalitions, log-rolling and other fuzzy attributes of political behaviour' (p. 62). Wolf distinguishes four types of non-market failure. First, there is a disjunction between costs and revenues, because of the difficulty of precise costing and the fact that there is no market exchange. Second, because public sector organisations lack objective measures of performance, they must substitute their own standards, which constitute what Wolf rather misleadingly calls 'internalities'. These standards do not necessarily bear any relation to the public good. The third failing of the public sector is the generation of derived externalities, that is unanticipated side effects resulting from public policies. The final failing that results from government intervention in the economy is distributional inequity, particularly of power and privilege, with advantage accruing to politicians, bureaucrats, and those whom they favour.

Le Grand (1991) has argued that the theory of government failure that is propounded by Wolf is neither particularly well specified, nor accurate in its description of public service organisations. It is difficult to argue that all the potential failings of the government identified by Wolf are inherent in the operation of the public sector, in the way that the failings of the market follow analytically from classical economic theory. As Le Grand says:

> . . . it is important to re-emphasise that a study of government failure does not imply that governments always fail, still less that markets always succeed. Whether a particular form of government intervention creates more inefficiency or more inequity than if that intervention had not taken place is ultimately an empirical question and one that is by no means always supported by the evidence. Governments sometimes succeed, a fact that should not be lost to view in the glare of the market's bright lights (p. 442).

Indeed, if it is the case, as those who have argued for the reform of the organisation and management of the public service along market lines maintain, that the efficiency of the public sector can be increased, then the pattern of failure is obviously not inherent in the fact of government activity. Wolf takes little account of the impact of organisational form and institutional structure on the performance of the public sector. Recent programmes of public service management reform in Britain and other countries have been based on the assumption that, given the right organisational and institutional framework, it is possible for government not to fail.

Conclusion

The key to efficiency in public service management is increasingly seen to be the separation of responsibility for the provision from that for production of public services (Koldarie, 1986; Savas, 1987). The government might take on itself the responsibility for ensuring that certain services are produced, but do so by using private sector or voluntary producers, for example by franchising or by putting work out to tender. Savas (1987, p. 61) makes the distinction between arranging for a service to be delivered, and actually producing it:

> The distinction between providing or arranging a service and producing it is profound. It is at the heart of the whole concept of privatisation and puts the role of government in perspective. With respect to many collective goods, government is essentially an arranger or provider - an instrument of society for deciding what shall be done collectively, for whom, to what degree or at what level of supply, and how to pay for it. Producing the service, however, is a separate matter. A government that decides that a service is to be provided at collective expense does not have to produce it using government equipment and government employees.

It is this model of the enabling state that is being adopted in Britain, and to some degree in other countries.

Monopoly need not be a problem. Vining and Weimer (1990) argue that the appropriate form of organisation of the production and delivery of public services depends upon the contestability of the market, not simply competition within it. A market is contestable,

according to Baumol and his colleagues (1982), if the costs of entry
and exit are low, because there are few sunk costs. Even if the
market is most efficient when operated in monopoly form, for
example because there are continually falling costs as the level of
production increases, there may still be competition for the market
itself. Vining and Weimer then argue (1990) that:

> If, given public financing, supply is not contestable, then the
> government should produce the goods itself. If, given public
> financing, supply is perfectly contestable, then government should
> procure the good through contracting.

The possibility of government control through contracts, regulation
and other mechanisms opens up the attractive opportunity of taking
advantage of market mechanisms within a context of public control,
and so gaining the benefits both of government and markets. Much
of the recent change in the management of the public service has
involved the attempt to gain the advantages of market mechanisms,
while still operating within the public sector.

There are five major approaches that have been adopted by
governments concerned to reform the management of the public
sector from within, as compared with outright privatisation:
introducing user charges for services; opening services up to
competitive tendering or putting work out on a contract basis;
introducing internal markets; devolving financial control; and
establishing parts of the organisation on an agency basis. User
charges have typically been used relatively little in the management
of the public service, but are now being more widely operated.
Competitive tendering and contracting have been the most common
approaches used in the attempt to develop market mechanisms,
being used for a wide range of local government, health and central
government services. The United States and parts of Europe, for
example, have long made use of contracting for specific services.
Internal markets have only recently begun to develop on any
significant scale, notably in the National Health service. Devolving
financial control has been used throughout the public service, but
perhaps the most characteristic cases are the attempts in a number
of countries to delegate budgetary control to schools. The
separation of policy from day-to-day service management and

delivery has long existed in certain cases, for example in Swedish central government, but is now being developed systematically as the major method for changing the nature of the British civil service, and even more systematically in New Zealand through the establishment of agencies for operational service delivery.

The various market mechanisms used in the public service are not wholly independent of each other. In the case of local government in Britain there has been a combination of competitive tendering for services with the establishment of internal markets and devolved budgets. If the local authority staff win the right to do certain types of work in competition then they must operate the internal contract on a market basis. Internal markets necessarily go with some form of internal pricing and charging mechanism. The development of an executive agency form can be combined with the operation of an internal market and necessarily involves some devolution of control. Generally each of these mechanisms is intended to provide a greater incentive to managers to manage, and to ensure that politicians play their role effectively. The use of market mechanisms for the management of the public sector varies from case to case within countries, and from one country to another. In continental Europe, for example, there has been relatively little competitive tendering, though contracting out is quite widely used. In New Zealand there has been a great deal of emphasis on devolution of financial control and the development of appropriate accounting mechanisms. Britain provides the paradigm case of marketisation in that all the methods of change have been used, and been used more systematically than in other countries.

The introduction of market mechanisms into the management of the public service involves more than simply the growth of a managerialist approach to the public sector. Certainly there has been a developing managerialism, but that can be traced back to the beginnings of government provision of services on a large scale. For example, in the United States of America, movements for managerialism in local government were part of very early attempts to reform local government more generally (Dearlove, 1979). The development of managerialism has intensified from the mid-1960s onwards, but it is only in the last decade that a systematic practical theory of an alternative approach to the management of the public sector has begun to emerge. It is different from the earlier managerialist movement in that it is based on the development of a new institutional approach founded upon the introduction of market principles. The new market-based approaches are seen as enabling governments to gain the advantages of market-based approaches, while avoiding their failures.

2 The Market Alternative

Proponents of the use of market mechanisms for the management of public services claim that they will help overcome some of its inherent failings. The essential problem is argued to lie in the motivation of those who work in the public sector and the difficulties in monitoring and controlling performance. There is an inevitable tendency to inefficiency in government, so the argument goes, because there is a lack of market incentives. Critics of government argue that technological possibilities for lowering costs, raising productivity, or realising economies of scale, will tend to be ignored or not fully exploited by public servants. The costs of change are seen as high, and making changes as troublesome. Lack of incentives would not be a great problem if it was easy to monitor the performance of the public sector worker, because then, at least, rewards and sanctions could be introduced to stimulate performance or punish failure. A central purpose of the institutional changes that are being introduced is that purposes should be clearer, and standards objectively defined, and that there should be more explicit approaches to the assessment of the extent to which they are being achieved with payment and reward being tied to output. The attempt is to introduce the market disciplines that operate in the private sector into the public sector.

The two key developments in the management of the public services in recent years have been the development of markets and the introduction of competition. There are practical and theoretical problems with the model of the market that is proposed. The move to the operation of competitive, market-based processes for managing public services cannot be expected to be trouble-free. It involves a fundamental change of institutional structure, and there will need to be an explicit process of institution building that addresses the difficulties that are involved. The move will not be to free and unregulated markets, but to what Le Grand (1991) calls quasi-markets, which are governed by their own rules and procedures. The introduction of markets and competition will not easily overcome some of the problems which are inherent in the nature of service and product complexity in the public sector, and the difficulties that arise in writing and monitoring contracts. Indeed, as products and services become more complex, these issues are arising in the private sector, leading to transformations in market and contract forms (Best, 1990; Clegg, 1990). It is increasingly common, for example, for companies to co-operate as well as compete, and to move away from rigid contracting processes. If care is not taken, the public sector, not for the first time, will find itself adopting approaches to management precisely at the time that they are being abandoned as ineffective by the private sector. In order to understand the issues and problems involved we will need to consider recent developments in law, economics and organisation theory. In the second half of the chapter, I outline the central issues and themes that arise in analysing the network of markets and competition and I will draw upon this to discuss the impact upon management.

Economics, law and organisation

Institutional change

Attempts to change the management of the public service have traditionally tended to concentrate on structural reorganisation or the introduction of new techniques and processes, for example restructuring departments or the development of planning processes. The introduction of market processes and competition involves a more fundamental change to the operation of the public services because a change of the institutional framework is involved. The changes are not intended to alter the organisational structures and frameworks within which public servants work but the governing norms, values and beliefs with which they operate. The purpose is to introduce new values of entrepreneurial managerialism. As John Major (1989) has put it:

> Our approach to the public services is based on the belief that the people who work in them should, as far as possible become full participants in the more competitive and demanding economy which now surrounds them. They will have less insulation from economic risk and uncertainty. But to the greatest extent possible in services with a strong monopoly element, they will have the

same opportunities and incentives and the same responsibilities for efficiency and success as elsewhere in the economy.

The new market-based institutional framework that is being put in place is seen as leading to the change in values and attitudes that is desired. Public sector managers, it is hoped, will not simply operate different systems, and work within different structures, they will also act and think in a new way.

The importance of political and social institutions in fostering particular patterns of action and sets of beliefs has been increasingly recognised by economists, political scientists and economic historians. March and Olsen (1989) for example, emphasise the importance of considering the impact of institutions in understanding the working of political systems, and North (1990) explains development in economic history in terms of institutional change and the way that different institutions contribute to stability. Students of organisation theory (Powell and Di Maggio, 1991) have analysed the way that institutional factors work within organisations to foster particular attitudes, beliefs, and patterns of action.

North defines institutions as:

.... .the rules of the game in a society or, more formally, the humanly devised constraints that shape human interaction. In consequence they structure incentives in human exchange, whether political, social, or economic. Institutional change shapes the way that societies evolve through time and hence is the key to understanding economic change.

Institutions provide structures both for behaviour and thought, and lead both to stability and to change. Developing new institutions is a powerful way of changing the way that the public service will operate. It is not easy to change institutions, because any change will be resisted by those who benefit from the existing institutional pattern, and because institutions exist not only as external systems of constraints, but also as internal patterns of interests and values. Resistance will not only be manifest but will also be unconscious in that people will operate with a set of taken-for-granted assumptions about the proper way to manage public organisations.

Tushman and others (Tushman and Romanelli, 1985) have distinguished between two forms of organisational change, convergence and reorientation. In the case of convergence, change takes place over the long term and involves slow and steady patterns of evolutionary development. The basic pattern of organisational structure and culture do not change, but there is a gradual development of internal consistency within the organisation. The 'fit' between its various parts becomes more marked. The organisation converges on what theorists have called archetypes (Miller and Friesen, 1984; Hinings and Greenwood, 1988), with strongly established and internalised institutional constraints and patterns of action. In periods of reorientation the fundamental character of the organisation is transformed, involving radical change in organisational structures and values. Change is rapid and disruptive. Institutional understandings and patterns of behaviour are systematically undermined. Reorientation involves revolution rather than evolution. In many ways the public service developments of the 1960s and 1970s were convergent changes, as the bureaucratic form became more explicit and firmly established. It is clear that the public service in many countries is now going through a period of rapid change which means a major reorientation of its basic institutional form. The contrast between convergence and reorientation mirrors two aspects of the operation of institutions, namely the way that they contribute to stability, but also create the possibility of change.

There are three crucial features to the pattern of institutional change in the management of the public service that we are concerned to examine. First, it involves an economic component in focusing on the classical concepts of competition, prices and markets. Second it involves the introduction of the concept of contract with its socio-legal connotation. Third it involves a change in the organisational character of the public service because it involves a break with the tradition of the self-sufficient, bureaucratic government organisation. There is a move towards a network-based system of management, rather than integrated organisations.

Economic arguments

Transaction costs

Markets and planning constitute alternative approaches to coordinating economic activities. The first involves exchanges based on the price mechanism, which acts as the means of providing information about variations in the valuation of, and consequently the demand for and supply of, particular commodities. People will adjust their actions in the market depending on the information that they get through the price system, and those actions, in turn, will contribute to price adjustments. The value of the price mechanism, according to Hayek (1944, p. 27), is that it is:

> . . . superior not only because it is in most circumstances the most efficient method known, but even more because it is the only method by which our activities can be adjusted to each other without coercive or arbitrary intervention of authority. Indeed, one of the main arguments in favour of competition is that it dispenses with the need for 'conscious social control' and that it gives the individuals a chance to decide whether the prospects of a particular occupation are sufficient to compensate for the disadvantages and risks connected with it.

The market produces coordinated results without conscious coordinating processes. Planning, by contrast, involves the authoritative allocation of resources to defined purposes, and the use of explicit processes of coordination. All political systems are a mixture of market principles and organised, authority-based planning, but the mix can vary greatly.

Williamson (1975; 1985) has addressed the general issue of the relative efficiency of using market mechanisms as opposed to bureaucratic forms of organisation. The basis of his argument is that the most advantageous institutional form will depend on the level of transaction costs, which are the costs involved in making exchanges, for example the costs of writing and monitoring contracts. Transaction costs may well be high when the process of exchange is difficult or complicated, for example if detailed contracts must be prepared and managed or if it is difficult to evaluate the quality of products. In these circumstances hierarchical organisation may be more efficient than market processes. Institutional patterns, according to Williamson, will tend to evolve in a way that will minimise the costs of transactions, with organisation being more appropriate in some cases and markets in others. Williamson argues that whether markets or hierarchies are the more efficient will depend upon a number of factors: uncertainty and bounded rationality, complexity, opportunism and asset specificity.

The level of uncertainty refers to the extent to which it is possible accurately to predict future circumstances, and bounded rationality to the limits to the computational and analytical abilities of individuals. The greater are uncertainty and bounded rationality, the more difficult it will be to carry out transactions in the market, because it will be difficult to develop agreements that will deal adequately with contingencies. If there was full knowledge of the future and unbounded rationality then it would be possible to write contracts that took account of every eventuality. Contracts would, as Williamson says, reduce to plans. Where there are high levels of bounded rationality and uncertainty, then it will be difficult to write contracts, and there are likely to be continual variations and renegotiations. In such circumstances, hierarchy will have advantages over markets because those in power in organisations will be able to react to unforeseen events by changing the pattern of organisation action. Adaptation will be more rapid and less expensive because it can be done without formal negotiation and can be more far-reaching. The labour contract is much more flexible than the standard contracts that are normally drawn up for market exchange, because it is more open-ended, allowing the organisation to exercise authority to change the work of employees.

The relative advantages of markets and hierarchies will also be influenced by the degree of opportunism that is possible and the degree to which there is a likelihood of it being exploited. Opportunism involves 'interest-seeking with guile', the traditional assumption that individuals will pursue their own best interests at the expense of others. When the parties to a contract have differential access to information, or one is stronger than another, for example in terms of wealth, then it is possible that the party with the advantage will be able to exploit the other, for example by breaching the terms of the contract, safe in the knowledge that the powerless partner can do little about it. Opportunism will also be possible by the systematic misrepresentation of intentions. If I can conceal my true interests and the way that I will actually behave, I may well be able to take advantage of others who have no means of checking the validity of what I say, or how I have acted. It is not necessarily the case that the parties to a transaction will all act opportunistically, but without perfect information it will not be possible to distinguish the trustworthy from those whose commitments are false.

The dangers of opportunism are enhanced where there is 'small-numbers bargaining', that is when there is imperfect competition in markets, because it will be difficult to drop those who have behaved opportunistically in the past at the time of renewing agreements. Even if you know that you are likely to be exploited you may have little choice but to contract with the potentially exploitative party. Opportunism on the part of the members of an organisation must be assumed, but it is easier for the organisation as a whole to control the extent to which its members can appropriate gains, to exercise sanctions for unacceptable behaviour, and to influence organisational culture and values in a way that may reduce opportunism.

Asset specificity arises when the producer of goods or services must make an investment in specialist equipment, knowledge or skills which cannot be used for other purposes. It leads to a situation of bilateral monopoly. Once the investment has been made it is difficult for the buyer to go to alternative providers and the person who has made the investment gains quasi-monopoly advantages. The market may not be contestable because of the existing supplier's control of the necessary resources. The seller may also face a limited market because the buyer is the only purchaser for the products of the specialised assets involved. Many government activities will tend to be characterised by bilateral monopoly because of the highly professionalised nature of many public services. Williamson argues there will be advantages to the organisation in owning or employing highly specific assets, because it avoids being the hostage of those who control the assets and does not have to face the bargaining costs that are involved in bilateral monopoly.

Williamson's argument is that markets will fail not only for the reasons that have led to the development of state provision of services, but also because of the costs of transactions. Markets will not instantaneously and perfectly reach equilibrium. The structure of information and the nature of assets will determine whether or not the market is an effective medium for conducting transactions. The firm is then viewed not as a production function, but as a system of governance. Where markets fail because of high transaction costs then hierarchical organisations are likely to be more effective. If transaction costs were zero then many of the problems of market failure, notably externalities, would disappear, since reaching appropriate compensatory agreements between winners and losers would be costless, and private agreements could resolve problems. In practice, as we shall see, the choice is not simply between the market and the organisation, but involves determining the appropriate mix of market and organisation, according to the nature of the activity involved.

Agency theory

Williamson's markets and hierarchies analysis shows that the choice between the market and organisation involves a complex range of issues. Agency theory has focussed more precisely upon the issues which arise when one party, the agent, carries out work on behalf of another, the principal, and it is assumed that the interests of principals and agents do not necessarily coincide (Ross, 1973). Where there is perfect, free information, then there is little difficulty, because the principal will be able to monitor the agent's performance and to design an effective set of sanctions and incentives. Failures in performance, and the reasons for failure, will be instantly and accurately observable. Without perfect information there will be monitoring and incentive difficulties. The principal may not be able to tell whether or not there has been a failure, or, if there has, whether that failure is the result of actions of the agent. Failure adequately to perform may be due to unforeseen and unforeseeable problems, that is the state of the world, but it may equally result from the actions of the agent, for example shirking.

The problems in relationships between principals and agents are likely to be greater the longer are organisational hierarchies, because there will be more such relationships involved. There will be many agents and many principals; in part the organisational world is one of agents without principals as Macneil (1980) puts it. There will be information loss because of the greater complexity of communication. The pattern of careers will have an influence on principal—agent relations. If individuals typically advance by moving between organisations, then they will have an incentive to act to maximise their attractiveness to others rather than act in the interests of their existing employer. They may do this by focussing on activities that have high external visibility, rather than those which are the most efficient and productive within the organisation.

Where the principal finds it difficult to distinguish between those results that follow from the actions of the agent and those that result from the state of the world, then there will be an incentive for agents to underperform, and attribute failure to circumstances which were outside their control. Contracts between principals and agents may be structured to take account of these difficulties, for example by attempting to shift all the risk onto the contractor or to leave it all with the principal. Where possible the principal will try to build incentives into the contract, for example payment by results or flat rate payments, in order to encourage effective performance by the contractor, or make truth-telling more likely. If the incentives of agents can be aligned with those of principals, then it can be assumed that they will act in accordance with the principals' interests, and monitoring costs will then be reduced. The most efficient form of contract is one that is self-enforcing, because performance is immediately apparent and can be related to reward, but it is unlikely that most situations will allow fully self-enforcing contracts to be written. There will be some trade-off between the structure of incentives and sanctions and the degree to which monitoring is necessary.

Agency problems arise both within organisations and in contracts with external bodies, and so cut across the decision as to whether markets or organisations are the most efficient means of organising transactions. The sorts of relationships into which agents will be willing to enter will depend upon their attitude to risk. Risk-neutral agents might be willing to take on contracts that involved payment purely on the basis of output, however much that may be influenced by contingent factors that they cannot control. By contrast, a risk-averse agent will only be willing to enter into contracts that involve some certainty of payment whatever may happen. The contract between principal and agent, if it is to be effective, will have to operate to distribute risk between them in an efficient and mutually acceptable way. Complete inability to monitor the behaviour of the agent will create problems in allocating risk in an appropriate or acceptable fashion, and in developing contracts. Either the market will tend to decay, as in the case of Akerlof's market for 'lemons', or either the principal or the agent will be able totally to dominate the relationship, and 'hold up' the other partner (Klein, 1992).

Particular problems arise in dealing with the issue of quality in contracts between principals and agents. It is often difficult to measure quality, or for those providing services to provide evidence of the quality of their work. This is particularly so for professionals such as doctors, lawyers or social workers. In such cases it is difficult to write contracts of the traditional form and there is a need for trust-based relationships. Trust in turn depends upon the ability of those carrying out the work to provide evidence that they are likely to do a good job of work, for example because their reputations will be at risk if they do not. Principals are able to feel more confidence in the actions of agents the more the latter have provided 'hostages', that is the more they stand to lose in the case of poor performance. Equally agents will need to feel confident that they cannot be exploited by principals, who may misrepresent the value of the work done, or claim poor work has been done when evaluation is ambiguous. Agents may then not come forward because of distrust of the principal. Much of the efficiency of market and organisational systems will depend upon the signals and evidence of performance that agents and principals can provide to each other. Third party monitoring, for example through certification systems for quality assurance, may help in establishing a viable relationship between principals and agents. Where they cannot trust each other, both principal and agent may trust a third party who does not stand to gain from misleading either of them, or whose own reputation may be at risk (Heimer, 1985).

Property rights

The debate over whether the government or the market should produce certain goods and services may be couched in terms that assume an overly simple understanding of property. The concept of property rights does not refer simply to possession or ownership, but to a broader range of relationships (Barzel, 1989). The simple contrast between government or private ownership does not capture the range of possibilities. The concept of property rights refers to the rights to use, exchange and alienate goods or services. Property rights theorists argue that the reason for many non-optimal outcomes and externalities in social relations is that property rights are ineffectively defined and distributed. The motivation and incentive to use resources efficiently requires that there be an appropriate distribution of property rights. Common property, it is claimed, is particularly likely to be overused, since any individual use makes little difference to total usage. The important consideration in the distribution of property rights is what it is that different groups and individuals are allowed to do with resources.

Clearly the privatisation of public utilities and other public services involves a redistribution of property rights, but the move to contracting and internal trading organisations and agencies also involves changes in the structure of property rights, even if only within the existing organisation. Private concerns may be given the right to alienate the profit or surplus that may be made in the production and delivery of public services, while using publicly owned capital, as in the case of competitive tendering. Governmental organisations may let franchises or concessions for the provision of certain services, for example the operation of water supply in France and other countries. Devolution of budgetary controls within the organisation, for example the delegation of financial control to schools or other public service delivery agencies, changes the property rights of budget holders. The development of market based approaches in the public service has led to the emergence of a more differentiated and complex structure of property rights. Whether the sort of market mechanisms now being introduced within the public service will operate effectively will depend partly upon whether the pattern of property rights that is being established creates appropriate incentives.

Economic theories: discussion

These various theories can obviously be further developed and criticised, but my purpose here is to highlight the issues they raise. Economic theories about the pattern of institutions and their impact upon performance identify a number of factors that are important in the development of new systems of public management. They illustrate the difficulties that arise in developing an effective system of contracts, whether in the market or within the organisation. They suggest the problems of controlling performance without perfect information. Finally they highlight the incentives that will be created by different patterns of property distribution. The theory of economic institutions points to the range of forms of governance that are available in getting work done, whether it is in the public or the private sector. Concepts of property rights, principals and agents, and transaction costs enable us to develop a perspective that is more subtle than the simple distinction between public and private ownership. The developments in public service management involve a blurring of the boundary between the public and private. Analysing them requires a set of ideas that are more developed than the classical theory of the firm operating in a perfect market.

Law and contracts

An appropriate legal system is fundamental to the development of an effective institutional framework for social action. Legal theorists have, obviously, always been concerned with the issues that are involved in the development of contractual forms, the nature of property rights and the management of transactions. Much attention has been given to the question of how efficient forms of contract, and particularly of remedies for failure adequately to perform, can be devised. There has been increasing concern with understanding the way that long term relationships are regulated. Perhaps the most important distinction that has been made is that between relational, or obligational, and discrete contracts (Macneil, 1980; Sako, 1992).

Discrete contracts, the focus of classical contract theory, are contracts in which there is an instantaneous exchange of rights and duties, and in which the parties to the contract do not have a continuing relationship. Such an approach emphasises clear contract conditions, and specific remedies should the parties to the contract fail to meet their commitments. The courts are the arbiters of the agreement, and each party is seen as holding the other strictly to the bargain. This approach does not recognise the nature of modern organisations or the complexity of much modern contracting, as Macneil (1980, p. 22) has argued:

> . . . complexity of modern technology calls for processes and structures tying even the most specific and measured exchanges into ongoing relational patterns.

Contract forms in circumstances where there are to be repeated exchanges within a continuing relationship – where there is an iterated game (Kreps, 1990) – will be quite different from those in which the game is played only once. The organisation, like the market, can be seen as a nexus of contracts or treaties (Aoki *et al.*, 1990), enabling an extended co-operative game to be played. Without an appropriate set of formal or informal contracts, and an institutional framework that makes them possible, the game will tend to break down.

Contracts involve commitments either to particular or generalised exchanges by the contracting parties. The contract relationship must be structured to ensure that commitments are met, since it cannot be assumed that the parties will naturally deliver if it turns out not to be in their best interests to do so. Where the costs of breaching the contract are less than the costs of meeting obligations there will be an incentive not to carry out one's obligations. Indeed economists talk of the 'efficient breach' (Crasswell, 1988).

Contracts involve more than promise, and are essentially a means of sharing risks, benefits and responsibilities, or, more abstractly, a means of 'making the future present'. The contract is a means of making future decisions more tractable, without knowing what the detailed nature of those decisions will be. It involves the creation of institutions that allow the postponement of choice. The different forms of contract will depend upon what can be observed and how much the observation of performance will cost. For example, if it is difficult to assess objectively whether or not the contractor has performed, then it may be necessary to build contract forms that incorporate trust and reputation. As North (1990, p. 55) argues:

> Reputations, depending on the cost of information, provided parties in long-distance trade and impersonal exchange a mechanism to enforce agreements. Kinship ties, various forms of loyalty, minority groups in society bound together by common beliefs in a hostile world – all provided frameworks within which living up to agreements was worthwhile.

Alternatively there may simply be a focus on performance (Ricketts, 1987), but sanctions-based approaches are only likely to be appropriate in fairly simple circumstances.

The stronger the supporting institutional social framework of norms and relationships, the easier it will be to manage through contracts. Anonymity and one-off relationships make contracting difficult. The contractual system needs an institutional framework that provides for stability of relations. It is unlikely that the formal legal framework will be an adequate institution for ensuring that contract obligations are met, for it is likely to be slow, inflexible and costly. Reliance on formal legal organisations, such as the courts, is not likely to be seen as flexible enough for the operation of continuing contract relationships. If contracts are to be efficient as a means of managing public services then more extensive trust-based relationships are likely to be necessary to underpin them. They must be socially as well as technically adequate (Heimer, 1985).

The form of the contract is also likely to vary with the nature of the exchange involved. Macneil argues that the more complex the exchange, the more the contract will need to order the relations between the parties, rather than detail what is to be exchanged:

> Planning how to do things and how to structure operating relations rather than simply defining what is to be exchanged has come to dominate a lot of modern contracts . . .

There is an increasing concern in legal thinking for what it is that contracts are intended to achieve, rather than for the detailed sets of rights and duties that they contain (Atiyah, 1979). The argument of legal thinkers who have studied contracts has increasingly tended to emphasise the importance of solidarity, reciprocity and trust rather than the formal rights and duties embodied in the written terms of a contract. The precise distribution of formal obligations does not reflect the reality of exchanges in which parties must maintain extended rather than discrete relationships. The contract then becomes the basis on which continuing relations are negotiated, rather than a detailed statement of the nature of the relationship. Empirical studies have also found that parties to contracts in business do not adhere to the letter of the agreement where it is felt that do so would damage relations or reputations. Problems tend to be resolved by negotiation rather than litigation (Macauley, 1963, 1985; Beale and Dugdale, 1975; Gordon, 1985; Vincent-Jones, 1989).

The extended nature of complex contractual relationships influences the way that contracts are monitored, the way that failure to meet responsibilities is dealt with, and the way that disagreements between the parties to the contract are resolved. The longer the contractual relationship is to last, the more likely it is to be self-enforcing since the parties will value the relationship. Co-operation is easier the stronger a shadow the future casts on the present, as Axelrod's (1984) work has shown. It is not necessarily the case that there will need to be more extensive contracts the more important the matters involved or the longer the contract relationship is to be. Colson (1975) argues that it is necessary for there to be a degree of ambiguity in order for social systems to maintain their adaptability; the same is true of contractual relationships. As Gordon (1985) argues:

> In bad times parties are expected to lend one another mutual support, rather than standing on their rights; each will treat the other's insistence on literal performance as wilful obstructionism; if unexpected contingencies occur resulting in severe losses, the parties are to search for equitable ways of dividing the losses; the sanction for egregiously bad behaviour is always, of course, refusal to deal again . . . expectations of mutual advantage (narrowly conceived), reinforced only by coercive state enforce-ment of property and contract rights, fashion insufficiently durable bonds to induce co-operative social action on any large scale . . .

The identity of the parties involved and the continuation of the relationship are important in contractual agreements of any complexity and permanence. The contract process is not anonymous and fully specified.

The meaning of contracts is not self-evident, and the way that they are interpreted will depend upon the institutional framework that is created to govern the relationships between the clients, contractors and others involved in the contract relationship. It is, in practice, rare to resort to legal remedies in order to deal with disagreements. The contract itself requires a framework beyond the purely legal system if it is satisfactorily to be maintained. North argues that informal constraints, such as socially sanctioned behavioural norms or internally enforced standards of conduct, will be important in ensuring that contracts are able to work effectively. The contract culture that is emerging in the public sector will need to develop within an institutional framework that seeks to minimise the costs of transactions by developing trust-based relationships. A move to contracts requires more than a formal change in the basis of relationships.

Organisation theory and networks

Organisation theory also has a contribution to make to the understanding of the more differentiated institutional structure that is now coming to characterise the management of the public service. The move to the decoupling of hierarchical relationships has been a means both of creating and managing more complex market-based structures in the private as well as the public sector. Markets are increasingly seen as chains of enduring relationships involving a variety of forms of exchange. Enterprises are using external sources for goods and services where they would previously have produced what they needed internally. There is a more varied range of contractual forms being developed in the management of labour, such as sub-contracting and the use of consultants. Some industries, notably the building industry, have long been organised through an extensive set of contracts and subcontracts (Beardsworth *et al.*, 1988). Eccles (1981) has characterised the organisation of the building industry as the creation of quasi-firms. Handy (1989) has argued that organisations will increasingly take a 'shamrock' form, comprising the three leaves of the core organisation, peripheral employees on less favourable contracts than those employed in the core, and external contractors bought in as and when necessary. Others have proposed the model of the flexible firm, arguing the need for functional and numerical flexibility of the workforce

John Child (1987) has provided a characterisation of the forms of inter-organisational relationship that are developing between companies in particular industrial sectors, distinguishing five types, in addition to the integrated firm:

The semi-hierarchical mode in which the organisation is divided into semi-independent sections, with the centre providing integration and acting as a holding company. The various sections of the organisation act at arm's length from each other, with relationships organised on a quasi-market basis.

The co-contracting mode, with a set of formally independent companies engaging in continuing relations with each other, and sharing information and costs.

The coordinated contracting mode, in which a prime contractor coordinates a range of other subcontractors, as in the case of Eccles's quasi-firm.

Coordinated revenue links, involving franchises, licensing and similar forms of relationships.

Spot networks, involving relationships between organisations that do not involve any recurring relationship.

New patterns of contract, such as 'turnkey' and 'build-operate-transfer' contracts, are being devised to make the new forms of relationship effective.

These developments in organisational theory and practice introduce a third concept that operates alongside markets and hierarchy, namely networks. It is traditional to think of organisations as having clear boundaries, but the sort of developments that we have discussed above involve a blurring of the organisational boundary, and emphasise the continual creation and maintenance of relationships. The focus of study shifts from the structure of the organisation to the process of organising and the network.

The more complex and specialised technology and knowledge become, the more difficult it is even for large organisations to be able to directly employ all the skills that they need to operate effectively. Strategic alliances will tend to be necessary where there are advantages to be gained by vertical integration, either backwards or forwards, and where there are economies of scale or of scope. The effective development of networks has shown that it is possible to realise the gains of integration and scale without engaging in the creation of large organisations. Networks are seen as lying between organisations and markets and making it possible to gain the advantages of both. The distinction between organisations and markets has become less valid as markets come to be structured in a way that makes them resemble organisations and organisations come to be structured in a way that makes them resemble markets.

Just as within organisations we can now conceive of various forms of quasi-market operating, for example through the use of internal trading processes, so the market can be understood as a quasi-organisation.

FIGURE 2.1   **The organisation–market continuum**

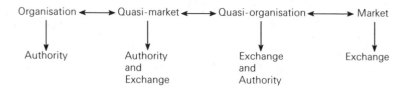

Market and organisation are then seen as being the ends of a continuum rather than binary opposites.

Networks are inherently less stable than the sort of integrated hierarchies that have characterised government organisations, and there will be a need to develop stabilising mechanisms to ensure that they do not break down. These mechanisms may consist, for example, of informal relationships between the members of different units in the network, informal rule systems or planning and information systems. Coordination may require the development of independent organisations that act to integrate the network or to provide information, for example audit, inspection and regulation bodies that monitor the quality of performance. The nature of networks is likely to be subject to greater change than the integrated organisation, and indeed they are more likely to be established in those sectors that are subject to rapid change. The sorts of markets that are being developed in the public sector will need clear mechanisms that ensure that the benefits of competition can be gained, and that will often mean the development of effective networks and networking mechanisms.

Institutional change

The organisational, legal and economic theories discussed above point to a number of problems that will have to be solved if the new institutional framework of public service management is to operate effectively. The key issues that arise relate to information, incentives, trust, quality and risk. The traditional approach to public sector management dealt with these issues mainly through an emphasis on professionalism, hierarchy, self-sufficiency, incremental patterns of planning and budgeting, and the departmental pattern of organisation. The culture of markets and contracts will require a different set of institutions.

Information

If information is free, complete, and equally available to all, then managing through contracts and market mechanisms will be relatively straightforward. It will be easy for the client to know whether the contractor has performed, and opportunism will not be possible for either side. Transactions will be relatively costless and the market more effective than hierarchy. Contracts will be easy to write and can cover every contingency. It is more likely, in practice, that information will be relatively costly to obtain, that it will be differentially distributed between their parties to an agreement, and that it will be incomplete. The greater is social complexity and variation, the more necessary it is that there should be detailed information for decision making, but the greater will be the cost of creating and maintaining information systems.

Where one party possesses information that is not available to the other, or is not available without high cost, then there are potential problems of moral hazard and adverse selection. Moral hazard involves the inability of the person letting a contract to be able fully to assess the extent to which results follow from the action of agents. For example, it may be difficult, without excessive levels of inspection, to determine whether the fact that streets are littered is a result of the fact that the person paid to clean them did not do so, or that they have been littered after having been cleaned. The greater the difficulty of making the judgement the greater the incentive for the agent not to carry out the work. Adverse selection refers to lack of knowledge before the event, when it may be difficult to know how potential contractors will behave. Poor performers will attempt to conceal the fact, and will be able to win some contracts.

Monitoring and incentives

Since it cannot be assumed that contractors, whether internal or external, will necessarily perform according to the terms of the contract, then principals will need some means of ensuring performance by agents. The principal may attempt to ensure performance by actually checking on whether the work has been done, through one or another form of inspection. Monitoring presents a number of problems. First, unless there is a clear physical product it may be difficult to tell whether or not the work has been done adequately, or, indeed, whether it has been done at all. If one orders physical supplies, it is fairly straightforward to tell whether they have been delivered or not, although it may still be difficult to determine whether or not they meet the required quality levels. The market for diamonds nicely illustrates the problems that can arise even when there is a very obvious physical product (Kenney and Klein, 1983). When diamonds are bought in their uncut form they are sold in 'sights', which are not examined in detail by the purchaser, because the difficulties of quality grading make that too costly to be undertaken. In this case the system operates on the basis of strongly developed trust between the buyer and the seller based upon repeated interaction. Similar procedures have been identified in other markets, such as that for wholesale fish (Wilson, 1980).

Quality monitoring is difficult in the case of many professional services. Clients may have great difficulty in knowing whether or not the lawyer who acts on their behalf has actually carried out the work required. Professional autonomy may enhance the problem, as, for example, in the case of doctors. Significant monitoring difficulties are presented in the case of services in which it is only possible to assess the degree to which the service has been delivered on the basis of judgement. What is to count as evidence of satisfactory performance will itself be a matter of debate in many cases, for example it is possible to engage in almost endless debate about the quality of education or of social care. Quality monitoring encounters additional difficulties in the public sector because its nature may be a justifiable matter of political debate. It is possible to see the same service as being either of poor or good quality depending on one's political values. Quality is likely to become a crucial battleground in the confrontation between the manager and the professional, and between politicians and public servants (Walsh, 1991).

It may be extremely expensive to monitor contract performance. A service that is delivered in a number of widely spread locations, and over an extended period of time, may require a large number of inspectors if it is to be monitored effectively. The costs of monitoring may be increased where the service requires technical or professional skill which is expensive to employ. The contracting out of professional services may require the employment of monitoring staff who have a professional training and who are capable of assessing the work of the contract professionals. One could, of course, contract out the monitoring, but there is an obvious danger of an infinite regress. The costs of monitoring services may be greater than any savings that are made as a result of the introduction of market processes.

The more effective is the structure of positive incentives for the contractor to perform, the less need there will be for monitoring and maintenance. Many of the changes that have been introduced in the management of the public service have been intended to change the motivation of managers and staff, so that less direct monitoring is necessary. The devolution of financial control, for example, is intended to give managers incentives to control their expenditure more effectively. If managers have the ability to use any money that they save in one year or to carry it to the next, then there might be expected to be more imaginative attempts to control spending than if they lose any money that has not been spent by the end of a financial year. Contracts will more easily be self-enforcing the more visible the output, and the clearer the relationship between inputs and outputs, and in such cases it will be easier to have a performance based approach to payment. The redesign of the public service along market lines will also involve a fundamental change in incentives, and, in particular, a move away from traditional notions of the public service ethic toward more commercial orientations. It may well be that these different motivations will clash one with the other, leading to ethical dilemmas, and clashes between differently motivated groups of staff.

Trust

Trust is necessary to the maintenance of all social relationships, and without trust there will be an ever-present danger of the development of anarchy. A contractual system will not be fully grounded in itself, and will need supporting social conventions and institutions, amongst which will be a degree of trust. Without trust there can be no confidence that future obligations and commitments will be met, unless contracts are complete and self-enforcing, which will rarely be the case if there is uncertainty, opportunism or bounded rationality. Paradoxically, argues Hirsch (1977), a world of markets and contracts needs a basis in values which it itself tends to undermine:

> Truth, trust, restraint, obligation – these are among the social virtues grounded in religious belief which are now seen to play a central role in the functioning of an individualistic, contractual economy (p. 141).

A world in which it had to be assumed that the motives of those with whom one dealt were always and everywhere of the most venal would not be one in which either the public or the private realm worked well. Trust need not require personal liking or close relationships. Indeed Axelrod quotes, as an example of co-operation based on trust, the way that the British and the Germans related to each other in the trenches in the First World War, so that the danger of death and injury was reduced. The great benefit of trust is that it is efficient; the more there is trust the less necessary it will be to engage in detailed and expensive monitoring of performance. Arrow (1974) points out that social trust is a public good. The more there is trust then the easier it is to develop long term relationships that are self-enforcing.

It is valuable to be trusted not for emotional but for purely practical reasons; without trust

> It is difficult to share risk, raising capital may be made more difficult, and there is likely to be little sharing of information about the conditions that are important in the production of service.

The development of trust, therefore, works in the interest of those amongst whom it is developed by reducing the costs which they face in managing their relationships with each other. This will be particularly important in the public service because it will often be difficult to measure effectively the levels of quality of performance.

It will be necessary for the purchasers of service to have some means of knowing that they can trust providers, through, for example third party audit systems of processes of quality assurance, and, perhaps, at a deeper level commitment to appropriate sets of values. The danger is that the more commercial, market-based approaches to service management can undermine the traditional bases of trust, dependent as they are on service-based commitments and professional organisational cultures.

Trust is as necessary to the development and maintenance of contractual relationships in the market as it is to authority-based relationships within the organisation, though the process by which it is created in each case will be different. Within an organisation the development of trust is based upon processes of recruitment and selection, the development of organisational culture and values, the nature of organisational careers and the ultimate availability of sanctions. Analogous processes will operate in the creation of contractual or quasi-contractual relations in markets or quasi-markets. A crucial feature of the development of trust in contractual relationships is the importance of reputation. The more importance the parties to the contract place on their reputations, the more possible it will be to trust them not to behave in an opportunistic way. The danger of loss of reputation serves as a brake on poor or opportunistic performance (Kreps and Wilson, 1982; Kay, 1993).

There is likely to be a closer relationship between the members of an organisation than within a network of organisations, though the effect of large organisational size will be to reduce the degree of personal knowledge. The process of trust development in a network will therefore be different from that within an organisation. It will be necessary to develop systems for signalling and recognising trustworthiness in ways that do not rely upon personal contact (Spence, 1972). Trust will be more difficult to develop at a distance than it is when there is direct personal contact.

Trust will be more difficult to develop the greater is the number of parties involved in the system, the less they interact with each other, and the less information is available. Investment in trust, as Fox (1974) has argued, if self-reinforcing. There are likely to be vicious and virtuous circles of distrust or trust; distrust leads to action that makes distrust more likely; trust is more likely in a culture of trust. Repetitive interaction between social actors will tend to lead to conventions, which in turn become established in institutions. Trust then becomes built into the system because one can rely on institutional conventions. Change is likely to disrupt traditional conventions underlying trust, and create the need for building new bases for trust.

Quality

The ability to monitor contractual performance will vary with the nature of the product involved. The more objective the product the more possible it will be to assess whether or not the contractor has met the terms of the contract. Economists distinguish three types of products, search goods, experience goods and credence goods (Nelson, 1970). It is possible largely or completely to evaluate search goods before they are purchased, that is before we enter into a contract. So, for example, we can evaluate the quality of many household goods, and even more complex goods such as houses, before we purchase. Experience goods cannot be evaluated before we purchase them, but only assessed in the process of use, as when we buy a meal in a restaurant, or visit the cinema or theatre. Credence goods may be difficult for us to evaluate at all, and we may simply believe that we either have or have not received a proper service on the basis of no clear evidence. Professional services will frequently leave the lay person in this position. The distinction between search, experience and credence goods involves two dimensions of the quality judgement, namely the degree to which it is possible to make an objective judgement of the quality of a product, and the time at which the evaluation may be made.

The more we are dealing with material goods the easier it is to make judgements on quality before the event, because it is possible to write more objective specifications and to assess whether or not the product matches up to them, for example by laboratory testing. In the case of services it is more difficult to give objective descriptions, and prior testing will be difficult because the product is experienced as it is used. It will also be more difficult to monitor the quality of services because the process of delivery and the relationship with the service provider cannot easily be separated from the service itself. The service provider and the service cannot be separated. Services are inherently goods that can only be assessed in the process of, or after, use and for which objective standards are difficult to state. There is relatively little experience of writing contracts for services, compared with that relating to the production of material goods, and a key issue that arises in the development of contracts and markets in the public service is that of how contracts can be written that will ensure that quality services are delivered.

Where it is difficult to develop effective measures of quality then it may be difficult to tell the difference between quality deterioration or improvement and efficiency effects. Quality may well be measured in terms of inputs, such as numbers of teachers or of medical staff. Under certain conditions, increasing competition may lead to higher prices and reduced efficiency, because increased expenditure is used to try to signal that one is providing higher quality than competitors, for example, in health (Donaldson and Gerrard, 1993). In practice this may simply mean that each of the providers is able to work less hard. The search for independent performance indicators is therefore an integral part of the development of a market approach to management in the public service, because it is necessary to distinguish between differences of quantity and of quality. The search for performance indicators is an attempt to move services from being credence to being search goods or, at worst, experience goods.

Quality judgement may be possible before the event, in which case it will be easier to make contracts, because the availability of information makes completeness more possible. In cases where it is only possible to assess the quality of goods and services after the event, then it may be difficult to make contracts. Warranty and guarantee procedures can serve to make contracts feasible where quality can only be assessed after the event, but there will be many instances in which such procedures are difficult, for example in many professional services or health care. The result of this difficulty may be that there is an increase in litigation as has happened in the case of professional services in the United States. The extent to which quality can be assessed before the event will also influence the nature of regulation and inspection. Where it is difficult for the users of services to assess quality, either before or after the event, there may need to be detailed procedures of audit and inspection. The quality issue has clear implications for accountability in a market-based system of public service delivery.

Risk

The development of markets and contract systems has the effect of creating distance between the parties to an exchange. Contracts may be written so as to leave all or the great majority of risk with one party or the other, and the distribution of risk will tend to have financial implications. The contractor who takes on greater risks will generally want to receive a higher price, and providing guarantees against risk will involve costs. The client is ultimately likely to bear the cost of risks, either directly, for example through the purchase of insurance, or indirectly through the costs passed on by the contractor. Contractors, faced with contracts that are based on performance standards rather than on carrying out work using a particular method with no guarantee of outcome, will charge higher prices to compensate for the risk involved and for the possibility that there will be extra work (Chapman *et al.*, 1989).

Those devising contract-based market systems must consider the most efficient way of dealing with the risk of contractor failure or inadequate delivery. Psychological studies of attitudes to risk tend to show that different approaches are adopted depending on whether the risk is one of making a loss, or one of not making a gain. The tendency is to minimise the maximum loss, and to maximise the minimum gain, rather than make decisions on the basis of objective probabilities.

Contracts need to be created in such a way that they will provide an appropriate set of incentives and reduce the risk that is faced by the parties to the relationship. The level of risk will be high in the early stages of the development of a new pattern of institutions because the initial experience is likely to be that of the destruction of a given set of restraints, without a new set being immediately available to put in their place. The detailed understanding of the pattern of risks involved will only emerge as the new institutional framework develops and patterns of behaviour become clear.

Conclusion

The creation of an effective, market-based system of management within the public service depends upon the development of an appropriate institutional framework within which it can operate.

The formal organisational system is to be seen as a second order development operating within an appropriate set of institutional constraints. It will be fairly straightforward to develop market-based approaches, but it will be more difficult to ensure that they operate in such a way as to create efficient and effective management. In particular it will be necessary for the framework to deal effectively with issues of information, monitoring and incentives, trust, quality and risk. These issues are not independent of one another, and the particular institutional framework that is needed will depend upon their interaction.

Given the number of variables that will need to be considered in developing an institutional framework for competition, it is to be expected that the patterns that develop in different countries and in different services will vary considerably. Variation will also follow from the existing institutional pattern and the distribution of power. Institutional frameworks are not only neutral mechanisms which ensure that human action follows certain relatively predictable patterns; they also serve to enshrine a particular pattern of political power and influence. In order to understand why the development of market approaches to public service management have taken the shape that they have it is necessary to examine the political issues that are involved. This involves not only considering the macropolitics of governments and their ideological commitments, but also the micropolitics of the distribution of power and influence within organisations, for example between managers and professionals.

3 The Political Dynamics of Marketisation

The transformation of the management of the public service has a number of roots, and is not simply the result of the rise to power of politicians influenced by liberal economic thinking. The market-based approach to public sector management has been important in countries such as New Zealand and Australia, governed by parties of the Left, as well as in right-wing regimes such as those of Margaret Thatcher and Ronald Reagan. Even in Sweden, the epitomy of the social democratic welfare state, there has been a growing interest in the development of new approaches to public management, such as contracting out, and the use of vouchers and user charges (Hallgren, n.d.). The development of market-based public sector management tends to accelerate under regimes of the Right, as has been the case following the election of conservative governments in Sweden and New Zealand in the early 1990s, but is not dependent on the existence of such regimes.

In many cases the reasons for change in the management of the public service were pragmatic, reflecting either the fact that the existing approaches were seen as having failed, or increasing fiscal pressure. Like it or not, change was seen as being necessary, or, as in many less developed countries, happened on a de facto basis, as public sector services simply failed to operate and private, often informal alternatives developed. Konig (1988) says of the German Social Democrats:

> The Social Democrats are fundamentally opposed to privatisation . . . This fundamental standpoint does not, however, prevent Social Democrats at communal level – albeit frequently after violent internal conflicts – from agreeing, under the pressure of shortage of funds, to the transfer of public tasks or functions to private individuals or firms (p. 547).

Much of the development of market-based approaches to public sector management was a result of the reaction to circumstances, rather than any change in basic values.

In most cases of change a significant process of learning was necessary, as governments broke with previous traditions and attempted to establish new systems. Learning between one country and another was important. The acceptance of the need for change depended upon the degree to which the existing institutional and political system was seen as having failed. It was much easier to argue the need for a new approach to the management of the public service if the previous system was accepted as having performed badly, though the greater the degree of failure the more difficult it may be to implement the change. In the communist economies of Eastern Europe and the former Soviet Union the previous pattern of public management had so palpably failed that the need for a change was widely recognised, though it will be difficult to establish an alternative system, because the political, economic and social destruction of the past fifty years has been so great.

The extent and nature of the change in the management of the public service was dependent on the existing institutional framework and the structure of the political and administrative system. For example in some European countries, such as France, there is a long tradition of contracting out for certain services, and widespread use of the voluntary sector and church-based organisations for the provision of social care. There is less resistance to the use of market mechanisms, and they do not necessarily have strong political connotations. The same is true of the United States and Japan, and in Australia the voluntary sector is recognised as the major provider of social care services. There is an existing organisational base on which to build. In other cases the institutional structure makes it difficult to create a coalition for change, because of the structure of interest representation, for example the influence of public sector trade unions.

The party political and ideological framework is also important in the process of change. The less established is the social democratic and statist pattern of government, the easier it is to change to a more market-based approach. In the United States, where welfare state institutions are weak, it is relatively easy to make changes, for example to use contracting out. In Europe change was easier in

Denmark or the Netherlands, for example, than in Sweden where social democracy was much more firmly established.

The ability of the government to change the nature of public service management is influenced by the organisation of the political system. In unitary systems of government, such as the United Kingdom, it is easier for central government to make changes throughout the public service, whereas in federal systems it is more difficult. The system of elections is also important in influencing the pattern of thinking and policy change, and in influencing the ability of politicians to put changes into effect, with proportional representation creating barriers to change, and plurality systems making it easier.

The pressures for change, acting in and through the existing institutional framework, have created different patterns of public service management. The effects are more explicit and more manifest in some cases than others. In the case of Britain the particular configuration of factors has been especially favourable to change, and it can be taken as an extreme case. Britain adopted the market-based approach to the management of the public service early and has taken it furthest. In other countries the change came later, or not at all, and has been less far-reaching. The only country that has gone through a pattern of development in the management of the public service that is close to the British experience in its depth is New Zealand (Boston *et al.*, 1991; Wistrich, 1992).

Changing ideas

The ideological basis of the development of market approaches to public service management lies in the ideas of the New Right theorists. The New Right espouses traditional liberal forms of thinking, emphasising the efficacy of the market as a method of passing information and aiding decision-making, as well as maintaining the freedom and rights of the individual. The New Right sees the market not only as a mechanism for ensuring efficient production and distribution, but also as a moral necessity in preventing the exploitation by the individual of another. The primary role of the state in a market-oriented system is then to guarantee the conditions of freedom, within which individuals can pursue their own interests without interference. The role of the state is a neutral one of enabling people to pursue their own idea of the good, rather than the forwarding of any particular form of social organisation.

There is a good deal of variation within the New Right about the appropriate role to be played by the state, from the anarcho-capitalists such as Rothbard (1973), to more measured theorists such as Brittan (1983). In extreme New Right thinking, which has had little influence on the world of practical politics, except perhaps in the United States, the state is seen as little more than a night-watchman, defending the property rights of individuals. More workable versions of New Right thinking argue the importance of reducing the role of the state, and of the influence of interest groups on government, and the need to establish a clear constitutional framework of constraints within which government should operate if freedom and efficiency are to be maximised. Public choice theorists such as Buchanan do not argue that there is no role for the state, but that careful analysis is needed to determine the constitutional form that it should take. The constitutional frame-work embodies the structure of rules and conventions within which both market and state operate.

The ideas of the New Right, harking back to traditional thinking in political economy, were overshadowed in the post-war years by the dominance of Keynesian economics and welfarism, which had come to be accepted to a greater or lesser extent in all western countries. In developing countries, too, the ideas that were dominant in the immediate post-colonial era laid emphasis on the positive role of the state in social and economic development. The essential base of these ideas was the growth of the economy, which enabled the virtuous circle of expanding private wealth, increasing public services, full employment and relatively low inflation to be achieved. Keynesianism was based in the notion that the state could manage macro-economic conditions in a way that would compensate for the inadequacies of the market. The micro-economic perspective that characterises the New Right was overshadowed by macro-economic thinking.

The expansion of the welfare state involved the extension of citizenship into social rights, on the grounds that full membership of society involved access to the basic goods that made effective involvement in social and community life possible (King and Waldron, 1988). The notion of citizenship that was developed was based upon participation, as opposed to the contractarian, exchange-based approach that has gained ground in the 1980s (Walsh, 1994). The degree to which Keynesianism and the institutions of the welfare state were adopted varied from one country to another, but the general result was the rapid growth of state activity and state provision of services. The basic policies of governments, whether of Right or Left, tended to converge on a common acceptance of the role of the state, both in managing the economy and providing public services. Planning and authority-based bureaucracy were seen as having, at the very least, an important part to play alongside the market. The pattern varied from the more market-based emphasis of the United States, to the highly state-controlled British case, but the direction of change was common (Esping-Anderson, 1990).

The overheating of the world economy in the late 1960s and the early 1970s and the oil crisis following the Yom Kippur War, undermined the traditional system of polico-economic management. Virtuous circles began to give way to vicious circles of economic decline. Unemployment rose rapidly, as did inflation, and the established certainty of the trade-off between the two, formalised in the Phillips curve, broke down. The result was 'stagflation', the supposedly impossible combination of recession and inflation. The effect on public services was particularly strong because the late 1960s and the early 1970s had been a period of especially rapid public sector growth, which had become built into expectations and patterns of budgeting. An assumption of growth had been established. The public service was also more affected by inflation than the manufacturing sector, because it was not so easy to raise productivity, or to reduce levels of provision.

The extent of the crisis varied from one country to another, being most severe in those, like New Zealand, Australia and Great Britain, which had most assiduously built the welfare state but given least attention to economic investment, and in the countries of the developing world. Public spending was widely argued to be a major factor in the economic failure of the 1970s, and the institutions of the welfare state came to be seen, and not only by politicians of the Right, as destroying incentive and weakening competitiveness. In other cases, such as Sweden or West Germany, where government provision of service had grown but the government had also encouraged industrial investment and development, the crisis was less severe, and the perception of the failure of state activity less marked.

The crisis of the 1970s was seen as one of politics as well as economics, the more so the greater the role that government had played in the years of post-war growth. The criticisms of the extreme Left and those of the liberal Right looked remarkably similar. The Left argued that there was a crisis of legitimation, because the role of the state had to expand to prevent the unrest that would otherwise threaten the capitalist economy, but that expansion required excessive limitation of the private sector's ability to make profits (O'Connor, 1973; Wolfe, 1977; Offe, 1984). The need for legitimatory activity by the state increased as the economy worsened, and public spending was increased, for example through spending on social security. The result was fiscal crisis, as the private sector tried to socialise the costs of capitalism but was increasingly unwilling to pay the price. There was also seen to be a legitimation crisis as political alternatives, within the existing consensus, became exhausted.

The Right argued that the growth of the public sector, by destroying the disciplines of the market, created inflation and long-term economic decline. Less radical critics argued that government was becoming overloaded (King, 1975), in trying to cope with too many problems; that excessive public spending and employment was crowding out the private sector (Bacon and Ellis, 1976); and that the state was becoming bankrupt (Rose and Peters, 1978). These various criticisms were essentially negative, not offering a clear alternative to welfare state spending and institutions, but rather arguing for less of the same. The focus in the latter half of the 1970s was on the reduction of public expenditure, or, at least, the reduction in the rate at which it was growing, which was not informed by any positive move to roll back the frontiers of the state in favour of the private sector, but simply a worry that the public sector spent too high a proportion of the economic product. It was only in the 1980s that positive alternative approaches, based on minimising the role of the state rather than reducing its spending, began to develop. They were based on the positive virtues of the market and not simply the failures of the state, and were most obvious in the policies of Margaret Thatcher and Ronald Reagan.

Margaret Thatcher was influenced by monetarist theory and libertarian thinking. Ronald Reagan preferred the optimism of supply-side thinking and even more extreme libertarianism, tinged with religious millenarianism (Krieger, 1986; Wills, 1988). The minimal state, in which both believed, was not to be a weak state, either internally or in international affairs, but its strength was not reflected in its size so much as in clear control of bureaucrats by politicians, protection of the rights of the individual, and preservation of the social system through restoring traditional moral values. Other countries, while tending to be less wholesale in their adoption of the ideas of the Right, could not ignore the new agenda of market-based management, faced as they were, to one degree or another, with the problems of financial constraint. Market-based ideas could not be ignored, given the apparent failure of the Keynesian, welfarist approach. The growth consensus, as King calls it, had disintegrated.

The role of ideas, and of those who propounded them, in transforming political approaches to public sector management was strong, and many politicians were greatly influenced by the brokers of new thinking and policies. The role of think-tanks was particularly strong in Britain and the United States, though they began to emerge in other countries. Individual thinkers played a considerable part, as tends to be the case at times of major change in ideas and institutions, when politicians need support both in formulating policies and in justifying what they wish to do. The writings of figures such as David Stockman (1986), Ronald Reagan's first budget director, refer frequently to the work of Hayek and other theorists. John Howard, who took over as leader of the Liberal party in Australia in 1985, was also strongly influenced by the ideas of Hayek. Politicians with a theoretical bent, such as Keith Joseph or Daniel Moynihan, were influential in making ideas palatable to less intellectually oriented colleagues. The changes that were adopted in New Zealand depended heavily on the ideas worked out by Roger Douglas, the Minister of Finance in the new Labour government in 1984, working with a small group of intellectual advisers. In developing economies rising generations were important as carriers of new ideas. Young technocrats were important in pushing new ideas about privatisation and the role of the market in countries such as Spain, India, Turkey and Mexico.

The role of theoreticians and theoretically informed politicians was both to provide ideas and to legitimate the action that was being taken by practical politicians. They were important in justifying the destruction of the mould of state action that had been developed in the post-war years. Many politicians who recognised or argued the need for change did not necessarily know what was to be done, and the officials whose interests were tied to the old regime were clearly not to be trusted to develop the new agenda. Those who could provide a plan for, or could justify action could exert strong influence in such a situation. They had both an intellectual and a rhetorical role in providing a language within which debate could take place as well as a justification of change.

Policy learning and imitation

While policy-makers might espouse the ideas of the New Right in general terms, and at a rhetorical level, it was not clear how they were to be put into effect in many areas of government. Ideas needed to be translated into practical proposals. Policies had to be developed, a process which involved an interaction of theory and practice. There was an initial process of learning by doing. Even privatisation, which became a major plank of its policy, was hardly mentioned in the British Conservative Party manifesto for the 1979 election, and there was no clear plan or programme for change in public service management when the government took office. Strategies tended to emerge from practice as much as from theoretical ideas. Experience with contracting and privatisation enabled governments to see how these approaches could be extended to a wider range of services. General policies tended to develop through starting with, and learning from fairly straightforward instances of their application, such as the privatisation of peripheral state enterprises, or increased contracting of services where there was already some experience of doing so. Experience also showed the limitations of approaches such as privatisation in certain contexts, for example in Norway and Denmark in the mid-1980s, where modernisation of the state was seen by the public as acceptable, but privatisation was not.

A key mode of learning was the imitation by one government of another, leading to a process of policy bandwaggoning. Britain has been the most obvious source of 'mimesis'; Ikenberry (1990) quotes the Thailand deputy minister in charge of privatisation:

We are moving slowly and at the moment I am trying to float off parts of one or two state corporations, one profitable and one not. So in a way we are starting to follow the policies of Mrs Thatcher which seem to have been very successful in Britain.

Policy imitation was also important in Australia and New Zealand, both in relation to each other and in taking ideas from Britain (Boston and Jackson, 1988). In part, as Di Maggio and Powell (1983) argue, it was necessary to imitate dominant themes in the international arena if public policy was to be seen to be legitimate and effective. In other cases, for example in relation to less developed countries and Eastern Europe, there have been explicit attempts to transfer policies, for example through the British government's Know-How Fund and the aid agencies, such as the World Bank. In these cases imitation was positively encouraged or even enforced. Adoption of policies for reasons of external legitimation might involve little real commitment. Cook and Kirkpatrick (1988) argue that in developing countries: 'Where privatisation is undertaken, it may simply reflect the policy-maker's judgement as to the token measure needed to secure the inflow of foreign assistance.'

In practice it is difficult to change underlying patterns of action, and the pace of development of the market in the previously communist countries and developing countries has been slow, with much surface imitation.

Managerialism

Past changes in the management of the public service have commonly followed attempts to introduce private sector techniques. In the United States there has always been a strong belief in the superior managerial capacities of the private sector, and private sector managers have routinely been brought in to manage public sector organisations. Ronald Reagan followed a fairly traditional path, though with greater commitment than, for example, Richard Nixon, when he appointed the Grace Commission – the President's Private Sector Survey on Cost Control (Goodsell, 1984) – which laboured mightily to discover waste, recommended privatisation and the use of private sector accounting and planning techniques, and imported more representatives of the private sector into government.

The import of private sector managers was not new in Britain either. The Heath government of the early 1970s brought private sector managers into government to some degree, but the effect was limited because of the shift to interventionism in the face of economic problems. Margaret Thatcher had more success. She started in a low-key way by bringing Sir Derek Rayner into government to conduct what came to be known as the Rayner scrutinies, searching for ways of reducing waste and increasing efficiency in the Civil Service. Another early development of managerialism was Michael Heseltine's introduction of the Management Information System for Ministers (MINIS) at the Department of the Environment, in order to allow politicians to know more clearly what civil servants were doing and to enable them to exercise greater control. These developments were essentially continuations of traditional managerialist approaches to public service management.

The new form of managerialism that has developed in the 1980s and 1990s has had a number of variants. First there was the attempt to gain greater political control over the bureaucracy, which was increasingly distrusted by politicians both of the Right and the Left. Because the policies that were followed by parties of different complexions were often not all that different there was not a great deal of difficulty, however politicians committed to radical change greatly disliked the traditional public official. Margaret Thatcher and Ronald Reagan were both hostile to civil servants, and attempted systematically to deprivilege them, for example through keeping pay down and changing pension entitlements.

The assertion of political control, and the development of new methods for monitoring the action of bureaucracies, was seen as crucial to changing the management of the government. In New Zealand the changed management of central government was intended to increase its transparency, through the development of a contract form of relationship between department heads and ministers and the specification of output targets. Officials would be held accountable to a much greater degree because they would be committed to specific targets, and ministers would be forced to be more precise in what they wanted. Australia introduced a similar system, as did some European countries, through in a less explicit fashion (OECD, 1990; 1992). More generally, performance-based management systems have been developed. The attempt to introduce transparency by separating politics and management is most explicit in the agency form of operation, in which the implementation of policy is placed in the hands of arm's-length organisations, with stated targets to be achieved. At all levels of government there has been an increase in the distance between the politician and the bureaucrat, and a search for greater transparency. A major difference between the new managerialism and that of previous eras is that it is based upon the reassertion of the dominance of the political level, following an era in which the distinction between the activities of bureaucrat and politican had become blurred.

The second aspect of the growth of managerialism in the public service in the 1980s was the development of decentralisation of financial control. At the macro level this delegation was reflected, for example in Reagan's new federalism, which attempted to shift responsibilities from the federal to the state and local level. Decentralisation was extensively used in the reforms of the public service in New Zealand. In the British civil service, Margaret Thatcher introduced the Financial Management Initiative, intended to delegate financial control and to bring about more effective accounting and financial management procedures. Australia introduced comparable changes through the Financial Management Improvement Programme. There has also been greater delegation of financial and operational control to schools in Britain, and, less systematically, in other countries. The changes in the British National Health Service following the Griffiths Report emphasised the allocation of clear management responsibility at a decentralised level, a development emphasised by the Resource Management Initiative.

The approaches to managerialism that were adopted varied between the Left and the Right. Parties of the Left were more likely to emphasise political control and service to the user than privatisation or contracting, because such an approach clashed less obviously with traditional commitments to collective provision and welfare. In a comparison of changing public management in Britain and New Zealand, Boston (1987) argues that:

It is the defence of the welfare state, and the desire to ensure greater equality of opportunity which, above all, distinguishes the dominant politics of the New Zealand Labour Party from the rhetoric of action of the British Conservative Government. Without this it would be questionable whether Labour could any longer be regarded as a social democratic party.

And in Australia managerialism can be seen as a means of gaining political control of the public service, rather than giving greater power to managers or introducing the market for its own sake.

In other countries, for example Sweden, where parties of the Left retained power or participated in coalitions, there was also more emphasis on the managerialist than the privatisation and contracting part of the agenda.

Political change

The development of market-based approaches to the management of the public service has been most marked in countries where the degree of political change has been greatest. In many cases the initial questioning of traditional approaches to public service management followed a change in political control from parties of the Left to parties of the Right, for example in Norway, Denmark and West Germany, Jamaica, and most obviously in Britain. It is not only change from the Left to the Right that has resulted in the adoption of new approaches to public service management, as the cases of Australia and New Zealand show. In both these instances the reforming Labour governments in the mid-1980s succeeded parties of the Right, which had adhered to traditional approaches to the operation of the state in the face of increasing political and economic problems. In New Zealand, for example, the Labour Party defeated Sir Robert Muldoon's National Party, which can be seen as representing the 'old Right'. Labour was aided by the fact that the New Right New Zealand Party took many of the National Party's votes. It was easier for parties of the Right to adopt the ideas of the new market-based thinking, but parties of the Left were also able to adopt the new agenda when they replaced traditional conservative regimes.

The new ideology of the market was more appealing the more the previous government, whether of Right or Left, was seen as having failed in the operation of more traditional approaches. In such cases, as Suleiman (1990) argued, privatisation can form the basis of populist appeals for support. In Spain, the socialist regime of Felipe Gonzales used market principles to counteract some of the policies of Franco which had involved building up the public sector. By contrast in Portugal and Greece (Bormeo, 1990) there was little development in this direction, following the return to democracy, because the dictatorships had favoured the private sector. In the Philippines President Aquino was able to introduce a radical programme of privatisation partly because of the disgrace of the Marcos regime which had favoured the public sector (Haggard, 1988). The development of a programme of privatisation in Turkey under the Ozal regime, though ultimately with relatively little success, had a similar background (Onis, 1991). Perhaps the most obvious case of the adoption of a market-based approach primarily as a reaction to past failure is that of Eastern Europe and the Soviet Union. Again, in these cases, the development of market approaches has a rhetorical as much as an economic purpose. The market has been an ideological category through which to criticise the past.

There has been less change in public service management where previous policies could not be argued to have failed. In Austria, for example, Keynesianism was adapted to deal with difficulties, and there was no conservative challenge, with the socialist party staying in power throughout the 1980s. The development of market-based approaches to management has been dependent upon a significant break in political continuity, and in many European cases there was not such a break in the 1980s. In the less developed countries it was also difficult to make changes while there was continuity of government, for example in India, where Rajiv Gandhi and his successors found that the need to hold together existing coalitions prevented any rapid development of market-based approaches to public sector management. Insofar as market-based approaches have developed in such cases they have been dependent on a slow, though steady, erosion of consensus, for example in Sweden and Norway. By the early 1990s the ideological atmosphere was beginning to change even in these countries, for example in Sweden where a New Right conservative party committed to sweeping away the welfare state was elected to power. In practice, without a significant break in political continuity, it is unlikely that there will be major change in the way that the public service is managed.

Political and electoral systems

The attempt to introduce new approaches to public service management was influenced by differences in political and electoral systems. In the relatively oppositional Anglo-Saxon polities of Britain, the United States, and New Zealand, which operate a plurality voting system, political control can be gained on the basis of a relatively small proportion of the vote. Confrontation between ideas is likely to be deeper and more explicit than in the more consensual, proportional representation-based, democracies of Europe, which are more characterised by coalition and compromise. The nature of the electoral system ensures that it is likely that there will be radical swings from one party and its associated ideas to another. In countries based more upon consensus, such as Sweden, and in which the voting system tends to lead to more representative parliaments it is less easy to develop oppositional programmes of government.

The extent to which attempts were made to change the way that the public service was managed, and the degree to which they were successful was strongly influenced by the institutional framework of government. It is much easier to change the way that the state as a whole will operate in unitary than in federal states. The extreme case is that of dictatorships which can introduce rapid and radical changes in policy direction if they are willing and able to suppress opposition, as for example in Chile and Iraq which both implemented privatisation policies. In unitary states the central government is more easily able to impose its will upon other levels of government and other public institutions. Britain and New Zealand present the most obvious cases. In Britain central government imposes its preferred policies upon local government, the National Health Service and other institutions often in the face of considerable opposition. Much of the reason for the very limited impact of the Reagan agenda on the way that American government is managed was a result of the fact that the United States federal government cannot influence the individual states and local governments in any direct way. Indeed, in the case of the United States, the relatively fragmented character of the federal government makes any change in policy difficult to implement even in Washington (Rose, 1988).

In Canada the Provincial system made it difficult for the central government to take a radical line, especially given the fear that any privatisation might lead to greater American influence on the Canadian economy. The development of market-based approaches, such as the extensive use of arm's-length companies in Montreal, has resulted from local initiative rather than national political change. In Germany the federal government can have relatively little influence at the subnational level. The degree of market-based developments in local governments in federal systems is generally a matter for the local authorities themselves. The difference between federal and unitary systems can be seen in the comparison between the approaches of Australia and New Zealand. In Australia the policy of 'micro-economic' reform has been concentrated at the federal level, and there has been relatively little impact at the local government level until recently. In unitary New Zealand the central government introduced an extensive reform of local government intended to change the nature of management to a more market-based approach.

It is not only in federal governments that the central government will have relatively limited influence, for even in unitary systems the position of lower tiers of government may differ considerably from one country to another. In the Scandinavian countries a great deal of emphasis is laid upon the importance of local self-government and its priority over other policies, such as the development of market-based management. Central government cannot, in practice, simply enforce change. In Europe more generally the importance of community and locality as the basis for government and decision is enshrined in the concept of subsidiarity. The position of local government as an autonomous institution, for example, is often established in the constitution. In other cases the character of the political system is such as to make wholesale change more difficult. In Italy, for example, the limited influence of government, the role of clientelist politics, and the fact that, in the past, contracting out has sometimes been mafia dominated, has limited moves to market-based management systems in the public service. Bruno Dente (1991) argues:

. . . privatization Italian-style is not privatization at all . . . even the measures drifting away from the welfarist ideal-type were not inserted in any sort of overall strategy but were more or less incremental changes devised to tackle contingent situations.

Generally, the more unified and centralised the system of political control and power, the easier it is to introduce new approaches to the management of the public service.

The institutional framework

The degree to which a particular institutional system of service management is susceptible to change will partly depend upon the strength with which it has been established. Weakly established institutions will be less resistant to change, especially where they can be seen as having failed. The more established any pattern of management the more it will be embodied in rules, beliefs, interests and values, the more force and pressure will be needed to carry through any change, and the less likely is internally generated change. It will be much easier to change conventions than fundamental values and perceptions that are deeply embedded in organisational systems. In the United States, for example, the adoption of procedures of contracting out services has been much more likely to take place in more recently established local governments of the south and west, rather than in the older cities of the north-east. In the more established systems the influence of interest groups such as trade unions has become more firmly based, creating significant barriers to change.

Institutional systems may also aid the introduction of market processes. It is easier to introduce change where an appropriate organisational infrastructure exists. In France it has long been the practice to contract out certain services, using large private companies, such as Societe Lyonnaise des Eau and Compagnie Generale des Eaux, to compensate for the small size of communes in the provision of services such as water. Relationships between the companies and the public authorities are close, and allow for the degree of political influence that is important to local notables. The debate over the use of contracting processes has, therefore, been less fraught. In Japan, too, there has long been a tradition of contracting out urban services and there is therefore less controversy about this approach to service delivery. Institutional patterns of organisation and public management will be more difficult to change the longer and more firmly they are established and the more uniform they are in character. Change will be easier where it fits in with a pattern of provision that is already established to some degree.

The existing institutional framework will influence the sort of changes that are possible in altering the pattern of public service management. There can be seen to be particular national models for the delivery of public services, such as the French model, involving close relationships between public authorities and private providers, or the German model, involving publicly owned 'companies'. The development of market-based approaches will vary with the specific ensemble of methods and approaches that have developed in each particular country for the delivery of public service, and the available alternatives. In many less developed countries, just as the privatisation of state agencies is difficult because of the lack of a capital market, so it would be difficult to contract out where there is a clear lack of a private sector market. In Eastern Europe similar problems to those that face less developed countries confront governments that are concerned to privatise and develop the market for the provision of public service. The result is likely to be a focus upon small-scale changes, for example the development of local enterprises such as public transport, or buy-outs for very basic services such as street cleaning. Alternatively services may be provided by large multinational companies, the export of privatisation, which is happening with water management in South America and parts of Asia.

In less developed countries private provision of urban services is as likely to result from the failure of existing institutional structures to deliver, as from active decision by the state. For example in shanty towns in Latin America, what services there are are frequently provided by self-help through an informal economy. Similar developments were apparent in Spain under Franco as urbanisation grew from the 1960s (Bormeo, 1990). In Egypt Islamic groups have been active in providing health, education and housing in the light of state failure (Sullivan, 1992). Urban transport systems in African and Asian cities, such as Nairobi, Manila, Abidjan and Bangkok are heavily dependent on a relatively informal private sector because the public service is so poor. The pattern of public service management that is developing is both constrained by and builds on the existing pattern of institutions, and the available alternatives.

Interests and public opinion

Interest pressures

Institutional patterns of organisation and management create structures of interest that will work to defend existing practice and resource distribution, as well as challenging interests that are concerned for change (Alford, 1975). In part those challenging interests may be created by the existing institutional framework. The successful establishment of a new institutional process creates legitimate actors who pursue their interests, which may lie in destabilising the institutional forms that established their position in the first place.

Dunleavy (1986) makes a similar point in his explanation of what he sees as the privatisation boom, in that many of those who lead the process are already in positions of power, where they can structure the form of change to their interests. Having risen they can kick away the ladder. Bureau-shaping becomes a means of pursuing personal career interests. Subordinate interests that are likely to favour institutional change are those that are not advantaged by the existing pattern of distribution. Equally reorganization is likely to be opposed by those who will lose most from change in the existing institutional framework, particularly producer interests and trade unions.

The obvious interest that has been anxious to expand the extent of private provision of public services has been the various industries involved, such as contract cleaners or caterers. They have been particularly anxious to open up the public sector because of the declining or static nature of the private market that they faced in the 1970s. In Britain, in particular, private sector companies have been anxious to persuade government to influence the market that they faced. Ascher (1987), in her study of privatisation, argues that:

. . . the contractors have directed their lobbying efforts almost exclusively at the political decision makers, particularly those at the national level. Their campaign has been low-key, often operating behind closed ministerial doors, and virtually invisible to those outside mainstream Conservative Party politics (p. 72).

Privatisation is generally more likely in countries with a strong private sector which can put pressure on the government, or where large international companies can have an influence, as for example in the case of French and British water companies in South America and South-East Asia. The greater use of market mechanisms in Spain, compared to Portugal and Greece, following the collapse of the various dictatorships, partly reflects the greater strength of the private sector and the banks, and their links to the other key Spanish institution, the Roman Catholic Church, through the organisation Opus Dei.

Contractors in Britain have been effective in lobbying Parliament through their ability to recruit Members of Parliament to forward their interests, and through the more general advocacy of backbenchers anxious to see market principles put into practice. Backbench pressure was particularly important in keeping the idea of competitive tendering alive when it faltered in the first half of the 1980s. Private companies have also tried to increase their ability to influence government by the recruitment of civil servants who have close knowledge of particular services. In other European countries the pressure on government from the private sector has generally been less than in Britain, either because there is less that central government can do or because there is already the possibility of carrying out government work. Large companies, such as Societe Lyonnaise des Eaux and Generale des Eaux do have powerful and well-established voices, but their interests are, in any case, taken account of within the system. The influence and organisation of the private sector has grown as the use of market mechanisms has expanded.

In many countries, for example the United States, parts of Europe, and Australia, the voluntary sector has had a strong say in provision because of its role as a major provider. The churches, as the sponsors of public service provision, can have a strong voice in the management of the public service. It is the larger and better established voluntary organisations that are likely to benefit. Voluntary agencies, for example those in Britain and the Netherlands, are worried by market-based approaches, because they are seen as eroding the volunteering ethic, and because small voluntary agencies will often find it difficult to operate in a world of formal contracts and other market mechanisms. Umbrella organisations that can support voluntary organisations, for example the National Council for Voluntary Organisations in Britain, are important in creating a voice for the voluntary sector, though with limited influence. Small voluntary organisations, which are least able to deal with market pressures, have the weakest voice. Large voluntary organisations are often well able to deal with the commercial world.

Where the private sector has a less direct influence in the development of market approaches, for example in the development of internal market procedures, then the dominating interests tend to be the academics and think-tanks, and individual specially created groups and units within the bureaucracy charged with changing cultures and patterns of operation. Academics and think-tanks should be seen as interests in their own right, concerned to forward a particular ideological or intellectual agenda. A key means of forwarding the new agenda for public service management has been the role of particular units and groups within the bureaucracy. In some cases this has been the finance department, as in New Zealand and Australia. In New Zealand the Treasury operated with a heavily theoretical approach, based on the thinking of Coase, Posner and Buchanan, principal–agent theory and the economics of contestability.

In the United States the Office of Management and the Budget under President Reagan played an aggressive role in forwarding contracting-out within the federal service, acting as a central reference point for change. There were also a number of specially created groups within the federal government charged with improving the management of government, such as the Cabinet Committee on Management and Administration, which had relatively strong support within government. In other cases, there is seen to be a need for specially created bodies that can act as proponents of the new management within the public bureaucracy. In Britain there has been the Audit Commission acting as a pressure on local government, and, more recently, the National Health Service. Other inspectorates, such as the Social Services Inspectorate, have played a significant role in bringing about change, for example through the publication of guidance and the monitoring of progress. In central government there has been the Efficiency Unit, created by Margaret Thatcher, sited in the Cabinet Office and reporting directly to the Prime Minister, and the Prime Minister's own policy unit. Australia formed an Efficiency Scrutiny Unit in 1987 and Canada formed an Office of Privatisation and Regulatory Affairs in 1986. In other countries, for example Sweden, part of the reason why change was slow in the 1970s was that there was no interest pressing for change within the bureaucracy, and existing civil servants were influential in representing existing agencies and structures and acting to minimise change. Reform is unlikely unless it has some leadership from powerful politicians who can make the bureaucracy move and unless there is also some source of pressure for change within the bureaucracy itself.

Much of the new public management is concerned with challenging the power of the producer and trying to give increased choice and responsibility to the client or user of the public service. It is inevitable that such an agenda will lead to some degree of confrontation with trade unions and professional representative bodies. Trade unions are particularly under threat where they operate through centralised bargaining systems which do not fit with or adapt well to the more decentralised patterns of control that are a major component of the development of the market-based approach to management. Again, the pattern varies from one country to another, depending upon the governmental attitude to the trade unions, their strength, and the degree of union involvement in the operation of the public service.

In Britain and the United States trade unions were explicitly excluded from decision-making at the national level in the 1980s. They had more influence in Labour-controlled local authorities in Britain and in the large cities of the north-east in the United States. In Europe the trade unions were more influential, especially in the corporate bargaining states of Scandinavia, in which labour interests are directly structured into the bargaining process. In New Zealand, and particularly in Australia, the influence of the trade unions is still relatively strong and has served to delay the implementation of micro-economic reform, particularly at the state and local level. Generally trade unions have not been a major force in the reform process, which is not surprising since many of the changes are being introduced to control labour and the unions more effectively. They have, at best, been able to delay changes.

Professional bodies, representing more prestigious groups of white-collar workers, have generally been more successful in delaying the impact of the market. Indeed, certain professional groups may benefit from the process. For example in the United States federal service, between 1980 and 1986, the number of manual workers fell rapidly, while the number of lawyers grew by almost half. In the British National Health Service the doctors have retained a considerable amount of power despite changes that were explicitly intended to control them more closely. Universities have succeeded in undermining some elements of managerial change in Britain. Other professionals have been less successful, for example teachers both in Britain and the United States have been subjected to extensive experiments in the introduction of market mechanisms of control, such as performance-related pay and delegated budgets. Even in this case, though, professionals can have a significant influence, as teachers opposition to the national curriculum and testing in Britain has shown. The evidence of contracting-out in Britain would suggest that professional and senior managers are often quite happy to lose the responsibility for the direct management of many manual operations. Professional staff are better able to defend themselves, at least in part, because of the difficulty in specification and control of the services they provide. It remains to be seen whether a determined government will be able to control such groups and subject them effectively to market processes.

Public opinion

Public opinion has not been a strong influence on the development of market-based approaches to public service management. Certainly governments may feel that they should not implement radical changes which go against what are seen to be strong public commitments to collective patterns of provision, for example in Scandinavian countries. In the United States the public attitude towards the market is more positive, making political approaches to change easier. In New Zealand it may be that the introduction of market-based approaches to management was made easier by the fact that core public values are: ' . . . not so much egalitarian as strongly attracted to the ideals of individual and entrepreneurial achievement' (Cleveland, 1986).

Public opinion has not been a source of positive pressure for change, though according to research for the Citizen's Charter Unit the majority do favour giving private firms the opportunity to show whether they can provide public services more cheaply (ICM, 1993). It is more influential, where it exists, as a force for opposition, for example over water privatisation in Scotland, but it has rarely been so.

In Britain the move to privatisation was not based upon any strong public commitment, and even after a considerable programme of privatisation there is still not a particularly strong commitment to the market. In certain cases, notably that of the National Health Service, the government must take great care to ensure that public attitudes favouring state provision are not offended. In most cases, though, the public is relatively neutral about the way that services are provided.

There is rather more evidence on the attitude to privatisation than patterns of management. Taylor-Gooby (1986) finds that there is no strong opposition to privatisation and some preference for private provision for example in health and education. He found that support for private provision co-existed with strong collectivist values. Saunders and Harris (1989) finds that there is strong preference for private provision of what are public services, such as health and education, which he expects to grow as the extent of private provision itself grows:

> As more and more people exit to the private sector, so those who remain will increasingly compare what they are getting with what is on offer elsewhere. This will be the case even if the absolute quality of state health and education services remains at the same level. Dissatisfaction with the state sector will increase and the desire to escape from it will strengthen (p. 28).

Saunders argues from these findings that what the state should do is move towards enabling people to buy on the market rather than directly providing services (Saunders, 1993). Evidence from other countries suggests neither strong support nor strong opposition to privatisation.

It is to be expected that people's views will tend to vary with their personal position, and that is the finding of the research that has been conducted by Edgell and Duke (1991). They find that there are generally majorities against privatisation, though there are strong minorities who favour private modes of provision. The position varies with the actual pattern of provision:

> Where state provision was the norm, privatization was rejected by the majority. Where private provision was the norm, privatization was more acceptable (p. 169).

Opposition to the private provision of health and social services in Britain was particularly strong. Attitudes varied strongly with partisanship, with conservatives tending to favour privatisation, and with sectoral location, with public servants being strongly against private provision. In Britain the Conservative Party was able to introduce market-based approaches to privatisation, in the confidence that they had the support of their own constituency.

In cases where public attitudes were likely to be particularly strong then the politicians were less likely to introduce change. In Britain the government was defensive over changes in the National Health Service, and in New Zealand the radical Labour government was slow to move towards outright privatisation, as opposed to changes in the pattern of organisation within the public service. In Scotland, where public opposition was strong, the government has had to be more careful about privatisation than in England and Wales. Generally, though, public pressure cannot generally be seen as a strong factor in explaining the development of a market approach, but equally has done little to check it.

Conclusion

The development of market-based aproaches to the management of public service have been based upon a number of factors, and the pattern of causation has varied from country to country. Britain and New Zealand are the extreme examples. In Britain a radical government, strongly led and influenced by New Right thinking, was able to develop a strategy for 'marketisation', partly on a learning-by-doing basis. Because it is a unitary state it was able to impose change on other levels of government, even against strong opposition, for example from local authorities, trade unions and professional interest groups. Think-tanks and academics, as well as political policy brokers were available to provide ideas and, in the intimate context of a relatively small London-based polity, were able to exert strong and highly focussed influence. The opposition was limited by the fact that it was widely seen as having failed when in government, and the public sector was generally accepted as inefficient and unpopular, though the evidence for inefficiency was limited. Specific agencies for the forwarding of market initiatives were strongly developed within government. Finally the government, given the nature of the British electoral system, was able to stay in power continually throughout the 1980s, and therefore to carry its programme through. A similar process is apparent in the case of New Zealand. In most other countries there was a less consistent set of factors leading to the development of market-based approaches to the management of the public service.

The process of change did not simply involve the implementation of a developed plan for reform. Rhetoric, learning-by-doing and imitation were as important as the direct impact of ideas. Rhetoric was necessary to bring about the acceptance of new ideas. New ideas became more acceptable as they were seen to have succeeded. Imitation was crucial to the spread of new ideas. The introduction of market mechanisms for the management of the public service can be seen as a process of policy diffusion and gradual institutionalisation, rather than a management revolution. It is necessary to make changes at the level of language before changing organisational processes and practices. Britain has been important internationally in providing the new market language.

PART II
THE MARKET IN ACTION

4 Charging for Public Services

Prices are the information mechanism of the market, which enable producers and consumers to make decisions on the comparative value of goods and services. In a perfect market, marginal costs and marginal values will equate to prices throughout the economy, and there will be allocative efficiency with the optimum pattern of production and consumption. Critics of the government as producer argue that there is too little use of the price mechanism in the public service, and that, where possible, the users of services should pay (Seldon, 1977). Price is seen as the most appropriate mechanism for enabling choices to be made and preferences to be disclosed, since it allows the direct comparison of one alternative with another through the use of money as a common measure, and makes opportunity costs clear. Pricing may be seen as difficult in relation to public goods which are collectively consumed, but few goods that are provided by the public service are unequivocally of this sort.

The public sector is seen as not making adequate use of the price mechanism even when it is easily available, and there are identifiable individual users and clear units of service. New technology makes the pricing of services more feasible, for example through the measurement of the extent to which individuals actually make use of roads. Even where it is considered that there needs to be redistribution of income in order to allow the disadvantaged to have access to beneficial services or to services to which they have a right, the price mechanism might be used through vouchers or other devices. Where it is not possible or efficient to use prices to charge individual users in a free market the proponents of change argue that there can be internal pricing mechanisms within public service organisations themselves, that will allow quasi-markets to operate.

It is surprising that the reorientation of public service management has not made more use of the pricing mechanism. Davies (1978) has argued that:

83

. . . the normative theory of pricing has had little impact upon the perceptions of politicians and others, and the concept of 'allocative efficiency' appears to be almost completely absent from their discussions.

The position has changed somewhat over the last decade, with the increasing influence of liberal economists, who must bear some responsibility for advocating the introduction of the ultimate charge in British local government, the poll tax, which was seen as a means of pricing for services on an aggregate basis. Generally, though, despite adherence to a market perspective, the use of explicit pricing has not been great. Where there has been development of the use of charging and pricing it has tended to be a secondary result of financial restraint or of the development of other market mechanisms. In the United States of America, for example, the passing of proposition 13 resulted in a wider use of charging, and the introduction of contracting has resulted in widespread use of internal prices and charges, but explicit confrontation of the issue has been limited. Where charging has been used the purpose is more likely to have been cost covering and revenue raising, rather than the creation of a full market relationship.

For and against charging

The theoretical case for charging is that, if services are provided free, people will use more than they would be willing to pay for, and there will be waste because of misallocation of resources. The production of free or subsidised goods will be greater than is desirable because the full opportunity cost will not be considered. The wastefulness will be enhanced because of the need for officials to run the system of rationing that is likely to develop, as a result of the difficulty of producing sufficient to meet an unwarranted level of demand. Public choice problems will be increased because of the lack of the information that effective prices would provide. Bureaucrats and politicians will be able to expand the supply of public services beyond the levels that would prevail in a price-governed market. The establishment of markets for public services, in which price was used to reflect demand, would reduce the need for rationing, eliminate the need for extensive bureaucracy, and reduce the power of the bureaucrats and politicians. Where it is not possible to privatise the production and distribution of services then mechanisms such as vouchers can be introduced to discipline the producers, through giving purchasing power to the service user. All goods have prices in practice, that is the values that are forgone in producing the particular good, and everybody is worse off if the wrong pattern of goods is produced. In theory, at least, the gainers in a more optimal system could always compensate the losers, with net gains in welfare resulting.

The lack of a set of efficient prices for public services can be seen as leading to unintended subsidy. As Rose and Falconer (1992) argue for the case of school meals:

> . . . the subsidy in meals sold well below cost is negatively redistributive giving a boon to children whose parents are deemed able to pay. The subsidy is largely financed by families without children or parents whose children do not take a school meal. Overall 52 per cent of expenditure on school meals subsidises children who are not in poor families.

Similar examples of unintended subsidy occur in most areas of public spending, often with the less well-off subsiding the better-off. In education, for example, it can be argued that the subsidisation of higher education from general taxation effectively involves a transfer of income from those who do not to those who do go on to university. Public transport subsidies may serve to subsidise those who are able to live in the suburbs at the expense of those who must live in the city. Clear pricing, according to its proponents, would make the subsidy apparent and lead to more rational decision-making.

The reasons that justify charging do not derive only from macro-economic theory. Seldon makes the argument in terms of the politics of the bureaucracy:

> Charging puts the suppliers – politicians and bureaucrats – face to face with the customers who feel the power of people who pay, who know they pay, and who know how much they pay. Politicians and bureaucrats have a more comfortable (because less demanding) and more powerful (because less accountable) life

when customers are more distant, less informed and less well placed to complain – that is when they pay taxes.

The existence of prices and charges creates greater transparency in the political system. Charging, on this argument, can be seen as making a contribution to the development of democracy, and the liberal Right would argue that the market, with its multitude of free choices by the consumer, is superior to the formal political process in the promotion of democracy. Charging serves to eliminate the phenomenon of over-supply of public services identified by public choice theorists. It will force the politicians to confront patterns of vested interest, which is seen as one reason why there has been little willingness to confront the issue of pricing and charging.

In practice pricing and charging can be introduced for reasons other than the development of effective market processes. Parker outlines a range of purposes for which charges may be used. Prices and charges may have a symbolic role, to express an ideological position. They may be used to prevent abuse through frivolous or wasteful usage, to reduce costs to the public purse through revenue raising, to deter usage, or to concentrate resources on priority services. Charges may also be seen as a way of reducing the stigma that might otherwise apply to the use of public services. They may be used to serve as signal of the quality of the service, since low valuation is likely to be placed on services that are free to the user. There is also evidence that people would generally choose, at least in theory, to have user charges imposed or increased rather than to pay increased taxes, even though in practice there may be opposition to any specific charge.

A major justification of the use of the price mechanism is that the individual user will exit from markets in which they do not consider that they are getting value for money, and that this change in demand will act as an incentive on the producer. The variety of consumers' marginal valuations is likely to change too rapidly and to vary too greatly between individuals to be managed through administrators' rationing decisions.

The arguments for pricing and charging are clearly strong. Even within a planned system it is necessary to be able to make decisions on the amount of various services that are to be produced even if the price mechanism is not actually used for distribution. Indeed, much of socialist economics has been taken up with the issue of how to determine shadow prices within a planned system. Within an essentially market economy the case for charging is even stronger.

The limits of charging

The case for charging and pricing is not self-evident and incontrovertible. Even where it is possible to establish charging it is not always obvious what the basis of the charge should be. Where there are very low or zero marginal costs in running a facility, as may be the case for parks or open spaces, then the introduction of charges may reduce efficiency, by leading to lower levels of usage while making little difference to net costs. Charges may also be inappropriate where they are low relative to the costs of collection, an argument that has been made for not pursuing those with low poll tax arrears. The cost of charging may be considerable.

The application of charging, for example in aspects of health provision, may lead to undesirable patterns of usage. Maynard (1988), discussing the National Health Service, argues that:

> . . . prices are an expensive substitute for taxation and may have ambiguous, if not perverse, effects on incentives and the behaviour of users and providers.

It is also possible to make a case against charging on a normative basis, arguing that it is wrong to charge for certain public services, however possible it may be. It can be maintained that some services are so basic that to charge for them would be morally offensive. The most obvious instance of this argument is the case of the National Health Service in Britain, for which the question of charges has been seen as involving fundamental ethical issues. Though it has been possible to make charges, and significantly to raise them, for prescriptions, dentistry, and eye testing, the core of the National Health Service, health provision in hospitals and by general practitioners, is free. The proportion of the costs of the National Health Service that has been covered by charges has always been less than five per cent. It can also be argued to be inappropriate to charge for services which people are required to use, for example schooling. Charging may erode altruism, as some evidence from the United States suggests, and create motives that undermine the commitment to the public interest, with public servants providing the services that maximise income rather than welfare.

It is also possible to make the case against charging on efficiency grounds. Charging may lead to under-use of merit goods, that is services that we want to encourage individuals to use to the benefit of all. It is feasible to argue that many goods that are produced by public services, such as education, health and social services, have a merit component. The universalist argument against means testing as a method of assessing the right to receive merit goods on a subsidised basis is that it will lead to social divisiveness and stigma. Those whom one would most want to use a service may be precisely those who are most likely to be put off by the imposition of a charge, for example the very poor. Charging for inoculation, for example, may create a disincentive to those most prone to disease. All are disadvantaged as disease then spreads.

Charges will only meet the criteria of economic efficiency where they have an appropriate relationship to the level of output, which, as some public choice theorists argue, will not normally be the case. Charges will only act in the way that prices do if there is freedom for the user to choose whether or not to use the service, and the individual's decision on usage actually influences the amount produced. If the charge is unavoidable, and does not vary with the degree of usage, then it is little different from a tax. Licences, for example the road-fund licence, are of this form. Perhaps the most extreme case of a tax masquerading as a charge was the UK Community Charge (dubbed the 'Poll Tax'), for which the payment bore little relationship to usage (Bramley and Le Grand, 1992): indeed, there is some evidence that there was an inverse relationship between payment and usage. Without competition, then, the public service provider may be able to provide more than is wanted, and charges may then simply be a method of raising the maximum revenue. If charges are to operate to control the market then there needs to be a relationship between price, demand and output.

A further argument of the New Right is that charges are rarely related very directly to the services for which they are levied, going into a common pool and being a method of thereby redistributing income. There is no spur to use charges as a means of making efficient decisions, because there is no residual claimant to the surplus of income over cost. Charges, that is, need to exist within an adequate framework of property rights, if they are to create an appropriate pattern of incentives. McChesney (1991) argues that there are two conditions which need to be met if user charges are to be optimal. First, the government must be a lower cost producer than the private sector; second, user charges must be set optimally. These criteria, he argues, are unlikely to be met, not least because government accounting systems typically lack the cost information that would allow the decisions to be made.

Payments, subsidy and vouchers

Opinion polls have found consistently strong support in Britain for the continuation of the provision of health services free at the point of use. Critics on the Right, though have argued that in supporting the provision of free public services, the public are being pragmatic rather than committed, and that the opinion polls conceal a degree of ambiguity in public attitudes:

> . . . most people are pragmatists. They want a good service, they are prepared to pay more to achieve it, they feel that they are more likely to get what they want by purchasing privately, but they are prepared if need be to increase their tax contributions to the state system since they are already paying into this and cannot, therefore, also afford to pay for private solutions. To take their answers as evidence of strong popular support for state collectivism is simply to misinterpret what they are saying (Saunders and Harris, 1989).

Certainly there is evidence that people are willing to pay for core public services, or at least to provide additional finance when faced with public expenditure cuts. There has, for example, been rapid growth in the extent to which parents provide additional funding to schools. The extent of private policing has grown in Britain and the United States as people have become concerned for security in their own neighbourhoods. Private insurance in health has increased in Britain.

If people are essentially pragmatists, they are likely to be indifferent between provision by the public or by the private sector. There is little evidence of a strong commitment to provision by the private sector. In practice it seems likely that views will vary strongly from one culture to another, both within and across countries. In the United States of America, where market principles are widely accepted, one would expect more extensive use of charging for public services. In Western Europe one would expect charges to be less used, though in some cases, for example refuse collection in Germany, there is a long history of charging. Public attitudes are likely to vary both with culture and past practice.

The effectiveness of charging depends upon the extent to which charges play the role of prices, and the extent to which those who are seen as having the right to a service will have access to it in the market. The pricing of public services necessarily raises the issue of distribution of resources, unless we are indifferent to questions of access. The more basic the goods and services involved the less likely we are to accept that questions of access are not relevant. Property rights cannot be seen as a direct reflection of the initial distribution of income if there are to be general rights to basic social goods. It is still possible to have pricing within a system that is concerned for the pattern of distribution, by ensuring that individuals have the resources that enable them to make choices, for example through the use of a negative income tax or other compensatory mechanisms.

Improving access may involve subsidising the user in the service, and general or specific subsidy. In Britain the National Health Service is generally subsidised, whereas in many other countries, operating insurance systems, the subsidy to health goes through individual users. In public housing in Britain it is individual users who are subsidised, through housing benefit and tax relief on mortgage interest payments. Subsidy may be operated either through the general redistribution of income, for example through tax allowances, or through targeted subsidy, such as free prescriptions. Individual, general subsidy will be more effective in enabling individuals to make choices about the pattern of services they are to use and therefore to make possible the introduction of prices. In systems of general subsidy it will be difficult to relate finance to patterns of usage through charging and pricing, as has been the case in the National Health Service, which is experiencing difficulty in ensuring that money follows patients. In practice British politicians have proved unwilling to trust individuals to make their own judgements, relying more upon general and ear-marked subsidies. Ear-marking creates the opportunity for greater political patronage and more direct manipulation of the system.

One of the key mechanisms that can be used to determine the pattern of distribution of public services is the voucher, which is seen as a valuable mechanism by many on the Left, largely because it is seen as limiting the influence of the professionals, as well as those on the Right. The simple voucher may be used to put purchasing power into the hands of the user, but vouchers may also be topped up to take account of income differences. The use of vouchers has been increasing: they are widely used by the American federal government in managing those services for which it is responsible, for example in the case of food stamps, though vouchers have been somewhat less popular under Presidents Bush and Clinton than they were under President Reagan. Local authorities in the United States make little use of vouchers, though there is increasing experimentation, particularly in day-care facilities and specialised transportation (International City Managers Association, 1989). There have also been a number of developments of vouchers for schooling in the United States, notably in East Harlem, where it is claimed to have improved the quality and variety of the education service offered (Chubb and Moe, 1990). In Britain the reform of education has involved allocating finance to schools in a way that makes the pupil equivalent to a voucher, though the explicit adoption of vouchers has so far been rejected. Vouchers have also been used for training, and some local authorities have experimented with vouchers for social care, though only at the margin.

Difficulties of pricing and charging

Public sector organisations rarely have the information that would be necessary in order to be able to set efficient prices that reflected market conditions. There is limited knowledge of patterns of use, of the reasons why people do and do not make use of services, and of the circumstances in which they do so, still less of the impact of any change in price on the pattern of use. Accounting systems are primarily intended to provide information for public reporting, and the sort of detailed management accounting information that would be necessary for unit pricing is often not available. Pricing and charging depend upon an organisational infrastructure of cost and management accounting. Much public sector reform, notably in

Britain and New Zealand, is aimed at creating such an accounting framework.

Even if the case for charging were theoretically accepted and the necessary information was available there are still reasons why it might not be used. There are theoretical problems in setting charges for services in which the fixed investment costs are very high, but the marginal variable costs are very low. Clearly this is the position that characterises former public utilities such as gas and electricity, but it is likely to be true also of aspects of health and other public services. In such cases a mixture of charges, for example a standing charge to meet the fixed costs, and unit cost to cover the actual amount used, may be necessary. Where the variable costs are very low they may not be worth collecting. The result is complex pricing systems that are not transparent to the user, and which make it difficult to make consumer decisions.

It is also difficult to set costs that take adequate account of the needs of future generations, because charges may be set purely in terms of the present, perhaps selfish, generation. In any case assessments of the future must be based upon assumptions that are certain to be inaccurate. In order to be able to charge effectively, the public organisation must allocate costs to particular time periods, but that decision is not one that is wholly objective. The prices that we should have charged will always turn out to be different from those that we have actually charged. We are, of necessity, ignorant of the valuations that others, or even we ourselves will make at another time. It may well be that in the future we will prefer that we had preferred differently in the past and, therefore, would prefer to have had a different system of valuation. Regulatory mechanisms, as has been apparent in the newly privatised public sector can go only part of the way to solving the problem because the information available to the regulators is limited, and they must make assumptions about the future. The introduction of markets introduces questions of valuation that are at least as difficult as those that confront a politically based rationing system.

It is difficult to determine the costs of many public services because of the nature of the production process. The technical relationship between inputs and outputs is difficult to determine in service industries such as education and social care, and it is therefore difficult accurately to allocate costs. Knowledge of unit costs has typically been limited within public service organisations, and there is often no market that can be used as a yardstick against which to measure the organisation's cost structure. Benchmarking techniques, which are common in the private sector, are difficult to operate, though the Audit Commission's Quality Exchange, which provides comparative cost information on local authority services, suggests methods that might be used.

The cost structure of the public service also makes accurate charging difficult. There tend to be large central administrative costs, and costs of bureaucracy and democracy, which it is difficult accurately to allocate to services. Johnson and Kaplan (1987) argue that the management accounting mechanisms of large private corporations do not work to allow effective decision making:

> The management accounting system also fails to provide accurate product costs. Costs are distributed to products by simplistic and arbitrary measures, usually direct-labour based, that do not represent the demands made by each product on the firm's resources. Although simplistic product costing methods are adequate for financial reporting requirements – the methods yield values for inventory and for the cost of goods sold that satisfy external reporting and auditing requirements – the methods systematically bias and distort costs of individual products. The standard product cost systems typical of most organisations usually lead to enormous cross-subsidies across products. When such distorted information represents the only available data on 'product costs', the danger exists for misguided decisions on product pricing, product sourcing, product mix, and responses to rival products (p. 2).

The public sector is more prone than the large private corporation to the problems of inadequate management accounting systems. Public reporting and probity have a higher profile, and auditing frequently plays the role that would be played in the private sector by management. Overheads are often high because of the strong role played by policy-making.

Much of the activity of the public sector is not directly related to service production, so that the distribution of non-productive costs and the methods by which it is accomplished are even more important than in the private sector. The strong relationships between the different parts of the public service mean that it is often the case that one organisation or part of an organisation cannot either control or know the full costs that it generates. One public organisation can create costs for another for which it is relatively unaccountable. For example people may be released from long-stay health institutions without any consideration of the costs that are imposed upon the housing or social service. The way that the police act will influence the costs that fall upon the courts, which will, in turn, influence the costs of the prison service. Central governments may make decisions that have cost implications for other government agencies without any real costing. The system character of the public sector, as a network of organisations, will have a strong influence on service costs.

The major problems that arise with pricing for public services are that the initial distribution of income is such that it will rarely be possible to allow the unalloyed operation of market mechanisms, and that consumers will rarely be free to use or not use the service. The first of these problems creates the dilemma of whether the public sector should be involved in the direct production and distribution of services or the creation of a distribution of income that will allow the price mechanism to operate effectively. Where that decision is not clearly made then it is likely that the pricing of public services will involve an ill-considered mixture of allocative and redistributive decisions. The welfare state has been dominated by the direct decision by producers about how products should be distributed, often with little knowledge of the pattern of need or use. Studies such as that of Le Grand have shown that patterns of usage are frequently very different from those that would be considered desirable, and those that are assumed, both by politicians and providers, to exist.

Redistribution raises political problems in that it confronts entrenched interests, both within and outside the public organisations. Politicians are relatively unwilling to confront the issue of prices and unintended subsidies, because of the difficulties of confronting the established patterns inherited from the past. As Rose (1989) argues:

> The simplest thing for the risk-averse politician is to leave charges as they are . . . The practice of charging in the mixed polity reflects an inheritance of past choices more than it does the logic of economic or political principle (pp. 283 and 285).

Changes in charging policy and practice will tend to be peripheral, and there is a tendency to change existing charges rather than introduce new ones. Politicians tend to be less willing to confront the issue of charging for the services that they deliver themselves, as opposed to those delivered by others.

Charging and pricing practice

The issue of charging for public services was of relatively little significance in the nineteenth century, when the activities of government were predominantly concerned with classic public goods such as foreign policy and defence. Even so, the unwillingness to consider charges in a rational way contributed to the slow progress towards the development of effective public health systems in cities in Britain and elsewhere. The expansion of the services provided by the state makes the issue of greater importance, because of its impact on distribution. Providing an increasing range of services which are not clearly priced, even if only on a notional basis for purposes of decision making, means that it is difficult to sort out the distributional impacts of the provision of public services. As Foster *et al.* (1980) argue:

> The question that must be asked especially when the range of goods being provided by the government, both central and local, increases is why should redistribution be in the form of goods rather than in the form of income?

There is much paternalism and condescension in the provision of services in kind rather than enabling people to make their own purchasing decisions on matters of public services. Even if there are political reasons for not pricing public services as part of the method of distribution, it is difficult to see how public organisations can make decisions about the way the services are provided without some knowledge of comparative costs. Implicit pricing of some sort is necessary if the public service is to be able to establish clear priorities.

There are a variety of ways of approaching the introduction of charges and prices for public services. A common distinction is between the use of charges and of fees. The former can be used where there is an individual user whose level of usage can be identified, and who has the choice of whether or not to use the service. The concept of charging can be used when there is no choice about usage, but in that case the charge is more like a tax. Charges are more commonly used where there is choice over the level of usage, for example for the provision of leisure services, and for many aspects of social services such as residential care or nursery provision. The fee is unlike a price in that it is not directly related to the level of usage, but is a standard sum that is paid by any user of the service, perhaps with subsidy of the poor. As Bahl (1984) argues, fees 'represent compensation paid to the government for expenses incurred in providing special services'. Fees may take the form of licences, for example for dog ownership or the use of skips. Charges in the form of fees are common for such services as the issue of passports or planning consents. In many cases what are described as charges are actually more like fees, as for example in the case of prescription charges in Britain which are standard and bear no relationship to the cost of the service provided. In many cases the level of the fee is set by central government, even though the service is operated locally, for example in the case of building control, and bears no relationship to the cost structure of provision or the nature of the market. Charges rarely have the full characteristics of prices, or operate within a clear market framework.

It is common to try to take account of distributional issues in the setting of charges by varying them in relation to income or other factors. Many local authorities will have special rates for providing services to people who are unemployed for the use of leisure facilities. Older people are often allowed to travel at reduced rate on public transport and receive free prescriptions. Residential care for the elderly and others in need is subsidised. Housing benefit is available for those on low incomes. There are free school meals for children from disadvantaged families. The decisions about subsidy in the public service are rarely made on the basis of detailed information about patterns of demand for the services involved, though the use of market research, for example in leisure and social services, is increasing. Objectives in charging systems have become a little more clearly established over the last ten years, partly as a result of financial constraints, and partly because public sector organisations have become more consumer conscious. There is still, in the main, a fairly unconsidered process of cross-subsidy, often inherited from past practice, so that the impact of the public services on distributional equity is as much accident as design. The issue of whether services should be provided on a universal or selective basis is particularly muddled, with an ideology of universality existing alongside widespread, but unsystematic means testing and de facto rationing.

The lack of any coherent approach to charging in the management of public services has long been recognised. In 1909 the Minority Report of the Royal Commission on the Poor Laws painted a picture of inconsistency and muddle; there was seen to be a:

> . . . chaotic agglomeration of legal powers, conferred on different Authorities at different dates, for different purposes, but all alike entailing on the individual citizen definite financial responsibilities, proceed upon no common principle. Moreover, the practice . . . is even more wanting in principle than the law; varying, indeed, from systematic omission to charge or to recover anything, up to attempts to exact an entirely prohibitive payment for the service performed.

Little has changed since this was written, and indeed the expansion of services has greatly widened the field within which confusion is possible. Judge noted that: '. . . the personal social services probably contain more variations, inconsistencies, anomalies and means testing than any other social service' (1978, p. 10).

Studies have found confusion and inconsistency reigning in other services. Bovaird (1981) in a study of charging by Dudley Metropolitan District Council found that there were rarely clear objectives for charging and anomalies in the approaches adopted. In recreation:

> It also appears that the logic of revenue raising and use regulation objectives have often not been followed through. Admission prices in most cases appear to be set well below revenue maximising levels; and regulation of demand by differential peak pricing has rarely been attempted.

Coopers and Lybrand, in a study of local environmental services, found that there was little information on which to base pricing alternatives and little understanding of the market for services. The approach to pricing was found to be incremental, at best adjusting for the effects of inflation. Pricing is done according to rules of thumb, or on a copy-cat basis. The Layfield Committee on local government financing argued that there was a need to reconsider the role of charging, and the UK government produced a consultative paper on the subject in the mid-1970s. The financial difficulties that have faced the public service in Britain since the 1970s have led to an increased emphasis on the use of fees and charges in order to raise revenue. The government has given increased emphasis to charging, and local authorities have shown interest in the extent to which they could raise extra revenue by reconsidering their charges. The White Paper (Department of the Environment, 1986) which introduced the poll tax argued:

> Charging users for a local authority service is an even more direct way of ensuring that local people can see what they are getting for what they are paying. Charging has benefits in terms of efficiency as well as accountability. Where consumers have a choice whether to pay for a service or not, those who provide the service can accurately judge the real level of demand. Realistic charging policies help to improve the efficient use of services (p. 53).

The interest in charging, though, has been neither strong nor sustained. By the time that the new council tax (Department of the Environment, 1991) was proposed, following the failure of the poll tax, the enthusiasm for charging was somewhat more muted.

> The new council tax will be the main locally set and collected source of revenue for local authorities. There are other local sources, in particular fees and charges. It has been suggested that local authorities which incur expenditure specific to their area might have access to other sources of revenue – perhaps through fees and charges or new minor local taxes. For example, tourists might be asked to pay more towards any extra local authority expenditure to which they give rise.

The view seems to be that the value of charges largely lies at the margin of services rather than as a central mechanism for the introduction of market pressures to the public service. None the less, by the 1990s, the use of charges for public services had become a consistent theme running through government thinking on public expenditure, particularly for local authorities.

The development of charging

The extent to which charging for services is possible is very considerable, and certainly much greater than the extent to which it has ever been used in practice. Rose estimated that about 75 per cent of public services were amenable to charging. Foster and his colleagues provide a rather higher estimate of about 90 per cent of local authority services amenable to charging. The level of charging in practice varies considerably from one country to another, but is well below these estimates of the levels that are possible. Rose (1989) provides the following information on a number of OECD countries.

TABLE 4.1 **Receipts from government charges as percentage of tax revenue**

Country	Receipts as percentage
Germany	8.3
United Kingdom	7.4
USA	6.4
Spain	4.5
France	2.6
Sweden	1.4

These figures suggest little, if any, relationship between national cultures and ideologies and the extent to which charges are used. As Rose argues:

Charges are relatively high in Germany, very much a mixed economy welfare state rather than aggressively free-market, and they are low in France, where historical difficulties in collecting income tax might be expected to encourage their use. Since public expenditure claims less than half the gross domestic product of nearly every OECD nation, charges appear even more shallow when they are measured as a proportion of the national product (p. 275).

Certainly charges are more used in the more market oriented culture of the United States of America and to a lesser extent Canada, but they are little used in some relatively market oriented systems, and extensively used in systems with very little orientation to the market.

In Western European countries, in services other than health, in which there is more use of insurance systems, the level of charging has not historically been greatly different from that in Britain, though the advance of charging in the 1980s has been more limited. The pattern is characterised by the same fairly unplanned and random pattern as is the case in Britain. In Japan there is rather more use of charging, particularly for local authority services, which probably reflects more the lesser distinction between the state and the community than a commitment to market forces. In New Zealand, despite the extensive reorganisation of the public services on a market basis, prices are relatively little used, as is the case in Australia.

In developing countries the pattern of charging, as in Britain and other industrial countries, is muddled and unclear. There is some tendency to charge for environmental services such as refuse collection. Charging is commonly used for transport and social housing and for the provision of some educational services, though often on a nominal basis, with little relationship to the value of the service or the level of usage. The relatively poor level of services in many cases does lead to the emergence of priced private sector alternatives, for example in the case of public transport.

Belief in the use of the price mechanism is now strong in Eastern Europe and the countries of the former Soviet Union, though the commitment is formal more than real, and the reduction of subsidies has proved difficult to achieve in practice. The public services in Eastern European countries lack even the most basic information to be able to introduce effective charging systems, even if they were willing to do so in practice, which is often not the case. In housing, for example, it is difficult to untangle past patterns of allocation. Past charges have recovered only a proportion of running costs, and the backlog of maintenance is enormous. It is difficult to develop an appropriate price in such circumstances. Much of the problem is one of property rights; as Blore and Devas (1992) argue in the case of Hungary:

Although local government has been given the technical rights of ownership previously vested in the state, these rights have been modified by the tradition of a generation which has been to vest substantial user rights in the tenants.

There is little willingness to confront the issue of change in a long established system in which the assumptions about property rights are quite different from the formal situation. Before a coherent pricing system can be established the institutional and organisational base on which prices can be based must be created. The formal ideological commitment to market principles often turns out to be fragile when it runs up against the reality of social disruption that would result.

Heald, after an exhaustive examination of the available statistics, found very little overall change in the level of charging in the British public sector in the 1980s. Rose found that there was little change in charging practice in European countries in the same period. There is strong variation in the extent to which different sectors use charging to fund services; using public expenditure categories, arts and libraries covers 29.9 per cent of its costs from charges, whereas the Home Office covers only 1.9 per cent. Change had occurred in specific sectors. In the National Health Service charges for prescriptions have risen more rapidly than the rate of inflation. The costs of dental treatment have risen significantly, with dentists covering a high proportion of their costs through charging. In public housing the rents of council house tenants have risen so that they are nearer to market rates and now cover fully, or more than fully, the costs of housing management, though, of course, many tenants receive housing benefit. Charges have been introduced for planning services and building control. Local authorities make significant income from parking charges, particularly in cities. Charges for public transport have been increased in order to reduce subsidies, rising considerably in many areas. In some cases there are charges for various aspects of police work. Generally charging can be seen to be widely spread but not to be deeply established in the public service.

The only case in which there is significant evidence that the use of charging has increased significantly in recent years is that of the United States. Income from charges and miscellaneous sources, according to Spicer and Bingham (1991), rose from 15.5 per cent of total income in 1970 to 23.4 per cent in 1987. (There is no obvious reason why the figures quoted should differ so significantly from those given by Rose, which is illustrative of the problem of getting accurate data on charging.) The rise in charging was particularly marked in the Reagan and Bush presidencies following their shifting of the burden or resourcing services to the cities. In the early 1980s charging was also used to replace the revenue lost following proposition 13 and similar votes to limit property taxation levels. Bahl quotes the following figures for rates of change in the revenues raised by charging in cities of various sizes in the United States of America.

TABLE 4.2   Increase in the use of charges – United States of America

		% Change 1979–80	% Change 1980–81
Small cities	– User charges	11.4	2.1
	– Fees and misc.	17.2	−6.8
Medium cities	– User charges	7.5	21.7
	– Fees and misc.	15.6	−9.7
Large cities	– User charges	4.0	11.6
	– Fees and misc.	18.2	−9.6
Largest cities	– User charges	2.4	8.2
	– Fees and misc.	26.6	3.1

These figures do not suggest any unequivocal trend toward charging even in the United States, and patterns seem partly to reverse between the earlier and the later period. Larger jurisdictions were less likely to increase the use of charges than fees in the earlier period, though they behave in the opposite fashion in the later period. Smaller cities were more likely to increase the use of charges in the first period though not in the second.

Overall there is little practical evidence for any clear trend towards greater use of charges in the United States. Even when they were hard-pressed local authorities in the United States did not generally see charging as the soltion. Charging did increase for some functions, but there was no general tendency to replace local taxes with user charges. This is perhaps an overstatement but seems broadly fair. Even in the United States, the country most likely to be favourable to charging, the degree of change has been, at most, limited.

Generally, despite the pressure on public finances, charges have been used more only where it has been relatively easy to do so, that is where there are already identifiable users paying for services that they use. The spread of charges has changed little. Where charges have been increased they have not generally been used as a pricing mechanism to limit the use of services but rather as a cost recovery mechanism. In most cases they are levied for services which people cannot easily avoid. In this sense the limited increase in charges has been the equivalent of a tax rise, since the user has no choice over the service or the quantity of it that they receive. There is no attempt to relate prices to marginal costs or values. Charges have been imposed more where the public sector has a monopoly advantage. This approach to charging has relatively limited effects on the behaviour of public service providers or politicians.

Internal charging

User charges have played little part in the reform of the public sector in the United Kingdom, and in most other countries, with the limited exception of the United States of America, because the focus of change has been in the organisation of production rather than in giving power to the user. The nature of the change has meant that there has been an increasing focus on internal charging, where the constituent units of public service organisations operate an internal market, with one part of the organisation paying for the services that it receives from another. Internal charging is crucial to the operation of devolved budgets, competitive tendering and internal markets.

The introduction of charging for central support services such as finance and personnel is particularly important. Previously these services were paid for on the basis of 'below the line' allocations to service delivery departments, which had little real implication for the service providers. In a complex, highly differentiated organisation the process of setting internal charges and prices is difficult, since the set of prices is inter-related, with the price for one service depending on the price it, itself, is charged for another. So, for example, the costs of accounting cannot be set without a knowledge of the computing costs that will be charged to the accounting service. The organisation must either go through a complex iterative process or resort to fiat (Audit Commission, 1994). As we shall see, a more direct method is to establish the market for internal services and let the prices emerge. This can be done by the devolution of the budgets for internal services to the client departments and allowing them choice over where they purchase services. They can choose to buy internal services and at what prices. What has so far emerged is a hierarchically controlled market. Even though it may not be possible to set prices that are uniformly equal to marginal costs within the organisation, the use of appropriate prices where possible can be seen as a second best solution. After all, the private sector does not normally set prices in the way that the economic theorists would suggest, and a system of administrative rationing is unlikely to be as responsive to the fluctuating valuation of the users of services as a price system, however limited.

There are difficulties with the determination of internal transfer prices, and there are no universally accepted accounting methods for doing so. Ahmed and Scapens (1991) argue that:

> The use of cost allocation in performance evaluation is, however, a very controversial subject. One view suggests that as overhead costs are a joint responsibility, all sections of the organisation should be aware of them. Furthermore, cost allocations can be used to motivate individual managers to exercise a degree of control over their consumption of central services. The alternative view is that such allocations move costs away from where they are incurred (and ought to be controlled), to other parts of the organisation where it is more difficult to exercise control. Although many accounting textbooks discuss these and other purposes for cost allocations, the academic view remains that costs allocation is a useless and wasteful exercise (p. 41).

The position may be argued to be different to the extent that organisational sub-units are free not to use corporate central services, but that freedom is limited. If there is no external market against which internal prices can be assessed then there is likely to be perceived unfairness.

The price-setting policy within the organisation is as much a political matter as a means to organisational efficiency, as Eccles's study of transfer pricing within industrial companies showed. Conflict of views and interests between providers and users can lead to highly elaborated systems, which are very costly to run, for example with complex and detailed time-recording and billing systems. Where there is an external market for the good or service involved then the internal charge is increasingly likely to approximate to that price, as long as there is freedom for purchasers to go to external suppliers. The difficulties are greater in the public organisation because there is no final market for many of the services that the organisation provides, and so it is difficult to follow the theoretical guideline of equating marginal costs with marginal revenue. Eccles shows that a variety of approaches have been adopted in practice, none of them in line with what strict economic theory would suggest.

Internal charges may be based upon actual or standard costs, though the former are unlikely to be effective in imposing market disciplines since they will only be known after the event. The purpose of internal charging is to provide an incentive to individual units of the organisation to improve efficiency and responsiveness, but also to ensure that individual units contribute to the overall purposes of the organisation. It is difficult for an internal charging system to ensure that both these ends are achieved. It may well be the case that what is in the interests of the individual unit within an organisation, for example the school or the hospital, may not be in the interests of the organisation as a whole. It may be possible for isolated units to obtain services at a lower than average price, but for the overall average price to rise. This has arisen, for example in the case of insurance cover where units which can get a cheaper price pull out of collective insurance policies, leading to large rises in costs to others. It would be possible to establish compensation procedures to deal with this sort of problem, but that may be difficult, costly or impractical, and the public goods solution may be best.

Capital resources have generally been poorly managed in the public service, at least partly because they are often free or inadequately costed. Managers have had little incentive to use capital resources effectively. Little thought has typically been given, for example, to the use of property, until relatively recently. The distinction between revenue and capital expenditure is often irrational, and the incentives to the proper evaluation of investment projects limited. This problem is apparent, for example, in the evaluation of information technology investment. An important feature of many of the changes in the management of the public services has been the introduction of internal charges for the use of capital assets. As Mayston (1990) says of the development of capital charges in the National Health Service:

> By providing incentives for the most effective use of capital resources to individual districts, it would provide maximum value for money of resources within the NHS, whilst still facilitating a second major objective of modern health care systems, that of the containment of total costs. This framework would also incorporate more automatic virement between revenue and capital expenditure at the district level in order to optimise the balance between the two (p. 175).

Developing appropriate systems for charging for capital expenditure is difficult and there are many pitfalls. In assessing depreciation one needs to be clear on the extent to which it results from use and the extent to which it follows from the passage of time. There are difficulties in making judgements where the services which an asset is used to produce are not themselves charged for. Judgments must be made about the values of generations to come, since they will inherit our investment decisions as sunk costs which they may have to continue to pay, perhaps for assets that are no longer wanted or which no longer even exist, as with some public service housing. There is the longstanding issue of the extent to which one can measure varying items of capital against a common yardstick. It is impossible to take the issue of values, and the need to make value judgements, out of capital accounting decisions.

There are clear gains from the introduction of internal charges for capital and central services as the basis of establishing a coherent pricing system, but it is difficult to create the information system that will make such a process possible. The development of systems that would allow effective management and cost accounting has proved difficult. There are also significant organisational barriers to change, notably the vested interests of those who are likely to lose as a result of the introduction of any system of internal charging. It is not only a question of barriers and opposition, but also of the cost and effectiveness of such services. The British National Health Service, for example, has seen a rapid rise in the number of accountants and other support staff that are necessary to manage the internal market. The organisational infrastructure of charging may itself be costly.

Conclusion

The use of charging as a means of introducing market mechanisms for the management of public services has been relatively limited. Certainly there has been an increase in the use of charging, particularly in the United States of America, but, even there, it has been used to a rather lesser degree than might have been expected if real markets were to be developed. The development of charging has been greatest where the pragmatic pressures of financial constraints have been greatest, and where the use of charges was already more firmly established, for example for health services in a number of countries. There are differences between Labour and Conservative local politicians in Britain, with the latter traditionally being more willing to make use of charging for services. The advance of charging as a method was most rapid in local government in the United States of America, where it faced less opposition. It has been difficult to introduce charges where they do not fit with inherited values or expectations. This partly explains why, despite formal commitments to increase the use of charging, as for example in the power taken by the Secretary of State for the Environment to require local authorities to set charges for a wide range of services, the degree of change has been limited in Britain.

The values that attach to the public service have a strong element of universalism, or at least are thought to do so by politicians, and they are unwilling to introduce charges, particularly for such touchstone services as health. It may be, as Saunders claims, that people would be willing to pay for better services, and there is evidence for the assertion, for example in the growth of private health insurance, but there is still strong commitment to the universal provision of service. In Eastern Europe there is a clear clash between formalistic commitments to a market-based ideology that would imply an increased use of prices, and patterns of inherited behaviour that make it difficult to do so. It is only where there is a clear pressure from external constraints, notably financial cutbacks, combined with a relatively favourable context of values and traditional experience, that there has been a significant growth in the use of charging. Charges, where they have been introduced, have typically been used to cover costs and raise revenue rather than to fulfil a market-style pricing function.

The development of charging and pricing for public services has also been held back by the lack of an organisational infrastructure that would make it possible. Put simply, public services have traditionally had little idea of their costs in a form that would allow them to create accurate prices. Budgeting is rarely done in a way that would allow a clear relationship to be established between the inputs to the service and the outputs, even in relatively simple services. Central and overhead costs are often allocated in a fairly random manner, distorting final costs. There is a good deal of unconscious cross-subsidy between services. Capital investment in building and plant and equipment has often not appeared in revenue budgets, as was the case until recently in the National Health Service. If there is to be a move towards the use of charging for service in the public sector, then before it can effectively be done there will have to be the development of an effective structure of organisational accounting that will make it possible. In the case of New Zealand the development of an accounting framework that would reflect real cost has been paramount in the reform of the public service. In this sense the development of charging can be seen as the final stage in a process that starts with the internal reform of the operation of public service organisations to ensure that they are able to set prices.

The development of internal charging and internal markets and of the devolution of budgetary control are stages on the way to the operation of real, price-based markets, though that end-point may never actually be reached. The possibility of using charges depends on the creation of the institutional framework that will make it possible, particularly the reform of the way that property rights are defined and organised, both within organisations and in the organisation's relationships with its users and other stakeholders. The development so far has been to establish prices as part of internal charging systems, within revised property rights allocations within the organisation. What has been given less consideration has been the way that property rights more generally might need to change in order to ensure that people have the opportunity to use public services, that is the question of the distribution of resources between users. The approach, so far, has been a rather unhappy mixture of universalism and selectivity. The more markets spread the more untenable this approach becomes. The development of market based mechanisms for the management of public services leads, willy-nilly, to the requirement to re-think the pattern of access and rights to service. The Citizen's Charter movement in Britain has begun to address this wider question, but the debate is at an early stage, and has focussed on individual rights to redress and the role of information. The debate over empowerment, prices and access is more fundamental.

5 Contracts and Competition

Contracts involve a move from a hierarchical to a market-based approach to the organisation of public services, in which the roles of principal and agent are clearly separated and property rights more explicit. The public sector, as client, commissioner or purchaser, contracts with those who actually provide the service, the providers or contractors. The responsibility of the purchaser is to define what is wanted, to let the contract, and to monitor performance; the provider is responsible for the actual production and delivery of the service. In the extreme the public organisation may employ few, if any, staff, contracting for all the services that it needs. Public employees find themselves faced with a move from status to contract. In the United States of America there are examples of local authorities that employ few staff and operate almost wholly by contracting for services, for example Lakeland in California, and similar approaches are developing in Britain in local authorities such as Berkshire, Croydon, Westminster, Wandsworth and Rutland. Contracting out can cover professional services such as law, accountancy and finance, as well as manual services such as refuse collection. The purchasing side could also be contracted out, so that the public organisation would not need to employ any staff at all. Contract, or at least quasi-contracts, can also be used as a mechanism within the organisation itself, involving an internal separation of purchaser and provider, as in social care and the National Health Service in Britain and, to a lesser extent, other countries such as Sweden and New Zealand. Indeed, to some degree contract has become a metaphor for the character of change in the management of the public services as a whole.

The public organisation may simply choose to contract services out to the private, voluntary or non-profit sector, or it may allow the internal staff to bid for the right to provide the service in competition with private contractors, the approach operated in competitive tendering or market testing. In the United States of

110

America it has been common to contract services out, particularly at the local level, and market testing of public services has been much less used. Legislation introduced to the United States Senate in 1987 applying to the federal government required that:

> . . . an agency may not start or conduct any commercial activity in the executive agency to provide goods or services for the use of or on behalf of the agency if such goods or services can be procured from any responsive and responsible profitmaking business concern (Lieberman, 1989, p. 31).

In Britain it is common to operate a competitive tendering system, with the public providers bidding against the private sector, though central government, in particular, has made a good deal of use of contracting out.

In other countries competitive tendering has been rare, and contracting has been used less for putting pressure on public services to become more efficient, and more as a means by which small public organisations can ensure that work which they could never do themselves is effectively performed. The contracting by small French communes with large water companies and other large private and semi-public organisations is an example (Lorrain, 1991). Other examples of contracting out include the majority of the fire service in Denmark and the trading standards service in the Netherlands. Interest in competitive tendering between the public and private sector is growing in New Zealand, Australia, the Netherlands, Sweden and other countries, though none have shown any willingness to go as far as Britain, in subjecting a large proportion of the public service to competition. It has, so far, been more used at central government level, but interest from local government is growing internationally.

The case for contracting

The argument for contracting hinges on the issue of whether it is better to produce goods and services within the organisation or to purchase them on the market, which, in the industrial context, would be seen as the make or buy decision.

The arguments that are made in favour of contracts for public services go beyond purely economic considerations. A central objective is to remove politics from the process of service delivery; politics would only enter into the setting of initial service strategy and the specification of the service. It would be separated for the production of public services. Graham Mather (1989), one of the strongest advocates of government by contract argues that:

It reduces the public choice phenomenon of lobbying for bureaucratic expansion by introducing built-in competitive pressures. It facilitates review of policy objectives by requiring regular reassessment and respecification within a democratic framework. It strengthens opportunities for quality control and concentration of resources on supervision and compliance. It regularises relationships between local authorities and competing agencies. It is a force for transparency of funding. It is compatible with earmarking of finance to measurable service delivery, developing the model of the community charge. It is compatible with specific remedies and new enforcement powers for individuals who have suffered loss by reason of government failure or by the failure of agencies granted monopoly or other enhanced powers by the state.

This is a formidable list of virtues, though there must be a degree of suspicion of an approach that sees benefit in the poll tax. What is being claimed is that the move to contracts allows clear separation of politics and management, and establishes the rights of the citizen to service as property rights, stated in service entitlements, with standards and processes of redress clearly laid down. In some cases British local authorities have explicitly developed contracts with local citizens over what services they will provide. The purpose of operating through contract is to make responsibilities explicit, and to create an appropriate pattern of incentives.

The contract process

The contract process involves the client in defining the service that is to be provided and the conditions that are to govern the contract.

There are two basic approaches to the specification of the work to be done. The first approach involves stating the outcome that is to be achieved, and leaving it up to the provider to determine how the work is done. In certain cases, such as the provision of a refuse collection service, it will be straightforward to state the outcome that is to be achieved. In other cases, such as contracts for health or social care, outcomes are likely to be much less specific and more difficult to state. Where it is not possible to state the outcome that is to be achieved then the client may state the methods that are to be used, for example the frequencies with which activities such as grass cutting are to be performed. Alternatively, when outputs are difficult to monitor, there may be a simple focus on results (Ricketts, 1987). The contract may simply state the workloads involved, for example the number of procedures to be performed in a health service contract. It is only rarely the case that it is possible unequivocally to state the outcome that is to be achieved by a contractor. There are inevitably issues that are obscure or purposes that are difficult to state unambiguously. The contract conditions will have to detail how lack of clarity and the inevitable incompleteness of contracts is to be dealt with. Generally contracts will be a mixture of method and performance, with the contract conditions stating how issues of interpretation and disagreement are to be dealt with.

The contract serves to create a distribution of risk and responsibility between client and contractor. A method-based contract will entail less risk for the contractor than a performance-based contract. The contractor will normally be risk averse, and will add a risk premium to the bid in a performance contract in order to cover the variable elements of work that may be needed to accomplish purposes in different circumstances (Barber, 1989). The risk faced by clients in performance contracts is that they will pay a higher price than is necessary, and that they cannot be certain of the quality of the service provided. It is often difficult, even for simple services such as cleaning, to assess the quality of services that has actually been delivered. For complex services, such as health or social care, the problems are fundamental. The client may prefer a fixed price contract, but must accept that where the possibility of variation in the work needed is high, it will only be possible to get a fixed price that includes a high risk premium. The appropriate form of contract will depend partly upon who can most effectively bear the risks that are involved, but also upon the relative power of purchaser and provider.

The most advantageous situation from the client's point of view is that in which the contract is self-enforcing, because it provides incentives to the contractor to maintain quality and efficiency, for example through profit-retention as in leisure contracts. The more the contract can be made self-enforcing the cheaper it will be for the provider to monitor performance. The contract is more likely to be self-enforcing the more the rewards to the contractor vary with their performance, the more their work can be checked, and the more poor work will damage the provider's reputation.

A further distinction that can be made is that between punishment-based and cooperative contractual approaches. The former are contracts that are based upon the assumption that the interests of client and contractor are opposed, and that the contractor will not act in the interest of the client without the threat of sanctions. Equally the client, if possible, will exploit the contractor. Where contractors fail to deliver then they will be punished, for example through delays in, or deductions from payments. The cooperative contract is based on the assumption that there can be a degree of trust between client and contractor, and that punishment is an inappropriate means of dealing with failure, ultimately because it is not efficient. It is assumed that failure to achieve the required result is as likely to result from the state of the world as the contractor's actions, and that the best response to failure is for client and contractor to work together to achieve results and overcome difficulties. Cooperative contracts are seen as more fitting when there is continuity in client and contractor interaction, rather than one-off spot contracts. In public service contracts for more complex services there is a good deal of emphasis on the importance of trust between client and contractor, because of the inevitable difficulties of checking performance, though punishment-based approaches are common in simpler services.

The dimensions of contracts

Contracts can vary greatly in size, formality, detail, variety and the length of time for which they run. Many of the contracts that have been let for public services in Britain have been extremely large. A

Department of the Environment study of contracting found that the value of individual contracts in local government often ran into millions of pounds (Walsh and Davis, 1993). The degree of formality in contracting has grown over time, though it varies from service to service, for example contracts with voluntary agencies for the provision of care in Britain are often relatively informal, but they are very formal for services such as refuse collection.

The level of detail in contract specifications varies with the importance and ease of specification. It may be difficult to write detailed specifications for many aspects of service, for example in health or social care, however important they may be. The more difficult it is to specify the service to be provided, the more interest will tend to shift to the contract conditions, and the structures and processes that they lay down for the management of contracts. In some more complex contracts, public organisations will only settle the detail of the service to be provided after the contract has been let, through a process of negotiation with the contractor. Variety relates to the question of the range of services that are included under a single contract, and will influence the degree to which there is disaggregation and fragmentation in the process of service delivery. An organisation can choose for example whether to let a contract for a total service such as finance, or to break it down into its component parts, payroll, exchequer, accountancy and so forth, and let separate contracts for each. Contracting tends to result in the elements of service being broken down, in order to allow separate contracts, because of the complexity of integrated approaches, with a consequent fragmentation of service.

The nexus of contracts

As the extent of contracting in the public service grows then the issue of subcontracting and of relationships between contracts becomes significant. Subcontracts have always raised questions about liability for default, increasing the difficulty of identifying responsibilities clearly. It may well be the case that one contractor or subcontractor can claim that a failure to perform effectively was the result of failure by another contractor, and that she or he bears no fault. It is common, for example, for refuse collection contractors to be bound by previously agreed contracts for the maintenance of refuse vehicles. Failure of the vehicle may then be blamed by the main refuse collection contractor for failure to collect. The complexity can be illustrated by the case of housing management in British local government. The local authority must contract for housing management and for the maintenance of public housing. It must also let contracts for professional support services such as finance. An organisation, such as a local authority, might then let a contract to a housing management organisation, which, in turn contracted with the housing maintenance organisation. Both would contract separately with the commissioning organisation, which would in turn, contract with the finance contractor. Figure 5.1 illustrates the potential linkages that might be involved.

FIGURE 5.1   The nexus of contract

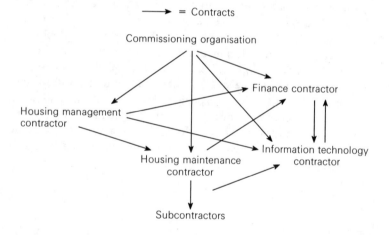

As more services become subject to contract, and the number of overlaps between contracts increases, these difficulties are growing. The move to contracts implies a degree of separability between the aspects of a public organisation's work that may not be realistic. The concept of the organisation as a nexus of contracts identifies rather than resolves the issue, and the relationship between authority and contract will need to be thought through in the new organisation of the public service.

Stinchcombe (1990) has argued that contracts can act to create relationships that are very little different from those that exist within an organisation. The contractor may be tightly coupled into the organisation, and the relationship between client and contractor more like one of internal employment than arm's-length control. As Stinchcombe and Heimer (1985) say:

> A structure with legitimate authority, with a manipulable incentive system for adjusting costs, quantities and prices, with a structure for dispute resolution, and with a set of standard operating procedures, looks very much like a hierarchy, very little like a competitive market. Yet all these features of hierarchy are routinely obtained by contracts between firms in the same sector of the market.

This is even more so when the contractors are internal to the organisation, as is normally the case in local government and the National Health Service. The tightly coupled relationship between client and contractor that exists in many cases, tends to lead to a reduced emphasis on legal rights and limited reliance on contract law. Reference to formal rights under the contract are seen as a last resort. More emphasis tends to be laid on the importance of trust and the maintenance of relationships, or as in the National Health Service in the UK, a resort to authority or power, that is the resort to the traditional organisational methods. The developing network of contracts also raises issues about the relationship between politics and administration, with the political role reduced to oversight rather than involvement.

The result of contracting is to increase specialisation, but to move its locus from the organisation to the interorganisational network. Even if contracting is internal, the organisation itself becomes a network. Different organisations within the network concentrate on specific activities in which they may have a comparative advantage. The management of contracts is then a management of networks, which may operate on a continuing or spot basis. A potential result of this is that relatively independent decisions in one part of the network may have implications for organisations elsewhere in the network, which are not adequately considered. Governance may then be more difficult. The decisions of electricity producers in Britain, and the implications for coal following the privatisation of the electricity industry, are an example. Decisions that seem to be an inevitable result of market forces and efficiency considerations may be the result of market forces and efficiency considerations, or they may be the result of prior decisions about how networks of organisations are to relate. Authority ensured a clear locus of decision, which is lost in an organisational network.

The development of contracting

Contracts have always been used by the public service for purchasing certain supplies and services, for example for major construction contracts, where the public organisation lacks the necessary skills. Basic supplies, lightbulbs, paper or whatever, were, obviously, largely purchased on the open market. The use of contracting has expanded greatly over the last twenty years, and it has been used for the provision of core as well as support services. The increased use of contracting has occurred worldwide, but has been particularly prevalent in Britain and the United States of America. In Britain almost every service that is provided by the public sector has been considered for operation on a contract basis, including such apparently unlikely cases as prisons and aspects of the justice system. The approach has been most used for those services that are obviously amenable to a contracting approach, particularly environmental services such as refuse collection and disposal. The contract mechanism is now spreading rapidly in health, social care and other social services, and not only in countries with a conservative government, being used, for example, in the Swedish health care system under a social democratic government. Contract, whether external or internal to the organisation, is seen as more or less universally applicable.

Contracts have long been used for the provision of certain services by smaller rural authorities in Britain, particularly for refuse collection, though on a very limited basis. The normal assumption, though, has been that provision will be made, through directly employed staff. The stimulus to change came with the election of a Conservative government and public sector strikes in 1979. Contracting with the private sector was seen by some local authorities as a means of reducing the power of the public sector unions, which they saw as having held them to ransom during the 'Winter of Discontent'. A small number of Conservative authorities, notably Wandsworth and Southend, contracted their refuse collection services out to the private sector. The voluntary contracting out or market testing of services continued over the next decade, though with limited impact because the contracts were small and for relatively peripheral services. Contracting was not generally seen either as efficient or a politically acceptable method of procuring public services.

The extent of competition outside central government was radically increased by legislation and government constraint, starting with the manual services. The Local Government Planning and Land Act 1980 required local authorities to compete for the right to carry out building and highways construction and maintenance work, an approach that had long been advocated, for example by the Chartered Institute of Public Finance and Accountancy. The ability to include this provision in legislation very soon after the Conservative election victory reflected the fact that work had already been done on it within the civil service. The initial impact was reduced by the exemptions for various categories of work and for smaller organisations, but the results have become very noticeable as the regulations have gradually been tightened. By the early 1990s local authorities had lost a significant proportion of their building work to the private sector and there was extremely tight competition (Walker, 1993).

In 1983 the Department of Health and Social Security required competitive tendering for ancillary functions in the National Health Service, that is catering, laundry and domestic work. As in the case of local government, this followed partly from dissatisfaction with the strikes of 1979, but there was also increasing pressure from Parliamentary backbenchers and pressure groups. The government started by encouraging voluntary tendering by health authorities, but when that was seen to have failed, it moved to compulsion. Health authorities were given a timetable for the submission of support service to competitive tendering. In other public services different methods were used to introduce market pressures. The deregulation of public transport allowed the private sector to provide bus services on their own initiative and to bid for subsidised services on a contractual basis. The government made extensive use of contracting out within the civil service, and the range of services covered was somewhat wider than in local government and the National Health Service. Central government services subject to contracting out or market testing in this period include fisheries, aerial surveillance, maintenance of the RAF's training aircraft, messenger services, research and development work, and radio communications work, as well as such standard support work as the cleaning of buildings.

The major expansion of contracting and competitive tendering followed the Local Government Act 1988, which required local authorities to subject a range of manual services to competitive tender. If the local authority won the right to provide the services then it had to do so on a quasi-contractual basis, operating an internal trading account, which could not be cross-subsidised, and had to meet stated targets that were set by central government. The services that were initially covered by the act were refuse collection, street cleaning, building cleaning, catering, vehicle maintenance, grounds maintenance and leisure management. Competition has been extended to a range of other local authority services, including professional services, such as engineering, law, finance, personnel, housing management and computer services.

The National Health Service and Community Care Act 1990 provides for the extension of contracting to the social services, with the local authority acting as a purchaser of service from its own internal providers, from the voluntary sector and the private sector. Many local authority social services departments had moved towards contracts on their own initiative, and a number had 'externalised' their own residential establishments, or set them up as internal companies with which they contracted (Wistow *et al.*, 1992). Market testing was introduced throughout the civil service from 1993, covering a wide range of services. By the end of 1993 £1.1 billion worth of civil service activity had been subject to competition (Prime Minister and Chancellor of the Duchy of Lancaster, 1994).

Other legislation had the indirect effect of putting the work of public sector organisations onto a contractual basis. The Education Reform Act 1988 introduced the local management of schools, whereby schools were given their own budgets with considerable freedom on how the money should be spent. Schools could then choose whether they wished to use the services of the local education authority, or buy them elsewhere. Further education colleges and polytechnics were given similar freedom. Schools were also enabled to opt out of local authority control and become grant-maintained, receiving their finance direct from central government, and contracting for services as they wished. It has become common for schools and colleges to contract for support services such as maintenance and payroll. Where services continue to be provided by the local authority, this is done on a contractual or quasi-contractual basis. Contracting has also been introduced for the provision of inspection services in education, with schools able to contract with registered inspectors.

There has been a move to contracts even in services that have been little affected by explicit legislation. In London the clamping and the storage of illegally parked vehicles has been contracted out since 1988. Police services, particularly support services, are increasingly operated on a contractual basis. The Audit Commission now subjects a proportion of its special studies to competition. Central government has increasingly contracted out to consultants work that would previously have been done internally, and government generally has become major client of consultants. A number of local authorities have contracted out their housing through voluntary transfers, either to existing housing associations or through the externalisation of their own housing department in the form of a newly established housing association. Voluntary contracting out and voluntary market testing are widely used by public organisations such as universities. In some cases this is done through competitive processes, and in others through floating off the internal providers, with a guarantee of the purchase of a certain quantity of service for a given period, though the latter approach is now less possible because of European legislation.

Contractual or quasi-contractual mechanisms of various sorts now affect the greater proportion of the public service. In others, such as health and local authority manual services, the contract culture covers almost the whole of the service. The patterns of contracting vary. The three major modes are purely internal contracting, competitive tendering and the contracting out of services. The National Health Service provides an example of predominantly internal contracting. In local government the dominant mode has been competitive tendering, though the use of straightforward contracting out is growing, partly as a means of avoiding the strict competitive tendering regime. Central government has made most use of contracting out without internal competition, though the market testing regime involves extensive use of competitive tendering.

The nature of contracts

The nature of contracts varies with the nature of the service. The forms of contract that have been let in local government for manual services have typically been large, highly formalistic and detailed. They have generally taken the form either of measured bills of quantities or detailed schedules of rates for individual jobs. Bills of quantities give the local authority a fairly clear idea of the costs that they will bear, although the costs of claims can be high in some cases. The danger of schedules of rates is that the contractor may engage in strategically opportunistic behaviour by putting in low prices for work that is not likely to occur very often and high prices for work that can be expected to arise commonly. In order to deal with this danger it is common for the organisation letting the contract to pre-price the schedule of work, and ask the contractor to state the percentage higher or lower than the given price for which they will carry out any job. This approach prevents the contractor making use of any specialist knowledge they might have of the pattern of work. These forms of contract are long established in the construction industry, and there has been a good deal of study of their risk and incentive effects.

Where possible the public services, which are highly risk averse, tend to try to develop full descriptions of the work to be done, and, as far as possible, operate fixed price contracts. The bill of quantities and schedule of rates approaches to contracting cannot be straightforwardly transferred to complex services such as health, leisure, housing management, social care or professional services. In the National Health Service and social care there are three basic forms of contract recommended in government advice: block contracts, which are simply agreements to provide a given range of services for a stated total cost with very little clarity on service quantity; cost and volume contracts, akin to bills of quantities, stating the cost of units of service and the number of times they will be provided; and cost per case contracts, where the price for a particular aspect of work is stated but there is no commitment to a particular volume of work.

In the case of leisure services local authorities have developed contracts that give a detailed description of the total work to be done, with the contractor bidding for a stated subsidy and sharing the income or profits above a certain level. The contractor generally keeps the larger part of any profit or income in order to encourage efficiency and maximisation of use. The complexity of such contracts illustrates the difficulties that are introduced in contracting when there is income from the work done.

In social care there is a pattern of two-stage contracting, with the social services department making a broad agreement to purchase from providers on a price per case basis, and making spot contracts for individual users as the need arises. The development of contracts for social care illustrates the complexity of multiple contracting that can arise. There is, effectively, a three way contract, involving the social services department, the individual user, and the provider. There may also be subsidiary contracts with third parties who may be providing for part of the costs of the care. Health authorities also become involved where there is a need for nursing care provision.

Contracts for professional support services such as finance, and for direct professional services such as housing management, have been little developed as yet. It is highly unlikely that the development of contracting for such services can be done using the sorts of approaches used for manual services. The approach adopted is likely to be some form of lump-sum pricing with statement of how prices are constructed. In some cases unit prices can be stated, for example the cost per hour, and more detailed approaches used. The major problem with professional services is that it is difficult to know the relationship between price and quality, since the standard of service provided is likely to vary with the individuals involved. Contracts for professional services are likely to lay a great deal of emphasis on the importance of the reputation of the provider.

The impact of contracts for human services, such as social care and health, and professional services, can be assessed by examining experience in the United States. In social care the contract mechanism has proved costly and bureaucratic (Kettl, 1993; Smith and Lipsky, 1993; Richardson, 1993; Gutch, 1992). In the case of health there have been many attempts to develop contract approaches that will control the rapidly escalating costs of the service (Smith, 1992). Post-payment systems have been replaced with prospective payment systems both for hospitals and for general practitioners, in order to give providers an incentive to control costs within the set price. The approach now is one that is based on the establishment of diagnosis related groups, which involves categorisation of illnesses into similar groups, for which there is a similar level of payment whatever the costs that the provider may incur. This approach has involved a very considerable technology of statistical and technical analysis that will establish reliable bases for payment. There have also been attempts to develop similar approaches in Britain, though with limited success.

Price, quality and risk

These various approaches to contracting involve different methods of dealing with risk and the problems of quality. The tendency has been for the client, being highly risk averse, to write the contract so that the provider bears the greater risk, even where it might be more efficient for the client to do so, for example in the case of voluntary groups bidding for small contracts in social care. The exception to this approach occurs when the client has to contract and there is a limited market. So, in the case of social care, those local authorities with a larger number of local providers have tended to write tighter contracts than those in areas where there are fewer providers and purchasers must to some degree take what they can get. It seems likely that the search for security and for the minimisation of risk has led to higher prices than might be obtained through some sharing of the risk, especially if the providers are also risk averse. As Chapman *et al.* (1989) argue:

> . . . clients who are more able to take risks than their contractors may be paying inefficient risk premiums if they are insisting on fixed price contracts. The bigger the gap between the ability to take risk in relation to the contractor and the client, the greater is inefficiency (p. 92).

The distrust of cost plus contracts as providing an incentive to abuse by the contractor has led to an excessive degree of search for a fixed price. Even in cases where there is income involved the public organisations have minimised risk, as in the case of leisure contracts, where the local authority gains if the contractor makes income, but has little to lose if there is a failure to meet income projections.

The economics of public service contracting would suggest that the government is an efficient bearer of risk. McAfee and McMillan (1988) argue that:

> What the government's attitude towards risk should be is clear cut. Like the shareholder who owns a diversified portfolio, the government is involved at any time in many independent activities; consequently it may disregard the uncertainties associated with any one activity. Moreover, because the risks associated with any one public project are borne by all the taxpayers, the cost of risk-bearing is insignificant: an unexpectedly high cost incurred on any one public project will make an insignificant difference to any one citizen's tax bill. For these two reasons, (risk pooling and risk spreading), the government should not seek to avoid risk; instead it is socially efficient for the government to choose its activities in a risk neutral way. The fact that the government normally self-insures against all risks to its physical assets is evidence that, at least in this respect, its policy is indeed to behave in a risk neutral way (p. 14).

This is an overstatement, since many governmental organisations may be small, and therefore limited in their ability to spread risk. Government will also need to take account of political issues, such as public perceptions of proper behaviour, whatever economic theory may say. At the same time McAfee and McMillan's analysis does present a useful warning of the dangers of excessive conservatism in letting contracts in the public service.

The fixed price contract is likely to have an effect on the way that the service is provided; if contractors cannot control the income they receive then they are likely to try to cut the cost of the work by reducing the quality or quantity of work done. In the United States of America, for example, there is some evidence that the setting of fixed prices for work, through prospective payment systems, leads to quality decline and early discharge from hospital, with patients going home 'quicker and sicker'. Contractors are also likely to search for an expansion of work that is not covered by the fixed contract price, making claims for variations to the specification.

There are great difficulties where quality cannot easily be defined and where it is difficult to observe. The more complex the service the more difficult it is likely to be to measure the quality of service. There may be interaction effects between services that are unpredictable. Intangible services are unlikely to be easily monitored. In many cases the results of particular services, such as certain types of medical intervention may only become apparent in the long term. It may be difficult to observe performance under the contract simply because work sites are widely dispersed geographically, or the work takes place out of normal working hours; both of these are problems, for example, in monitoring performance on cleaning contracts.

Monitoring and control

In monitoring the quality of the service that is provided under contracts, much will depend upon the information that is available to the provider before and after the event. As Propper (1992) argues:

> . . . the impact of contract specification depends on the extent to which providers have greater information than purchasers . . . opportunities to circumvent price controls exist if there is an unregulated sector or clients whose fees are not regulated alongside the regulated sector and providers have discretion over the patients they treat and the location of treatment . . . if quality is not fully observable, opportunities for cutting quality exist under both price and cost-plus contracts (p. 18).

The more likely it is that the contractors will try, and be able to avoid their contract responsibilities, the more the client is likely to introduce inspection and other forms of contract monitoring.

A variety of monitoring processes may be used, for example checking of a random sample of work, inspection of a fixed proportion of work, or the use of public complaints. It is not always the case that there is more contract monitoring when the service is more complex or more difficult to observe. There is some evidence that the level of monitoring is lower the more complex is the contract and the more difficult it is to assess quality. The most complex of the local government services that have been subject to tender under the Local Government Act 1988 is leisure management, but it has relatively low monitoring costs. Social care is extremely complex, but there is little in the way of detailed monitoring. In these cases monitoring is replaced either by attempts to shift the risk of failure onto the contractor, by the development of a more trust-based relationship between client and contractor, or by requirements for quality assurance.

In some cases the service is easy to specify both in quantity and quality terms before the contract is let and it is easy to know whether or not there has been effective performance. It is rarely the case that the work to be carried out under a contract can so easily be stated, even in the case of manual services; building cleaning and vehicle maintenance contracts, for example, are subject to significant specification difficulties. It is difficult to state the nature of the work for most professional services, indeed professionalism frequently exists precisely because it is difficult to state the nature of the work to be performed. In such cases it is likely that providers will dominate the contracts because only they will have an understanding of the work. The more difficult it is to state the work that is to be done before a contract is let the more necessary it is to be able to manage service variation effectively. In practice variation procedures are often poorly managed and contractors are able to make significant claims.

There are three approaches that can be adopted in order to control contractors in situations where it is difficult to specify the work, and, perhaps, to monitor whether or not it has effectively been performed. Purchasers can introduce mechanisms that are intended to ensure that the commitments of the contractor are credible. They can try to ensure that contractors hold the same values as purchaser and are committed to the provision of a good service. Finally the purchaser can try to deter failure by making it subject to penal sanctions.

The establishment of credible commitments can be attained through performance bonds or company guarantees, through ensuring that the contractor has a reputation which is at risk if performance is poor, or through requiring quality assurance systems. Performance bonds require the contractor to provide an insurance against failure, by guaranteeing an amount of money that can be claimed should the contract be terminated or the contractor go into liquidation, and are commonly used in contracts for manual services. Such bonds are normally for 10 per cent of the value of the contract. Bonds have rarely been claimed except in construction work, and are of little help when the market is limited, or involves voluntary or other agencies without strong financial foundations. Bonding may do little more than raise the price of the contract, since the contractor is likely to add the value of the bond to the tender price. All the same bonds are commonly used in local government.

Guarantees by parent companies are generally seen as more useful, where they can be used. Reputation is more likely to be at risk for professionals than for manual services. Quality assurance is now strongly emphasised in the letting and managing of contracts. Quality assurance systems are managerial procedures that are intended to ensure that the service will be effectively produced. The client can then reduce surveillance because they can rely on an audit of the contractors quality assurance system. The establishment of a quality assurance system in itself can be seen as a contribution to the credibility of the contractors commitment, since it involves investment in a relatively specific asset, making it more difficult for the contractor to exit from the market.

Clients can try to ensure the commitment of the contractor by attempting to align the values of the contractor with their own. In the case of contracts for community care a great deal of attention is typically given to ensuring that the contractor's philosophy is in line with that of the purchaser. Internal contracts tend to rely more upon the alignment of values than those with external providers, and the internal contractor may be required to follow defined policies on matters such as equal opportunities, training or staff conditions. The extensive use of contracting in French local services is dependent in part upon 'self-limitation of power by the private company' (Lorrain, 1991, p. 107), which recognises the needs of the client organisation, and is based upon long-term contracts. It is easier to ensure commonality of values in long term contracts, and if the contracting organisation is not primarily oriented to profit. Commonality of values may be maintained if the contractor takes over the staff of the organisation after winning the contract, though the evidence is that attitudes can change very rapidly to reflect new patterns of incentives, for example after management buyouts from the public service.

Contracts typically contain provisions allowing the client to exercise sanctions when the contractor does not perform effectively. These sanctions may involve the issuing of default notices, deductions from or delays in payments, bringing in other contractors to carry out the work and charging the contractor, and, in the extreme, termination of the contract. Clients may also use retention money, whereby a proportion of the contract price is withheld until the work is properly completed. In some cases other contractors may be brought in to do the work if the contractor fails, though this is relatively uncommon.

There are difficulties in any sanction process. The value of the sanction may be lower than the saving that the contractor makes by not carrying out the work, so that they have an incentive not to perform and simply accept the deduction. It is not uncommon for this approach to be adopted in building cleaning contracts. It may be difficult to ascertain the level of damages that result from failure to perform. The cost of administering a system of penalties may be greater than the money that is recovered. Clients tend to be unwilling to terminate contracts because of the difficulty of finding an alternative provider and the costs of going through tender processes involved. The experience of contracting shows that relatively few contracts have been terminated because of the failure of the contractor. The establishment of contracts tends to involve sunk costs which the clients are unwilling to write off. There are also legal difficulties surrounding the use of sanctions in contracts, such as defining the liability of the contractor and ensuring that sanction systems are not penal and therefore unenforceable.

The means of ensuring that contractors carry out their responsibilities under contract vary from service to service. They normally involve some combination of the above approaches, but the pattern varies. In the case of manual services in British local government, such as refuse collection or building cleaning, the use of default, deduction of money and delays in payment is common, but the actual level of deduction is low. In social care there is little use of sanctions. Monitoring of social care contracts tends to rely on requiring that providers are quality assured, and termination of contracts is rarely used. In other countries there are similar patterns. In the United States deduction of money is not common, except in health care. In Europe there tends to be reliance on regulation and alignment of values, rather than financial penalties or strong surveillance. The emphasis in contract management tends to be on ensuring good relations with the contractor.

Completeness and hierarchy

Contracts are never complete. There are always matters that cannot be precisely stated and covered in contract conditions and specifications before the contract is let. A major purpose of the contract is to ensure that issues of incompleteness can effectively be dealt with in the contract management process. The incomplete contract needs effectively to be completed at the time at which potential difficulties or differences of interpretation arise. This is rarely done by resorting to the courts, because it is expensive and tends to make the future relationship of client and contractor difficult. Even when there are fundamental disagreements, it is rare for either party to be willing to take legal action. Most contracts do contain some formal arbitration mechanism, though, again, it is rarely invoked. Where there is resort to arbitration it tends to be done on a relatively informal basis or perhaps by the use of private arbitrators, with both sides committing themselves to accept the decision of the arbitrator.

Specific sections in the contract are designed to deal with problems of incompleteness, notably clauses that deal with variation and the ability of the client to direct the work of the contractor. The use of variation clauses is very common, for example in cleaning and ground maintenance work, and often involves fundamental changes to the nature of the work that is done. In effect a degree of hierarchy is built into the contract, allowing the client to direct the work of the contractor. The operation of public service contracts supports Stinchcombe's argument that contracts are to some degree hierarchical documents.

The greater the uncertainty faced the more difficult it is to create mechanisms that will deal effectively with unforeseen contingencies. The result in public sector contracts, as with those in the private sector, is that there tends to be considerable emphasis on the development of trust. The evidence from the contracts instituted under the UK Local Government Act 1988 is that trust was seen as important in dealing both with external and internal providers. Indeed, in many cases, trust is argued to be more important in relating to external providers because it was not possible to resort to hierarchical authority. Typical statements made by contract managers were:

> The idea was that you draw up a specification and put it out and got a price and agreed a contract and then held them to it in a penal way. That's rubbish. You can't adopt a penal approach. You need to agree with the contractor what is to be done and work together to provide the service.

> If it's a long-term contract then the only way of getting a good service is working with the contractor. It means an appreciation of how a contractor thinks and operates. It needs an appreciation of what is fair and reasonable in the nature of the contract. They need to be fair and reasonable in the way that they read the letter of the contract. If they stick to the letter of the contract then you get opposition. (Quotes from local government employees interviewed as part of ESRC projects.)

Trust tends to be more emphasised in those contracts that deal with services that are more difficult to specify. Trust is not easily developed, and there is evidence that relationships at the beginning of contracts are often poor, when the parties to the contract know less of each other.

Private and public providers

There is some difference in the way that internal and external contractors are dealt with. Research on the services contracted under the Local Government Act 1988 shows that there is more use of sanctions and more termination of contracts with private contractors. This pattern may result from the private sector providing a worse service, as defenders of public provision claim. It may equally result from the unwillingness of public organisation to punish their internal providers, or because those organisations that are more willing to contract with the private sector are also more willing to exercise sanctions. Despite the claims of the trade unions, there is little evidence that private contractors provide a poorer quality service than the internal provider. They do seem to be more capable of protecting their interests, because they are more used to managing under contractual relationships, and are likely to push the client harder. Nevertheless, clients seem to be as happy to deal with private providers as internal contractors. Local units such as schools, when they have been given freedom to choose who shall provide services have been largely indifferent when choosing between public and private providers.

Dunleavy's bureau-shaping hypothesis finds support in the frequency with which managers and senior clients say that they prefer to deal with external contractors, because they know how to manage under a contract and the relationship is clearer. The internal organisation is also relieved of the burden of managing large numbers of internal staff. As one social services officer said discussing the impact of the introduction of the mixed economy of care:

> Very quickly there will be no internal provision because care managers will want the freedom that comes from choosing from a range of external contractors. (Interview undertaken as part of ESRC project.)

There is certainly significant opposition to public service contracting, but the more senior the managers involved the more likely they are to be indifferent or to favour the private sector.

The pattern of provision

The degree to which service is now provided by the public or the private sector depends largely upon whether the process adopted has been one of contracting out or competitive tendering. In the United States contracting out has dominated, so that there tends to be more provision by the private sector. The pattern for local government in the United States is shown in Table 5.1.

Osborne and Gaebler (1992) state that the average city contracts out 27 per cent of its activities. The services contracted out, as Rehfuss (1989) says, are those which are least politically sensitive, the more technical services, and those that involve high start-up costs. There is a tendency for contracting out to be applied to more sensitive services such as prison management in recent years. In

TABLE 5.1   Provision of public services by the private sector in the United States of America – City and County services

	Percentage of government contracting cut
Vehicle towing	78
Day care	73
Cultural programmes	52
Hospital operation	50
Legal services	50
Drug/alcohol treatment	48
Mental health facilities	47
Paratransit operation	44

Source: International City Managers Association, 1989.

social services in particular there is a strong tendency for contracts to be between different levels of government.

The Congressional Budget Office reported a 10 per cent increase in the value of federal contracts in the United States between 1983 and 1987, most of the increase coming in the Department of Defence. About half of the cost comparisons made under Office of Management and the Budget Circular A-76 result in contracting out. The United States federal government had contracted out $196.3 billion worth of work by 1987. At the local level the main growth in contracting out came in the 1970s, although the pressure rose again in the late 1980s because of increasingly tight finance.

Contracting out can be expected to continue to advance in the United States. Osborne and Gaebler argue:

> Competition is here to stay, regardless of what our governments do. In today's fast-moving marketplace, the private sector is rapidly taking market share away from public organisations. Public schools are losing ground to private schools. The postal service is losing ground to Federal Express and UPS. Public forces are losing ground to private security firms, which now employ two-thirds of all security personnel in the nation (p. 107).

This is an overstatement, but there is clearly a trend to greater use of the private sector.

In Europe there is relatively little provision by the private sector except in France, with its tradition of using large private and semi-public companies for the provision of infrastructural and environmental services. There has been some extension of contracting out in France, predominantly in services, such as street-cleaning, where it was already well represented. In Italy there has been a growth in contracting out, both at central and local government level, for example in the collection of taxes, but there is no consistent pressure for change. In other countries the use of the private sector is very limited, and where it exists has a long tradition of provision. In Germany, for example, refuse collection is performed very widely by private sector firms, but there is little tendency for the involvement of the private sector to grow. There has been some very limited growth of contracting in New Zealand, though the pressure has increased since the election of a conservative government in 1990. In Australia the move to contracting only began in the late 1980s, though it is now growing rapidly and there have been only limited experiments with contracting in healthcare. The Department of Defence in Australia is also widening its use of contracting. Contracting at the local level is limited. There has been some increase in contracting out in the Netherlands, since central government recommended the approach. In Sweden there is an increasing use of contracting in local government and social care, under the pressure of a conservative government, though the rate of change is slow, and the private sector has made little advance.

The impact of the contracting out of services at the central government level in Britain can be seen in the reduction in the level of employment in the civil service which fell very rapidly in the first half of the 1980s. Private contractors have won about 30 per cent of the contracts let under market testing. In the National Health Service private contractors have been relatively more successful in winning contracts for domestic services, and much less successful in laundry and catering. By 1988, of a total of 871 contracts let, private contractors had won 176 (20 per cent). The pattern since the late 1980s has, if anything, been that private sector contractors have been somewhat less successful. Contracting out of health services is now beginning to advance, though slowly.

There has been considerable growth in the proportion of local authority services provided by the private sector following the introduction of the Local Government Planning and Land Act 1980 and the Local Government Act 1988. In building and civil engineering the proportion of work done by the private sector increased, as can be seen from the market share figures in Table 5.2. The pattern varies considerably from one part of the country to another depending upon the level of competition, and the impact of economic factors such as unemployment.

The success of the private sector following the introduction of the Local Government Act 1988 varied considerably from one service to another and from one part of the country to another. The figures gathered by the Local Government Management Board are summarised in Table 5.3. The private sector tends to win the smaller contracts, so that the proportion of the total value of the work that has been won is much less than the proportion of contracts won. Contractors are more likely to bid and win contracts where the authority is more favourable to contracting out, and there has been almost no success in the Labour-controlled authorities of the North of England and Scotland. The success of the private sector in contracting has increased little since the early stages of the process, though most people in local government expect that it will increase over time.

There is little evidence, as yet, about what the impact of competitive tendering for white-collar and professional services will be. The experience of the United States suggests that there is likely to be a significant level of private sector interest. There is also growing evidence that there are firms willing to enter the market, for

TABLE 5.2   **Percentage of local authority building maintenance work by value undertaken by direct service organisations in Britain**

1982/83	64
1983/84	55
1984/85	52
1985/86	55
1986/87	52
1987/88	52
1988/89	49
1989/90	47
1990/91	51

Source: Walker, 1993.

TABLE 5.3   Local authority contracting under the UK Local Government Act 1988

Activity	Percentage of contracts won by private sector	Percentage value of contracts won by private sector
Building cleaning	48.5	20.5
Refuse collection	28.1	25.7
Street cleaning	29.7	20.7
Vehicle maintenance	21.8	12.1
Education and welfare catering	9.4	2.3
Other catering	24.7	14.1
Ground maintenance	33.0	16.7
Sport and leisure management	16.0	17.3
Average	31.9	17.0

Source: Local Government Management Board, 1993.

example for legal and financial services. It is unlikely that the private sector will have the success that it had with manual services, but there is likely to be a slow but steady advance.

Conclusion

Management by contract involves a move from hierarchical authority to control at arm's length, with either internal or external providers actually providing the service. Paradoxically though, much of the development of contract management, especially for complex services, involves the re-creation of management systems that are essentially hierarchical in character. The arm's-length nature of the relationship tends to be modified by the development of trust-based mechanisms. Certainly the move to contracts has led to an emphasis upon the development of measures of performance and monitoring. The contract state is a more evaluative state, but at the same time the introduction of contract does not imply a move towards a world of uncomplicated specificity and precision. Contract requires an appropriate institutional framework if it is to operate effectively, as does hierarchy.

As Harden (1992) says:

> The further one moves from the model of a discrete exchange between private actors, the more abstract the notion of a contract becomes and more work has to be done to construct a framework capable of delivering the intended results in a specific context. Contract offers no ready made mechanism for organising public services (p. 36).

The institutional framework is fairly simple to develop in the case of relatively uncomplicated services such as refuse collection and street cleaning. More complex services require a more extensive framework, one that will cope effectively with risk, uncertainty, and changed patterns of accountability. Trust is generally regarded as crucial to successful operation under contract, but it is not easily developed, at least in the short-term.

Developments so far have minimised the degree to which contract has changed the organisational pattern of the public service. Contracts have been large, and the private sector has won a relatively small proportion. The relationships involved have often mirrored the past where there have been management buy-outs, or other forms of contract, such as facilities management, in which the same staff have continued to provide the service. It is difficult to take this approach the more that the services that are subject to contract involve individuals as people, and the more they affect the core services of the organisation. Housing management, community care, and increasingly health care, as individual general practitioners come to play a larger purchasing role, require different approaches to the management of contract if the rights of the individual are to be adequately considered. The use of contract has only begun to affect the core of the public service, and when it comes to have its full effect is likely to require fundamental changes in organisation and culture.

6 Internal Markets

The development of internal markets is a key feature of the changing management of the public service in Britain, and to a lesser extent in other countries such as New Zealand, the Netherlands and Sweden. It is most commonly being developed in health services, in order to try to limit the independent power of the producers of health care, to create pressures for efficiency, and to increase responsiveness to service users. It is only in Britain that the internal market has been widely introduced on a compulsory basis, though other countries are adopting it on a voluntary basis, for example Swedish local authorities. The British government sees the internal market as the means of creating market pressures when, for political or practical reasons, it is not feasible to introduce privatisation. In general terms it is intended to apply the internal market to all services that remain within the public sector. The separation of purchaser and provider roles is an attempt to deal with the problems identified by the public choice school, particularly tendencies to overproduction, by ensuring that there are principals motivated to keep the bureaucracy small. It is an attempt to introduce the values of the market within hierarchical structures through clarifying principal and agent responsibilities.

Internal markets may be a component of other changes in the management of the public services; they play a part, for example, in the devolution of financial control and the operation of competitive tendering in local government. Internal markets have played a major part in the changed approach to the government of education in Britain, for example in the purchase of further education courses by Training and Enterprise Councils, and through allowing schools to decide what services they will purchase from the local authority. In the Civil Service the creation of agencies has involved the development of internal markets to some degree. Local authorities have, in some cases, chosen to establish services on the basis of internal market processes, sometimes as part of a more general movement towards the development of externalisation or privatisation. The Audit Commission (1994) has reported that about 20 per cent of local authorities operate internal trading agreements for support services such as finance. Services that remain in the public service are gradually being moved onto a trading basis, where they must earn their income from sale of services to the client side of the organisation.

The argument for internal markets

The internal market involves three key features: the creation of explicit and separate roles for the purchasing and supply of services; the establishment of internal quasi-contracts and trading agreements between these separate roles; and the development of charging and accounting systems. In a fully developed internal market system the internal provider will start the year with no finance, having to earn enough to cover costs and any surplus that is required. The basic mechanism of budget maximisation, which public choice theorists argue is at the basis of public sector failings, is partially eliminated, through reducing the significance of budgeting. In a complex organisation providing a wide range of services, such as a local authority, there may be a large number of purchasers and providers, and the same organisational unit may be purchaser in one relationship and provider in another. Such a reorganisation of the system inevitably creates fundamental pressures for change in the management of the financial system within public service organisations. The purpose is to ensure that budgets are not allocated by right, but are related to some pattern of demand, with a more clearly established pattern of property rights within the organisation.

It is possible to distinguish between what Mullen (1990) calls Type I and Type II markets, the first involving individual users as purchasers, and the second public organisations or professionals such as doctors operating on behalf of the ultimate users. In Britain the majority of markets for public services are of Type II. In some other cases, notably Sweden, there has been more establishment of choice on the part of the individual user (Saltman and Von Otter, 1992). Internal markets differ in the extent to which they use the price mechanism as a means of decision making over the levels of production and consumption. In the British National Health Service price was little used at first for the majority of services, which were provided under block contracts; in community care price has a major impact on the survival of providers. There are also major differences in the extent to which internal markets are regulated. Control in the National Health Service has been strong, with the Secretary of State for Health being relatively unwilling to devolve power and discretion. In the case of schools the degree of regulation governing purchasing has been relatively limited (Audit Commission, 1993a). There is little indication that there will be any move towards Type I markets, and the main effect of the introduction of internal markets has been to shift control from one group of professionals to another, the professional purchasers.

The arguments for internal markets are that they lead to a clarification of responsibilities, ensure that the different aspects of service management are effectively developed, and that they create pressures for efficiency. The creation of explicit responsibilities for purchasing and the requirement that producers operate on a trading basis is argued to reduce the ability of the providers, particularly professionals such as doctors, teachers and social workers, to dominate the service. Poor, or excessively expensive providers will be driven out of the system by the choice mechanism, even if it is exercised indirectly. Internal markets can be argued to lead to increased accountability, since the responsibilities of principal and agent are clear and separate. The duties and responsibilities of each side are specified in contracts or quasi-contracts, as are performance targets, and providers can be held to account for their performance. Means of redress for failure can also be laid down in contracts.

Purchasers, also, are forced to be explicit about the decisions that they make, particularly over the rationing of service. There may previously have been implicit rationing in the pattern of activities that were chosen by professionals, but it was often divorced from policy. In practice a great deal of discretion lay with street-level bureaucrats. Internal markets are intended to separate policy and implementation, and ensure that the latter reflects the former. The aim of the internal market is to increase the degree of transparency in public services, so that all can be held accountable for their actions. Rationing will be made explicit and the power of street-level bureaucrats will be limited.

The structure of internal markets, like that of other markets, can vary, particularly in the degrees of monopsony and monopoly, in the degree of freedom given to purchasers to choose where they go for service, and in the extent to which providers are allowed to trade. In the National Health Service in Britain, for example, the initial structure was one of bilateral monopoly, with health authorities dealing with large hospitals, but, as the number of general practitioners who are fundholders and who purchase services increases, the internal market will become more differentiated, though change may still be limited because there is a tendency for purchasers to stick with existing patterns of referral. As the Audit Commission (1993d) finds: 'GPs may wish to stick to traditional patterns of referral even if high prices and charging providers may lead to a lot of extra contract referrals.' Glennerster *et al.* (1994) argue that GP fundholding has had a beneficial effect on competition, reducing the monopolistic power of hospitals, though they fear that action may be taken to limit its influence.

In the case of schools and colleges, operating with their own devolved budgets, there are many purchasers and many potential providers. Schools and colleges are largely free to decide where they will purchase services and there are many providers for such basic support services as building cleaning and ground maintenance, and, increasingly, even for professional and educational services. The power of local authorities to trade is usually limited, on the assumption that the public sector should not provide services on the free market, though there are increasing examples of trading across public services, for example local authorities working for health authorities. This pattern of trading between government organisations is common in other countries, notably the United States of America. The structure of the market, and the mode of payment, will affect the way that both purchasers and providers operate, just as they do in normal markets. There is, for example, extensive evidence, from the markets for health care that have operated in the United States of America, that competition may lead to increased as well as reduced costs, depending on the framework of rules under which the system operates.

The development of the internal market brings out the need for management of services which previously may have received little if any attention, for example support services such as the cleaning of buildings. The creation of a trading relationship and the explicit pricing and internal sale of services, focusses the purchasers' attention on what they will and will not accept. The establishment of a purchaser role means that someone is given the explicit responsibility for deciding what service it is that is to be provided. The establishment of a provider role, with a separate trading budget, is argued to give providers the incentive to increase their internal efficiency through setting financial targets, and, perhaps, allowing profit to be earned.

Performance based pay goes along with internal markets in many cases, in effect giving public sector managers the sort of residual claim on surpluses that is common in the private sector. In local government, for example, about one third of managers of trading units are on performance related pay, and about 25 per cent of authorities have adopted performance pay more widely. Internal markets may also involve a focus on the resources that are used, for example through changing the pattern of property rights and responsibilities. Purchasers such as schools can use any money saved from one service for other purchases, in contrast to traditional annuality based budgeting systems, where any unspent money was forfeited, and the ability to move finance from one purpose to another was limited. Hospital trusts may also make surpluses though there are limits on how they may be used (Bartlett and Le Grand, 1994). Internal markets are argued to create incentives both for allocative efficiency, because of the purchaser's interest in effective patterns of provision, and technical and X-efficiency, because providers have residual claims over surplus and need to maintain markets, and so are anxious to determine optimum methods and minimise waste.

The development of an internal market may or may not be combined with the establishment of competition for services. In the case of British local government many of the internal markets that have been developed for the provision of professional services, such as law or finance, have allowed the service purchaser to have little or no choice, at least in the early stages. The internal market is based on service level agreements on the services that are to be provided by professionals, such as accountants, and the operation of zero-based trading budgets. There is a gradual but slow movement towards giving internal users greater freedom of choice, and powers to use budgets in an unrestricted way. The separation of purchaser and provider is still argued to be valuable in clarifying responsibility, even if exit from the internal market is not possible. As the internal market has developed in the National Health Service and other public organisations the level of competition has tended to increase. There is a tendency to move from the position of there being a single purchaser and a single provider to the establishment of many purchasers and many providers.

The model, frequently cited, for the purchaser–provider split is that of the retailing company, purchasing supplies for sale. The example most commonly quoted is that of Marks and Spencer; as Ham (1992b) has argued:

> The model we should be working towards is that which exists in a number of commercial organisations where purchasing and manufacturing are separately run. I am thinking, for example, of Marks and Spencer which buys all its goods and services from outside suppliers. The relationship between Marks and Spencer and its suppliers is one of interdependence in which the success of the purchaser depends upon the success of the providers and vice versa. This creates a common interest in working together to meet the demands of customers.

The analogy with retailing organisations may be misplaced in that the role of the public service organisation is much more like that of a manufacturer than a retailer, which would, at most, contract out only part of its activities. Internal trading in manufacturing industry, as Eccles (1985) has shown, is frequently the source of conflict. More generally the character of relationships between purchasing and supplying organisations varies strongly from one culture to another, and from one institutional context to another, and the assumption of transferability is questionable. The sort of tight relationships between networks of organisations that may exist in Asian capitalism may be based on cultures and traditions which it may be impossible to copy.

The characteristics of the context in which internal markets can be seen to work reasonably well are comparable to those in which external markets would work equally well, namely that the product should be reasonably easy to specify, that performance should be reasonably easy to monitor, and that providers and purchasers should not be able to take advantage of each other. Where the provider has the ability to decide what work is to be done, and whether it has been done to a satisfactory standard, then it is likely that the market will fail, at least in the short term. The internal market, then, raises the same issues as does the use of an external market, namely whether the purchaser has either the knowledge or the skill to manage internal contractors. If the market is to work effectively then there must be an ability to assess the relationship between price, quantity and quality. As Donaldson and Gerard (1993) show in their review of the evidence on the use of market mechanisms in health provision, it is difficult to reach any firm conclusions where the interaction between the three is hard to observe. It is not surprising, therefore, that the development of internal markets has gone along with the development of performance measurement and attempts to develop quality management, and that the result is increasingly complex organisational and interorganisational systems.

Internal markets in health

The most explicit attempts to develop internal markets for the provision of public services have been in the health sector. In New Zealand there was a proposal for the establishment of Regional Health Authorities which would purchase care on behalf of patients from a range of providers, both public and private. Surprisingly, in view of the market orientation of the New Zealand government, the proposal was rejected in favour of a less explicitly market-oriented reorganisation. In Leningrad, and some other areas in the USSR, there was an experiment in the 1980s with an internal health market on a local level, in which primary health providers held the budget for patients and bought from hospitals (Sheaff, 1990). Reform of the health service in the Netherlands along internal market lines has been proposed; there have been changes along similar lines in Sweden and to a lesser extent other countries. There have been experiments with various forms of market in the United States of America, for example health maintenance organisations which purchase health care on behalf of their members, and prospective payment systems, though these are more external market than internal market systems.

The most explicit case of the development of an internal market for health services is in the British National Health Service. The argument for the internal market was initially made by Enthoven and taken up in the Prime Minister's review of the NHS, established in 1988, as a result of what was seen as a funding crisis in the service. The idea was appealing in that it offered some of the benefits of the market, while preserving the public, tax-funded character of the service, which it was not politically possible to abandon. It fitted with the government's suspicion of the power of the professionals, and the perceived need to introduce market-based management approaches. The results of the review were published in *Working for Patients* in early 1989. At the same time a new contract was introduced for family practitioners. The proposals completed the move away from planning that had begun with the establishment of general management, following the Griffiths Report in 1982. The various managerial developments of the 1980s, general management, improved budgeting and resource management, the reallocation of resources in line with needs, and improved information management, could be seen as coming together under the banner of the internal market. In a planning system attempts to make major changes, for example to close hospitals or reallocate resources from one part of the country to another, are highly political issues, because they involve explicit decisions. The development of the internal market held the promise that such adjustments would emerge from the decisions of individuals in the market, and not require direct political involvement.

The White Paper proposed that the health purchasing role should be separated from that of provision. The providers, notably the hospitals, were to be allowed to take up trust status within the National Health Service, becoming independent of the District Health Authority, and reporting to a board of trustees. Trusts would operate independent trading budgets, and would have to cover their operating costs, including charges for the use of capital, through the money they earned for work done. Providers that did not take up trust status would operate as separate directly managed units within the health authority. The funding of district health authorities as purchasers is based upon the resident population with weighting for need. General practitioners in large practices were to be allowed to be fundholders, with budgets allocated on the basis of weighted patient numbers, and to purchase care directly from hospitals and other providers on behalf of their patients. The link between purchasers and providers was to be established through contracts, which would be quasi-legal documents. The purchasers and general practitioners who were fundholders were to be allowed, with some limitations to purchase services where they wished.

The contract form has also been introduced into the primary care sector as well as for hospital-based care. General practitioners have always been independent contractors, but the nature of the contract has now been made more explicit, with doctors paid according to tasks performed as well as on the basis of capitation. Family Health Service Authorities (FHSAs) act as the purchasers for primary health care in Britain, funding general practitioners on a contractual basis. The option available for family practitioners with larger practices to become budget holders creates a two-stage contracting relationship, since they are contractors to the FHSA, and themselves purchase from hospitals. FHSAs are playing an increasingly active role in monitoring the activities of GP fundholders. A complex nexus of contracts is emerging.

In the first year of the internal market in the NHS, when authorities were required to avoid radical change in patterns of provision, the large majority of contracts were between the DHAs and directly managed units or local trusts, and were of the block form. Health authorities contracted for about 20 per cent of the service they purchased with NHS providers outside the district; contracting with the private and voluntary sectors took up only a very small proportion of the total. The use of single block contracts for the purchasing of the majority of service reduced the transaction costs of contracting within the authority, but this was countered by the high costs that were involved in the development of a much larger number of smaller external contracts. The number of purchasers has increased as the proportion of general practitioners who are fundholders has grown and more services, for example community health services have moved on to a contracting basis. Though the proportion of total NHS resources held by fundholders is limited they have a very significant effect at the margin, and it is the margins that have proved most difficult to manage. The explicitness of trading has also increased as the number of hospitals and other health units that have taken up trust status has increased, and has been strongest where financial pressures have been tightest.

The forms of contracts operated in the NHS have become more sophisticated as experience has grown, with attempts to move away from the block contract towards forms that are more sensitive to the amount of work done and its unit cost. Change has been rapid; the percentage of services purchased under block contracts with floors and ceilings grew from 46 to 61 per cent between 1991–92 and 1992–93, and the proportion of work purchased under cost and volume contracts rose from 2 to 10 per cent (Appleby *et al.*, 1992). The UK National Health Service Management Executive (1993) has said that simple block contracts are no longer acceptable. GP fundholders do operate longer term contracts with hospitals, though they are also more likely to use spot purchasing than the health authorities, and more fundholder contracts are of the cost-per-case form. The role of fundholders is widely seen as making the operation of the market more unpredictable.

The experience of the National Health Service has shown some of the problems of running an internal market for complex services. There is a need for much more information than in a hierarchical organisation, in order that the system can be controlled effectively. Purchasers need to be able to make judgments of need in order to be able to create specifications of the type and amount of work that is to be done. The purchasers' difficulties are increased by the need to pursue government defined priorities, for example those laid out in *Health of the Nation* and the *Patient's Charter*. The recognition of the need for purchasers to be able to buy services that reflect health strategies has led to an increasing emphasis on the broader commissioning role, but the level of sophistication in the development of the purchasing role is low. Local health authorities are only beginning to develop the methods for analysing need and assessing the effectiveness of health procedures that are required for making informed choice between priorities. The move to explicit purchasing will make clear the choices between priorities, and the rationing decisions that have to be made, but its effectiveness is dependent on the development of adequate information and strategic planning systems by purchasers. Purchasers need to have clear prices available to them if they are to be able to make fully informed decisions on the cost–benefit ratio of particular purchasing patterns, but cost information systems rarely allow such informed decision making.

The development of effective commissioning requires sophisticated information both on the demand and the supply side, which is not available. It is equally difficult to judge whether apparent changes in performance are real or are the result of variations in recording practices. It is not surprising that purchasers have not been willing to switch between providers on the basis of price alone (Audit Commission, 1993d). The ambiguous relationship between price and quality would suggest that decision making by purchasers will be difficult (Hirschman, 1970).

The approach adopted by purchasers in converting broad priorities into detailed specifications has varied greatly from one health authority to another. In some cases there is a great deal of detailed description of what is to be provided, with quality standards stated. In the majority of cases the level of specification has been limited, with only broad statements of indicative levels of demand. The experience and expertise of the purchaser side has been limited, especially in smaller authorities. The provider still has considerable information advantages and 'decision authority' (Jensen and Meckling, 1992). The internal market, in the early period of its development, has operated without great purchaser–provider conflict, which can be expected to grow as the system moves away from the steady state that has dominated the first years of contracting, and as the purchaser attempts to control what is done more closely. There is some evidence of growing conflict and attempts to develop more claims based contracts.

The running of the internal market for health care demands a good deal of management time, and the majority of managers consider that it has resulted in excessive time being spent on administration (Appleby *et al.*, 1994). There is relatively little explicit checking of the quality of services, and the majority of managers tend to feel that there are major information difficulties in the management of contracts. Individual GP fundholders do tend to take a detailed interest in the nature of the services provided, and act more directly as monitors of contracts. The formal aspects of the system tend to be time consuming, for example the invoicing procedure and the management of adjustments to the contract. Budgets become much more difficult to manage because there are two parallel budgeting and financial management systems, one for the purchaser and another for the provider, which must be managed alongside and reconciled with each other. There have been major issues over the reconciliation of financial information, and the introduction of internal markets has shown the inadequacy of management accounting systems, for example in dealing with commitments. Information demands have greatly increased, and there have been problems in managing finances, particularly of higher cost providers, notably the London teaching hospitals.

The result of the growing complexity and formalisation of the organisational system is that there has been a considerable increase in the number of managers and accountants employed in the National Health Service in Britain. The development of the internal market makes it more difficult, in theory, to fudge decisions, and in that sense improves accountability, but transparency is dependent on the availability of effective information, which has proved difficult to develop. The complexity and proliferation of management may actually reduce accountability by increasing layers of management.

The operation of internal markets changes the pattern of motivation of purchasers and providers, both specifically and generally. Purchasers have an incentive to maximise the amount of work that they get for the money they spend; providers complain that purchasers are likely to use their monopsonistic position to impose higher levels of provision within given resources, and demand efficiency improvements when contracts are renewed. In the second year of contracts nearly 80 per cent of purchasers intended to increase the amount of care demanded for a given amount of money by more than 10 per cent, which many providers saw as a diktat, and the exercise of power without responsibility. There is less tendency to use the traditional market response of going elsewhere in the face of high cost or poor quality, than to use power of a quasi-hierarchical kind to obtain more favourable conditions. Providers have an incentive to 'cream skim', that is to pick the relatively easy cases, and to minimise the amount of work that they put into any particular case. The producer, for example, has an incentive to maximise throughput, and therefore to discharge people 'quicker and sicker', particularly if they are paid on a case by case basis. Most of reduction in length of stay follows from changed practice and technological improvement, but the incentive to discharge early may have an effect. Producers also have an incentive to take those cases that bring in extra resources, for example spot purchases from GP fundholders or other health authorities, rather than patients who might fall under a block contract, and who will not bring in extra finance when treated.

It is difficult to ensure that patterns of spending by purchasers and providers match budgets, and in each of the first two years of the operation of the market in the NHS there were frequent reports of hospitals having fulfilled their contracts well before the end of the year, and purchasers having no money to purchase further service. Renegotiation of contracts is common; the National Association of Health Authorities and Trusts in a survey in Autumn 1992 found that 38 per cent of the responding authorities had renegotiated contracts during the year. More than 80 per cent of authorities had experienced difficulties as a result of higher levels of activity than had been expected. In early 1993 a survey in the British Medical Journal found that 26 out of 30 large hospitals had over-performed on some contracts, and that 9 had to cut down on activity in order to stay within budget. A Royal College of Surgeons survey in 1993–94 found that 44 per cent of surgical units had to curtail or stop some activity. A similar survey in the previous year found a figure of 62 per cent. In part this is a result of the difficulty of planning finance within a differentiated system, but it is also a reflection of the nature of the market. The total size of the market is more or less decided by the overall level of spending determined at central government level. The efficient producer has only limited opportunities for growth, especially since purchasers tend to contract with providers in the district, and one hospital can only increase its production at the expense of another. Any adjustment of levels of provision across health authorities takes time.

Changes will also be needed in the rule systems embodied in contracts to cope with the relationship between costs and levels of provision. For example tapering prices could be used as levels of activity increase in order to cope with the way that fixed costs reduce as a proportion of total costs, a system operated in an internal market experiment operated in Stockholm. Such systems are difficult to develop when there is poor knowledge of the costs of services. Without the development of more effective pricing and costing systems the service is likely to be distorted by the perverse incentives of an inappropriate payment pattern.

The difficulty of predicting and controlling levels of activity undertaken by providers illustrates both the advantages and disadvantages of internal markets for complex services; at a deeper level it reveals the paradoxes that are inherent in the establishment of markets that are cash-limited. The achievement of higher than expected levels of activity can be seen as an indication of increased efficiency, with hospitals increasing their throughput of patients. At the same time it may indicate that capacity is too great. The market should operate to reduce capacity, as resources flow to the cheapest or best value providers, and there are readjustments, for example through ward closures in the course of the year, but the nature of contracts makes change difficult. The service is lumpy, making continuous adjustment impossible to achieve. The market reveals the need for change, but its character makes that change difficult to attain. There has generally been stability in the distribution of resources between different forms of care with some local variation. There is still a strong emphasis on acute services, and to a considerable extent patterns of resource distribution have been reinforced. Charge is, at most, incremental.

Extra contract referrals, for work ordered outside the standard contract, comprise only a small part of the spending of the British National Health Service, about one per cent, but illustrate some of the key difficulties with the operation of the internal market. Extra contract referrals are of two kinds: elective, where there is a referral by the District Health Authority or by a general practitioner; and emergency cases. The pattern of extra contract referrals is difficult to predict, given the lack of accurate historical information, and health districts have put aside about 1.5 per cent of budgets to cope with them. The total number of such referrals in 1991–92 was about 330 000, about 4 per cent of the total number of cases treated. The transaction costs of dealing with extra-contract referrals is high compared with the management of contracts, and, in the early stages of contracting in particular, managers claimed to spend a high proportion of their time dealing with them.

The effective operation of the internal market depends upon the accuracy of prices and the degree to which they reflect differences in costs. A major cause of the variation in prices is the cost of capital, which is now being charged to trust budgets. In the first year of the operation of the market, providers received enough resources to cope with differences in capital costs, but the link between finance and capital charges is now being broken by regional health authorities in their distribution of resources. The impact is significant because capital charges can vary from 5 to 30 per cent of total costs. Costs can vary widely from one hospital to another and from one health authority to another simply because of the impact of capital costs.

More generally the ability to set accurate prices is limited by the lack of accurate knowledge of unit costs. The various information and resource management initiatives of the 1980s did serve to improve the information available to managers, but the costing of health care is still extremely difficult and complex. It is as likely that many of the variations in cost between one unit or trust and another are random, or simply mistakes, as that they reflect real differences. Certainly they reflect different information, and costing methods, for example in the approach to fixed costs.

Purchasers are concerned for the quality as well as the quantity of service provided. The development of methods for the monitoring of standards of performance under contracts has so far been limited. There has been some pressure for Community Health Councils, the bodies established in the UK to represent users, to become involved, and family practitioners who are fundholders have shown a close interest in quality. Many contracts make reference to quality and require quality assurance systems, but active management of quality is limited, and few internal contracts specify methods by which failure to meet standards will be dealt with. The reforms introduced by *Working for Patients* did emphasise the importance of medical audit and other quality procedures, but these are not specifically related to the operation of contracts. Quality of service is still a matter that is left largely to the provider and the professional.

The market for health care is clearly a managed market, and various approaches for controlling the market are emerging. There are consortium purchasing arrangements between health authorities, family health services authorities, general practitioner fundholders and, increasingly, local authorities. At the same time, forms of locality purchasing (Ham and Spurgeon, 1992) are developing as authorities try to ensure that the needs of different areas and client groups within the population are adequately considered. There is increasing consultation of local people and communities in the development of purchasing plans, but there are great variations in the extent and effectiveness of consultation. Central government is also involved in the process of regulation.

The interest of the Department of Health is increasingly represented by outposts of the National Health Service Management Executive at local level. The overall pattern of management of the health market is not yet clear. Ham and Spurgeon have argued that there is a need to develop a more effective global framework for the market:

> What is clear is that there does need to be an agency capable of overseeing the operation of the market on behalf of ministers and in a position to intervene in appropriate circumstances. Such an agency would be responsible not only for resolving disputes between purchasers and providers but also for setting the framework within which competition develops. More specifically, the agency would play a part in determining the size and shape of purchasers and providers, planning for education and research requirements, overseeing the distribution of specialist services, including the availability of expensive high technology, and ensuring that access and equity were not undermined as competition increased.

The issue then is one of how hierarchy and planning can be combined with the operation of a market. The pattern that is emerging is one of managed networks using some market-like mechanisms rather than markets operating freely.

Local government

The development of internal markets in UK local government went along with the introduction of competitive tendering following the Local Government Planning and Land Act, 1980, and the Local Government Act 1988. Authorities are required to operate separate trading accounts for services subject to competition, and to meet financial targets set down by the central government. Separate accounts are required for each service subject to competition, in order to prevent cross-subsidy, and distortion of prices compared to costs. Where the local authority fails to make the required rate of return on capital, the Secretary of State may take action, for example requiring that a service be subjected to re-tendering, perhaps with the local authority being forbidden to tender, or that the trading organisation shall be closed down, as has been done in a number of cases. Local authorities are also developing internal trading on a voluntary basis for services not subject to tender, partly as a result of pressure from those services that are subject to the legislation.

The separation of purchaser and provider within the local authority tends to be more complex than in the National Health Service or community care, because there are a large number of inter-linked clients and contractors all trading with one another. When few services, notably those related to building and highways construction and maintenance, were subject to trading, the process was relatively simple because one could easily identify the relevant clients and contractors and separate their accounts from each other; when almost all parts of the authority are organised on a trading account basis then the process becomes much more complex. Local authorities have increasingly had to change their financial regulations and information systems, management accounting procedures, and budgeting systems to accommodate the more complex management accounting demands of the new system.

Developments in the management of specific services have added to pressures for the development of internal markets. The Local Government and Housing Act 1989, provided for the separation of the finance of housing from the financing of the rest of the local authority, commonly referred to as the ring-fencing of the housing revenue account, and required local authorities to meet net expenditure on the service from government subsidy and rents. Rent levels must be set by the authority to balance the account without any contribution from the general fund of the local authority. Housing managers were thereby given an incentive to keep the charges to the housing revenue account for central services and other support services, such as grounds maintenance, to a minimum. The development of local management of schools also created pressure for internal trading of services. Schools are now free to purchase or not to purchase, and education departments are being reconstituted in order to be able to operate as business units selling services to schools. The development of companies for waste disposal means that services provided to them must be at arm's length and operate on a trading basis.

The first result of this pressure for change in the way that local authorities were organised has been the creation of service level agreements, charging procedures and some user choice. Service level agreements are quasi-contracts for the provision of support services within the organisation, normally involving a statement of the service that will be provided, and its cost. Charges may be operated on a unit basis, for example the cost per invoice dealt with, on a block basis, for example a retainer charge for accounting, or on a daily or hourly rate, for example a charge per hour for legal advice. The budget for a service is calculated on the basis of historical patterns of usage, or on a more general formula basis as in the case of schools. In the early stages of the development of service level agreements within the local authority the budget allocated for central support services was normally ring-fenced. So the direct service organisation, for example, would be allocated an amount of money for the purchase of, say, legal services, and would only be able to use that money to purchase such services within the local authority.

A second approach to the management of support services was to devolve the budget for the purchase of central services to the direct providers of service, and allow them to decide how they wanted to purchase support services, with some requirement to purchase services such as financial audit, which were seen as important from a corporate perspective. The devolution of finance may go along with freedom to go outside the local authority to obtain services, and freedom to use the money allocated for purposes other than the purchase of central services. The line budgeting approach is then abandoned. Providers start the year with no certain income, and must earn what they need from trading. This approach has been adopted in local authorities such as Cambridgeshire and Warwickshire. The degree of freedom for purchasers is normally limited, for example through requiring a period of notice before they are allowed to withdraw from an agreement to purchase. In practice, in the early stages, users have generally stayed with the internal providers and have not changed their pattern of usage greatly, but differences do emerge over time. Schools, for example, have changed their patterns of purchasing markedly in many cases.

The separation of client and contractor roles is more difficult to operate at the elected member level than the officer level. The problems of potential conflicts of interest are increasingly leading to members being represented on one side only of the client/contractor divide, though this becomes more difficult the greater the number of services that are subject to contract, and the more contracts interact with each other. Generally the reporting of the client and contractor sides of services is being separated. On the contractor side many local authorities in Britain have established boards, which are generally smaller than traditional committees, have stronger powers, and operate more informally. About 40 per cent of local authorities have established such boards for services subject to competition, and comparable mechanisms are being established for services where they choose to operate an internal market. The division between members who are on the client and contractor sides has led to conflict in some cases, though most authorities have found it relatively straightforward to operate such systems.

As with the operation of the internal market in the National Health Service, the operation of the internal market in local government has led to greater internal management costs, in preparing specifications, monitoring services, and operating systems of invoicing and payment. On the contractor side there are costs in maintaining records of the way in which staff spend their time, so that it can be appropriately charged. Generally there are increased costs of information and management accounting systems. The development of internal markets is seen as ensuring better knowledge of costs and quality, but involves its own cost and bureaucracy. The result of the development of the internal market has been greater formality in relationships, particularly in the resolution of differences, though there is strong emphasis on the need for informality and trust.

The degree to which the operation of internal markets creates real freedom for purchasers is often limited. Where the amount of service purchased is low the costs of switching may make buying from an alternative provider uneconomical, even if the internal service is poor. The provider may then be able to ignore the needs of minor users who will not find it worth the effort of switching. There is evidence that this is happening in internal markets in local authorities. There has so far been little switching to external providers, and in many cases internal purchasers are unsure of their powers to change. In practice traditional relationships tend to persist for some time, with only gradual change. Organisational inertia provides a considerable advantage to existing providers. Internal purchasers are often unaware of the fact that they may be formally free to go elsewhere to obtain services.

The fact of multiple interlinked internal contracts in the local authority creates difficulties for the annual budgeting procedures that are required in the public service. One department cannot determine its prices until it knows the costs that will be charged to it by others, involving a process of potentially infinite regress. The normal way of dealing with this is to allocate the costs of the major internal providers first, and to accept that total working out of the process is not possible. The process of negotiating patterns of usage before the beginning of the year takes up a good deal of officer time. It would be possible to overcome this need for negotiation, to some degree, by giving purchasers the money for services, and allowing them to buy on a spot basis, but this would lead to great instability, and make effective budget planning impossible. Again, the local authority case illustrates the need for a mixture of market and hierarchical principles in order to ensure that the internal network of purchasers and providers can operate effectively. Most authorities have found that a clear organisational framework of rules is needed to ensure that the internal market can operate effectively.

Community care

The Griffiths Report (1988) suggested that social services departments should separate themselves into purchasers and providers, and the development of a market for care in Britain was provided for by the National Health Service and Community Care Act 1990. Local authorities have the responsibility for determining the needs of the local population, and meeting them either through purchasing services or by their own direct provision. Though it was not made a statutory requirement it was expected that there would be a purchaser/provider split:

> It will be essential at an early stage for local authorities to separate clearly the purchaser and provider functions so that those responsible for purchasing services on behalf of clients do not also have a direct interest in providing them (Department of Health, 1990a).

The degree to which the development of internal trading has been taken up has varied greatly from one authority to another. In some, for example Berkshire, there has been strong separation, while in the majority the development has been more limited. By 1993, 46 per cent of social service departments had made a purchaser/provider split and another 46 per cent were planning or considering change (Young and Mills, 1993).

Government guidance suggested a number of possible approaches to the purchaser/provider split within the social services department. There might be a central strategic purchaser, with the rest of the department established as a provider. Alternatively the social services department might be split into purchaser and provider divisions at second tier level. Finally the department might only separate into purchaser and provider roles at the local level, with individual care managers purchasing from either internal or external providers. The most common pattern seems to be that the division between purchaser and provider is being made at a relatively high level. Wistow *et al.* (1992) found that the majority of social service departments were relatively cautious about making radical changes at an early stage, and the depth of the purchaser/provider split is, as yet, relatively shallow.

As with the internal market in the NHS, the separation of purchaser and provider in community care raises issues about the balance between the needs of individuals and populations, the effectiveness of a market under cash limits, and the information on which to operate the market. The market for social care compared to that for health is much more one of spot purchasing. There are often many providers, though the position varies from one part of the country to another. Local authorities are required to operate a needs-led planning system, in which individuals have choice over who shall make provision, at least in the case of the care of elderly people. Care managers will have a key role to play in determining the needs of individuals and ensuring that they are met. In many cases this is likely to be dealt with by devolving budgets to care managers. Those authorities that have devolved budgets have found that there is a need for much more effective management information than under a centralised approach, and also that there is a need to be able to exercise certain reserve controls at the centre. If the system is purely decentralised there needs to be accurate knowledge of the pattern of demand, otherwise budgets and patterns of need will not match. As Jensen and Meckling have argued the organisation needs to balance the greater accuracy of decisions that decentralisation brings with the need for effective control. There is a need for centralisation and decentralisation at the same time.

The internal market for social care is at an early stage, but it is already clear that there will be marked differences in the way that it will operate from one local authority to another. Those authorities with a large number of local suppliers can behave differently from those where there are few. There is likely to be a balance of central and local control in all cases, for example with the centre operating an overall commissioning role and local managers operating detailed purchasing. In the longer term the major issue is whether the purchasers will want to continue with internal provision, or feel that they will gain greater freedom by purchasing from a wider range of provider. The wishes of local purchasers for freedom is likely to clash with the authorities perceived need for planning.

The implications of internal markets

The development of internal markets and purchaser/provider splits in the public service has a number of elements. First it requires that the purchaser has the ability to specify the service that is to be provided, and preferably be able to monitor the quality of service delivery. In practice this can pose difficulties particularly for professional services of which the purchaser may have little knowledge or experience. It may be difficult to specify the service before the event, because of the need to respond to circumstances. Even in the case of simple manual worker services there may be the need to specify what is to be done as the contract goes along rather than in a specification before it is let: grounds maintenance work, for example, is subject to substantial variation. Professional services are all the more difficult to specify, especially for the lay person. This difficulty has been dealt with in a number of ways. There has been a tendency to duplicate professional skills on both client and contractor sides, so that the purchaser can specify and monitor the service. Alternatively the purchaser side can buy in specialist expertise as necessary. In most cases, though, for example the UK National Health Service, the pattern of detailed work is decided by the contractor. The more difficult the service is to specify, the more likely it is that producer control will continue or that the purchaser will exercise power in ignorance of the nature of the work. Difficulty of specification on its own is not enough to ensure producer control.

Other factors such as the number of clients, the availability of substitutes, and the importance of the service will also be important.

The separation of purchaser and provider has led to a concern for the development of quality assurance systems as a means by which the provider can give a guarantee of the quality of service. Providers tend to argue that, if they have a quality assurance system, then there is less need of supervision by the purchaser. Many public organisations have looked to get their quality systems certificated by a third party such as the British Standards Institute. About 70 local authorities in the UK had had quality assurance systems certificated by 1993. Many contracts in local government specify that contractors shall develop quality assurance systems that are certificated under British Standard 5750. Twenty four per cent of authorities have included the requirement to achieve certification under the British Standard for one or more contracts, and a further 13 per cent require quality assurance systems without certification.

Attitudes towards quality assurance in the public service are strongly divided, with some feeling that it is a technique that may be appropriate to the manufacturing sector, but has little relevance for the public service, while others are strong advocates. Certainly the focus of quality assurance is on the procedures of the organisation, rather than the service that it produces. The spread of certificated quality assurance systems has been greatest in manual services such as catering and vehicle maintenance, but there are examples in social care, health and education. Certificated quality assurance is perhaps best seen as what Williamson has called a hostage, that is an investment that is specific to the service being offered that could not be recovered if the provider left the specific relationship. Quality assurance may have limited substantive value, but serves as a mark of good faith.

The separation of purchaser and provider raises the issue of how conflicts are resolved. The internal market operates with quasi-contracts, rather than real ones, since an organisation cannot have a contract with itself, and the normal legal mechanisms for dealing with contract incompleteness, imprecision and dispute are not available. Mechanisms have either emerged, or explicitly been established to deal with the issue. In the British National Health Service the Regional Health Authority oversees contracts and resolves disputes, which in the extreme can be referred to the Secretary of State. An arbitration unit has also been established, though it is not extensively used. In the local authority, differences are typically referred to the head of a department that has both purchaser and provider arms, or the chief executive, or another central officer. It is rare for problems to be referred to elected members. In the majority of cases, in practice, problems are generally worked out on a more or less formal basis between the purchasers and providers, as is the common practice in the case of full contracts in the private sector.

The development of contracts has the effect of leading to formalisation, duplication and pressure on trust-based relationships. There is a need for systems that can specify the services to be provided, monitor the quantity and quality of provision, order work, and deal with invoicing and payment procedures. Trust is still necessary, particularly where it is difficult to specify quantity accurately, but it is increasingly based within a much more formalistic framework. The balance of emphasis on trust will vary with the degree to which service failure is identifiable and with the availability of sanctions. In the case of local authorities, for example, there is much more likely to be an active system of monitoring and penalties the simpler the service.

The ability to operate an internal market requires information and systems that are neither needed nor available in the traditional public sector organisations. Under the traditional hierarchical approach to the organisation of the public service the manager's responsibility, once the budget for a service had been decided, was simply to ensure that there was no overspending. There was little if any concern with income and the account automatically balanced. Many costs were outside the accounts, for example the costs of central support services, and the costs of capital were rarely charged within the accounts. Trading accounts are increasingly coming to reflect full service costs, both to ensure that there is comparability with the costs of external providers, and also because the move to putting all services on a trading basis means that they must all be reflected in the management accounting system. In effect, until the advent of trading accounts there was little effective management accounting in the public service, and even now it has very limited effectiveness. Knowledge of unit costs, for example, is often very limited. The patterns of management accounting that are operated are still very much based upon allocating out non-operational costs to the direct costs of service delivery, rather than working from operational needs to costs (Johnson, 1992), though there is a slow shift towards costing that is more bottom-up than top-down.

Conclusion

Organisational developments in the private sector in the last decade have involved attempts to create networks that integrate activities between companies trading and even competing with one another. Similar processes are apparent in the internal markets that have been created in the public sector, for example the development of consortia and locality purchasing in the British National Health Service. The case for managed markets has been most strongly made by Saltman and Von Otter (1992):

> In the search for a new health policy paradigm for publicly operated health systems, planned markets have the capacity to integrate neo-classical economic and traditional planning approaches into a new synthesis – into a normatively as well as economically bounded health care paradigm.

The level of institutional development of a new system is low, and little of the detail has yet been filled in, but some of the major issues are clear. The first relates to the nature of the customer. The development of internal markets has, so far involved the ultimate service user very little. Patterns of consultation and involvement have begun to emerge, though experience, for example of the Oregon procedure for setting health care priorities, has shown that it is difficult to create effective procedures. A second issue is the trade-off between markets and hierarchies in the management of internal markets, with both being used in different circumstances. Third, there is the difficulty of developing the organisational infrastructure of information and procedures that is necessary for the effective management of trading within organisations.

Enthoven argued that there were six conditions that were necessary for the effective operation of the internal market:

- Incentives to make cost-effective decisions
- Suitably trained managers
- A culture of buying and selling services

- Reasonably precise cost information
- Supply of information on how to improve efficiency
- Freedom from conflict of interest

These conditions are not fully met in any of the internal markets that have been established for the operation of public services in Britain, though this is hardly surprising given the early stage of development. The internal market will take a considerable time to become effective. The central issue is the balance between the use of straightforward market processes and planning. Unregulated markets are unlikely in most cases. What we have at present are often markets in which there are few individual customers and limited use of the price mechanism.

7 Agencies and Devolved Control

The argument for devolved control is that the problem of producer dominance can be overcome by the separation of the political and the operational levels of public organisations. Service providers can be established as independent units, having control of their own budgets, and, preferably, acting in competition with one another. Politicians can set goals and can effectively monitor the performance of the bureaucrats by establishing systems for determining whether targets are being met, and perhaps, paying by results. Public organisations are separating the political and managerial levels through the creation of devolved budgets, with strong levels of independent control at the local operational level. Some of the developments of independence of operational units are, in effect, processes of privatisation within the public service, with the establishment of stronger property rights for managers as the basis of incentives, and control exercised through the establishment of clear performance-based regimes.

Performance measurement and targets have been central to the development of the newly decentralised system of control within the public in Britain, and the number of performance measures in the National Health Service and the civil service, in particular, has grown rapidly. The number of performance indicators in the National Health Service increased from 70 in the early 1980s to 450 in 1988 (Flynn, 1992, p. 109), and the number of indicators specified in the public expenditure white papers from 500 in 1985, to 1800 in 1997, after which 'no one was counting any more' (Carter *et al.*, 1992). Local authorities are now to report on a number of performance measures laid down by government, and monitored by the Audit Commission. Performance-based pay has become increasingly common in the public service, particularly at senior levels.

There are two main ways in which the political and the managerial can be separated within government: devolution of financial control to managers at lower levels of the organisation, and the establishment of internal agencies within the public service, operating as relatively autonomous units. The difference lies in the extent to which the traditional hierarchical links are broken. In the early 1980s the former approach dominated, as the emphasis on managerialism grew, and cost and profit-centre based systems of organisation became more common. More recently there has been an emphasis on the establishment of agencies and other bodies with considerable autonomy within public service organisations. The distance between politics and management is steadily increasing, with politicians being defined as having a strategic and monitoring role, and only very limited involvement in day-to-day service issues. There has been a growth of inspection procedures to check on whether managers are attaining their targets and working within defined strategies.

The development of financial devolution has been most popular at central government level, notably in Britain and New Zealand, but has also been developed in Australia, the Netherlands, and many other countries. It is also used increasingly at local government level, particularly in Britain, in education and in the management of health. Experience has shown that unless it involves very significantly changed power structures, the devolution of control, on its own, will have only a very limited impact, and autonomy will tend to be subverted. In the Civil Service the executive agencies have seen their autonomy continually eroded by ministers, senior civil servants within departments, and the Treasury. Schools, by contrast, have been given genuine increases in power and have so far been able to exercise their new freedom. Even there, though, there is some evidence that central government is asserting control over schools, replacing the local education authority with a new framework of funding agencies and direct central government control. Financial autonomy is not easily established.

Financial devolution

Devolved finance involves giving managers increased control over the budgets for which they are responsible, frequently combined with explicit targets either at the individual or the organisational level or both. At its simplest, devolution can take the form of limited cost centre management, with managers being given more freedom in the way that they control their budgets, for example over the purchase of materials or limited virement between budget heads. In practice, such devolution has often been limited by requiring managers controlling such budgets to operate within tight rules that limit their practical freedom. It is rare, for example, for cost centre managers to be given freedom in the recruitment and grading of staff or the purchasing of materials.

The level of devolved control has, in many cases, gone much further than this limited form of cost centre management. In Britain there has been the Financial Management Initiative in central government, the Resource Management Initiative in the National Health Services, and the formula funding of schools, with local management of school budgets. Individual local authorities, such as Surrey and Berkshire County Councils, have also established their own programmes of delegation of finance. New Zealand has operated an extensive programme of financial delegation, for example in health and education. Schools have been given increased financial control in many countries, for example, New Zealand, parts of Canada and the United States of America. Australia had its own version of the Financial Management Initiative, the Financial Management Improvement Programme and the Programme Management and Budget, as have many other countries.

The financial management initiative

The Financial Management Initiative (FMI) may be seen, at one level, as a rather narrow exercise in changing the way that accounting is done in central government, but that view neglects the degree to which changes in the rules of accounting can have radical results. As institutional theory suggests, changing the rules about the way that basic resources are controlled and allocated can have fundamental effects on people's behaviour, through the way that it affects incentives, beliefs and understandings. Managers with devolved budgetary control do come to see the resources that they control as belonging to them, and want to have the freedom to decide how they are to be used. Even if the real degree of financial delegation is limited, it will create pressure for organisational change.

Decentralisation of budgetary control in the civil service threatened the traditional, highly centralised, Treasury control of finance in British central government. It was intended to focus attention on the relationship between spending and service that becomes obscured in a highly centralised system. The initiative had its origin in the Management Information System for Ministers (MINIS), introduced by Michael Heseltine at the Department of the Environment, which was intended to enable politicians to understand and control the use of resources, and relate them to policy objectives. The intention that underlay the Financial Management Initiative was to extend the principles of this approach throughout government. Ministerial support was mixed, but there was strong support from the Prime Minister, which was crucial to the spread of the initiative.

The White Paper, *Efficiency and Effectiveness in the Civil Service* (Cmnd 8616), specified three elements in the Financial Management initiative. Each department should have:

(a) a clear view of their objectives and means to assess and, wherever possible measure outputs and performance in relation to those objectives;
(b) well-defined responsibility for making the best use of their resources, including a critical study of output and value for money; and
(c) the information (particularly about costs), the training and the access to expert advice that managers need to exercise their responsibilities effectively.

Pious as these statements may seem, they presented a formidable agenda to a large, slow moving organisation like the British Civil Service. The FMI can be seen as no more than the extension of management by objectives to central government, but, given the failure of previous attempts to introduce similar systems, this was a substantial change. The Fulton Commission had recommended establishing clearly accountable service units, which would work to clear objectives, but it had little effect on practice. The Financial Management Initiative had much greater impact.

The role of the centre of the individual government department was to be planning, setting targets, allocating resources and monitoring performance, with policy formation and implementation clearly separated. Each department was expected to produce an outline development plan, to develop an information system that would provide appropriate intelligence for managers at all levels, to specify the responsibilities of managers for resources and outputs, to develop a budgetary control system for administrative costs, and to develop performance indicators and measures. Managers were to be responsible for total costs, including capital expenditure, not simply variable costs. According to the National Audit Office (1986):

> The essential advances in the FMI proposals are the placing of budgets within integrated management systems, the assignment of comprehensive budgets to units of accountable management systems and the association of the budgets with measured outputs.

The aim of the Financial Management Initiative was to create improved management through more effective control of local managers as agents, through identifying and clarifying the role of ministers and senior departmental staff as principals, and through improving the information available. The system was to make the relationship between action and results more transparent, and to enable politicians more easily to fulfil their responsibilities as policy makers and controllers of the bureaucracy.

Managers were to have greater freedom to determine how they met their targets, and there was to be a reduction in the degree of direct hierarchical control. The change was opposed, as management changes in the civil service traditionally are, by a combination of inertia, the disbelief system, and action. Resistance to the Financial Management Initiative came from middle and lower level managers as much as senior managers, because they felt that they were likely to be held responsible for costs which they had little power to control. There was particular concern about the degree of control over pay gradings, staffing levels and accommodation costs. The Treasury was reluctant to reduce the centralised control that it operated, and generally there was concern about the possible erosion of the traditional concept of the civil service as a unified body.

The development of the Financial Management Initiative required the creation of a system of cost centre management, and a management accounting system that was adequate to allow managers to control expenditure. Both of these requirements were slow to develop in practice. The limitations to the development of Financial Management Initiative followed not only from resistance by those who wanted to preserve traditional approaches, but also the inadequacy of the technical systems that were available. Accounting systems were not capable of generating the information needed, for example in relation to accounting for capital or the development of accrual accounting, which has developed much more rapidly in New Zealand. The significance of the needs for information that are generated by the more managerially oriented public service is illustrated by the rapid growth in expenditure on information technology in central government, and the recruitment of more accountants.

The Financial Management Initiative emphasised the importance of management, seen as the efficient use of resources to attain defined purposes, as opposed to the professional specialism that has dominated the civil service. In bringing more responsibility under the individual operational manager the attempt was to strengthen accountability, and to relate it directly to performance in service delivery, rather than to internal purposes. The increased discretion of the line manager was a challenge to the traditional dominance of the policy stream within the civil service. The focus on results also gradually led to a shift of emphasis from the intra-departmental control of expenditure, to the control of spending across departments on whole programmes. As Metcalfe and Richards (1987) argue:

> With the gradual realisation that administrative overheads were only a fraction of the total costs of managing programmes, the spotlight shifted to programme expenditure as a whole. As a result, the management of relations between departments, and the networks of non-departmental bodies through which public services are delivered, moved to centre stage. Managing programme expenditure efficiently and effectively depends on managing the inter-organisational network through which services are delivered. This is one of the major ways in which the FMI is bringing attention to bear on managing change at the inter-organisational level (p. 191).

The Financial Management Initiative did not lead directly to a bottom-up approach to management accounting (Johnson, 1992), but it did move the focus away from the centre and unified control, and made clear the inadequacy of traditional information and control systems for management purposes.

The effectiveness of the Financial Management Initiative was constrained by the relative failure of performance indicators, which, as many studies have shown, are subject to limitations. Managers will tend to manipulate the system to ensure that they are seen in the best light. According to Carter and his colleagues, many managers simply represented existing indicators as performance measures:

> . . . departments tended to re-christen existing statistics of activity or costing information as performance indicators or measures of output (p. 20).

Perhaps the most basic limitation of the success of the Initiative was that there was no change in the way that overall budgeting and financial planning operated. The public expenditure planning process was not changed to make the Initiative more effective, by, for example, building budgets from the bottom upwards, rather than squeezing outputs into preconceived expenditure totals. The Initiative left the essential structure of control relatively unchanged, and though it made principal and agent roles clearer there was little change in the property rights of managers within the organisation. Managers had as much incentive to manipulate the system as to make it work. There was nevertheless genuine advance in the measurement of results and the information generally available to manage performance. It is easy to criticise the development of the Financial Management Initiative as simply the belated adoption of traditional Taylorist managerialism, but that is to ignore the commitment to the exercise, and the fact that it took place within an explicit framework of ideas about the relationship between resource control and incentives.

The resource management initiative

The Resource Management Initiative in the British National Health Service can be seen as having a number of roots, going back to the

1970s, in attempts to develop more effective accounting and management information and closer cost control. It was based particularly upon the attempt to develop clinical budgets, and better arguments for devolved management budgets. The initiating document for the Resource Management Initiative stated that its purpose was to:

> . . . enable the National Health Service to give a better service to its patients by helping clinicians and other managers to make better informed judgements about how the resources they control can be used to maximum effect (Packwood *et al.*, 1991, p. 11).

The approach differed from the Financial Management Initiative in being less orientated to control by principals of agents, and more to improving knowledge of the link between inputs and results at the local level. The main purpose was to improve the transparency of the management of resources through making detailed information more widely available. The point was not so much to control professionals, as to involve them in the process of management and performance assessment, and enable them to manage the resources that they controlled more effectively. The initiative also differed from the Financial Management Initiative in being introduced on an experimental basis on a limited number of sites, rather than throughout the service.

The impact of the Resource Management Initiative is difficult to assess since it later became enmeshed in the development of the internal market in the National Health Service. The evaluation by Packwood and his colleagues did find that it had beneficial results. It had led to changes in the organisation and quality of service, and in some cases to increases in the level of activity. It had also improved the ability of managers and professionals to manage change. The development of the Resource Management Initiative illustrates the long period that is necessary for change to take hold in a complex organisation such as the National Health Service. It is also indicative of the difficulty of making fundamental changes within existing structures, and it is not surprising that, just as in the central government, where agencies superseded the Financial Management Initiative, the internal market overshadowed attempts to introduce budget-based management changes in the National Health Service.

The Resource Management Initiative was more successful in community than acute units, which Perrin (1988) attributes to the fact that they faced an easier financial situation and to their simpler organisational structure. In the more complex areas of the service, notably in acute care, it is extremely difficult to identify and analyse expenditure in the way that is wanted, for example according to client groups and specialities. The main difficulty faced by the Resource Management Initiative was the autonomy of the professionals, the doctors, rather than the degree of central control. The Initiative tried to deal with doctors and other professionals by involving them, rather than trying to develop control systems based upon performance management. The aim was that there should be greater ability to analyse performance at a devolved level, rather than to control it. The limitations on the Initiative were more to do with the technical difficulty of developing effective systems to provide the sort of information that was wanted, and in the form in which it was wanted, than resistance. They illustrated the way that all changes in the management of the National Health Service have been limited by the lack of effective management information, despite the many attempts at improvement.

Local management of schools

It is in education that the most radical changes in the way that public organisations are financed and controlled have been made, with major changes in the extent to which schools control their own budgets. Traditionally there has been little budgeting on the basis of the individual school or college; the local education authority controlled resources, distributing them to schools and colleges on the basis of relatively unclear principles, only partially based upon the number of pupils or students in the institution. The Burnham system did allocate points to schools on the basis of weighted pupil numbers, which had some effect on resources, for example the pay of teachers and the number of promoted posts available, and a similar system operated for colleges. The local education authority was, nevertheless, left with considerable discretion and control over the allocation of resources, increased by the lack of transparency in the system. The determination of the way that expenditure varied from one school or college to another has been difficult to determine, since budgets were not calculated in that form. There was, as a result, little knowledge of unit costs in education, and schools and colleges could do little to influence their budgets.

A small number of local education authorities experimented with the devolution of finance to schools in the mid-1980s, notably Cambridgeshire and Solihull. Pilot schools were given their own budgets, with freedom to spend within certain limits. The experiments were limited, and, though they had some success, there was no systematic evaluation of the experience, and it is unlikely that it would have been taken up widely by other local education authorities without government legislation. The Education Reform Act 1988 made financial devolution to schools compulsory, and gave them considerable independence in the way that they controlled their funds. The policy for the local management of schools finance was based upon the distribution of revenue resources with local education authorities retaining control of capital expenditure. Education authorities also retain a proportion of total funding for dealing with authority-wide services, for example meals, administration and transport, though that proportion is continually being reduced.

Finance is allocated to schools on the basis of a formula which is devised by the local education authority, but which has to be accepted by the Secretary of State for Education. The formula is based largely upon pupil numbers, with age-weighting, and with some account being taken of special needs and other factors. As Thomas (1988) has argued, the heavy dependence of the formula on pupil numbers effectively makes the pupil into a voucher and schools have a clear incentive to attract pupils in order to increase budgets. The intention of the government was that schools should feel the pressure of the market, through parent choice, and the tying of budgets to pupil numbers would lead to school closure, where appropriate, as numbers fell.

The purpose of formula funding from the point of view of the government is to limit the discretion of the local education authority, and the local management of schools therefore differs from the Financial Management Initiative, which made no changes to the way that activities were funded. The local management of schools was not oriented to control so much as creating a changed pattern of incentives for headteachers and governing bodies through giving them stronger property rights over their resources. The difference of the local management of schools from most other initiatives in devolved budgeting was in creating a genuine pattern of bottom-up control. It was not so much changing the relationship between principal and agent as creating new principals and agents.

The devolution of financial control to schools involves the separation of income from expenditure, so that budgets do not automatically balance, and schools must become concerned for their income as well as controlling their expenditure. Schools can not only increase income through attracting more pupils, but also through commercial initiatives. They may, for example, earn income through the letting of school facilities. Again, this is significantly different from the Financial Management Initiative and the Resource Management Initiative, both of which were oriented only to expenditure control. Under the previous system there had, in effect, been no individual school budgets; the local education authority calculated an aggregated budget, and allocated resources to schools according to various indices of need. The only reason why expenditures would not match budgetary plans were unforeseen circumstances or poor budgetary control by the local education authority. Spending decisions were made during the year in allocating the global budget for such services as day-to-day maintenance of the fabric of the building, with central local authority officers in control. Schools themselves could do relatively little to cause over-spending, and the balancing of income and expenditure was not their responsibility, but that of the local authority. In the new system there is no reason why the finance allocated should match historical expenditures.

Schools that were not full faced particular problems when budgets were devolved, and the new system exposed the higher unit costs that they faced. There are particular problems with small schools and teacher costs. There is substantial evidence that unit costs, both in relation to teaching and non-teaching costs, are related to school size, with small schools being significantly more expensive. Local Education authorities were traditionally able to compensate schools for the problems of size to some degree, commonly through the allocation of a lump sum, with a sliding supplement, to cope with relatively high fixed costs, and salary protection. Such approaches increased markedly during the period of falling school rolls in the early 1980s, which had led to curriculum-based staffing systems.

Growing constraint on local finance makes the protection of schools difficult. The smaller the school the more likely it is that its budget will be severely disrupted by staff sickness, or unforeseen expenditures. Attempts to build up a sensitive global formula from sub-formulae have had limited effect. In some cases local education authorities have established insurance systems to protect schools against unforeseen contingencies, but this has been difficult to achieve because of the unwillingness of schools, and particularly larger schools, to co-operate. It is also difficult to maintain collective provision of services that were previously operated on a wholly centralised basis by local authorities, such as school library services, especially as the proportion of the budget held at the centre declines. The schools must make individual decisions and there are incentives to free-ride on provision for others, and simple difficulties in making collective decisions. There are clear incentives to underinvest in collective services, or for the pattern of expenditure to be more variable from year to year, so that continuity of service is difficult.

A problem that was much debated at the time of the introduction of devolved budgets was the impact of differential teacher costs, over which schools were seen as having limited control. As teachers grow older they move up the salary scale, so that a school which had older teachers would face higher costs. Despite much argument that schools should only have to budget for average rather than actual costs, possibly with the local authority acting as a banker to ensure balance of the total system, the government resisted. Schools have an incentive to hire younger teachers, since, given a fixed budget, they will thereby release funds for spending other than on teachers. Some schools have used early retirement and fixed term contracts to manipulate the costs of the teaching force. The impact of the cost of teachers with higher than average salaries is greatest in primary schools, and relatively limited in larger secondary schools, because of higher level of turnover and the effects of scale. Experience has shown that the effect of differential teacher costs is significant.

The result of formulae for the distribution of finance to schools has been that some have lost while others have gained. Arnott and her colleagues found that 21 per cent of schools had lost 3 per cent or more of their budgets following the introduction of the local management of schools, and that 20 per cent had gained by 3 per cent or more. Others have found large gains and losses. The impact of the system was reduced by the phasing in of change over a four-year period. The devolved budget is managed at the local level by the headteacher and the school governing body, and there is very little limitation on the freedom to choose how money will be spent. The government's view is that schools have an incentive to spend their money effectively because parents are free to place pupils in any school which has a place, and pupils were expected to go to the more effective schools, which would then attract more finance. It can be argued that the result has been to free up one side of the market only, the demand side, and that if there is to be more fundamental change there would have to be greater freedom to open new schools, as is the case for example, to some degree, in Denmark. The development of local management of schools has had the effect of making headteachers and governors more active in attracting pupils, and there has been a growing emphasis on the marketing of the school. The degree of choice available to parents is still small because of the effects of geography, and the effect of market pressures on schools has been markedly different depending on the range of provision, and the extent of over-provision in the local area. There is a high degree of local monopoly, and schools can therefore choose pupils as much as parents can choose schools.

The devolution of budgets to schools has been generally welcomed by headteachers and governors. The introduction of local management seems to have led to significant increases in the level of administration in the school. There has been less clarity over whether the devolution of finance actually does anything to improve the standard of education. There is also some concern in schools that operating the internal market will distract headteachers and governing bodies from their primary educational responsibilities. The increase in administrative costs has led to a decline in the resources devoted to direct teaching in many cases.

The pattern of behaviour under devolved budgets has been influenced by the fact that it has taken place within the context of severe financial constraint in public sector spending. Schools have generally been cautious in spending decisions. Marven and Levačić (1992), in their study of the first year of the operation of local management of schools in one shire county, found that the majority of schools underspent, and the total carry-over was £6.8 million, although much of this was committed to future projects. The Audit Commission, in a later study, found that many schools were holding balances of £100 000 and more. British Government figures showed that schools were holding balances of nearly £400 000 000 million in 1993. The work of Arnott and her colleagues suggests that the underspending was not the result of planning, and followed from a mixture of caution and difficulty in budget management.

The structure of the devolution of finance to schools is only loosely comparable to that in the National Health Service and the Civil Service, since the school is relatively independent of any hierarchical control. There is no system of planned financial targets, though the school must work within the context of the national curriculum and publish its result in national testing systems. National league tables of secondary schools, based on examination results, are now regularly being produced. The difference between the management of finance in the education system and the Financial Management Initiative in the civil service is akin to the different styles of strategic control exercised in multi-divisional companies. Goold and Campbell differentiate between strategic planning and financial control, the first involving a general framework with very broad targets, the latter a much more detailed set of financial targets with tight controls. Schools operate within a system of very broad strategic planning.

Different balances between professionalism and hierarchical control are emerging within schools. The governing body has gained power, but its influence is often limited compared with that of the headteacher, and as the degree of hierarchical control by the local education authority has declined, that within the school has increased. The relationships within the local education system now have the form more of a network, with the local authority retaining some very limited residual quality control responsibilities, allocating resources, though with very limited discretion, and selling services, for example library and psychological services, on an internal market basis. The major issue has been how to retain services in which there is some economy of scale. Schools have largely continued to purchase services from the local authority, rather than on the market, but have made significant changes in their patterns of expenditure. Purchasing patterns are slowly beginning to change, for example through the purchasing of services from other than the home authority, and from the private sector. Organisations specifically oriented to selling services to schools are beginning to emerge.

The impact of the local management of schools has been to devolve genuine financial control and create a system of bottom-up financial management. The role of the local authority is not now that of principal, but rather of supplier of support services on a market basis. Schools are gradually beginning to vary more as they make individual decisions about how resources shall be used.

Devolved budgets

The move to devolved budgets, with the establishment of cost centres and internal, semi-autonomous business units, involves a break with the tradition of the hierarchical bureaucracy. The change is analogous to the move from the uniform to the multiform organisation that has developed in the private sector since the 1920s. This development raises significant problems of co-ordination which are particularly important for accountability and responsiveness, and which will be considered in the next chapter. The significant different between the devolution of finance to schools and other experiments in devolved control lies in the greater degree of freedom for schools and the ability to carry surpluses from one year to the next. In the case of the Financial Management Initiative in the UK, the purpose was greater control, but schools have been given genuinely greater property rights over their finance. The impact of devolved budget holding in the National Health Service has been limited; as Owens and Glennerster found (1990):

> The nature of budget holding therefore is extremely randomised and idiosyncratic in the current structures, both old and new, which means many managers are functioning in a veil of ignorance.

These limitations are always likely to occur when the devolution of control takes place within organisational frameworks that are still strongly hierarchical.

The impacts of delegated budgets vary with the pattern of authority. Where there is devolution of financial control within a framework of central control the result will be different from cases of greater autonomy. As Milgrom and Roberts argue (1988):

Our general proposition is that any centralisation of authority, whether in the public or the private sector, creates the potential for intervention and so gives rise to costly influence activities and to excessive intervention by the central authority. The costs need to be weighed against the benefits of centralisation to determine the efficient extent and locus of authority (p. 87).

The point is that decentralisation alone is not likely to be powerful enough to overcome the inherent central control of organisations, and, where central control persists, managers will spend a greater part of their time trying to influence those with control than would be the case in a more devolved context. They are also more likely to try to manipulate the process of target setting where they are held to account on a performance-related basis. The distinction is easiest to see if we consider the cases of the Civil Service and the National Health Service in Britain compared with the local management of schools. In the case of education the power lay with the schools, effectively creating an internal market in which the local authority acted as a supplier of services. In the case of the National Health Service the attempt at control was limited, and the aim was simply to provide better information for local managers and professionals. In the Civil Service the process involved in the Financial Management Initiative was clearly one of decentralisation within a framework of central control, and the result was that local managers were still oriented to the senior controllers of the organisation rather than outward to the user.

Agencies, trusts and companies

Countries operate with varying degrees of separation between policy-making and implementation, but many governments have been moving to greater differentiation between the two functions over the last decade. The development of agencies has been the keystone of the changed approach to the management of central government in New Zealand. In Sweden there have been moves to increase the independence of the agencies which have been the traditional mode of operating the administrative aspects of central government. There have been changes along similar lines in many European countries, such as Denmark and the Netherlands.

Denmark has operated a 'free agencies' experiment. In the Netherlands:

> Agencies are more independent parts of the civil service and are considered to be ideally suited for ensuring that the emphasis is switched from resource-oriented authority to performance-oriented accountability. Agencies typically have greater management powers and responsibilities than normal civil service departments – for example, broader facilities for handling the budget, possibly in combination with the accrual accounting and commercial book-keeping (Organisation for Economic Cooperation and Development, 1990, p. 63).

In Britain the development of independent agencies has been central to the reform of the civil service and, in one form or another, has characterised reorganisation in health, education, and other services such as waste disposal.

Much of central government is now organised on an agency basis. In the National Health Service the large majority of bodies responsible for the delivery of service are being established as trusts, which are independent of the District Health Authority, though they remain within the Service. In education polytechnics (now with the status of universities) and further education colleges have been given independent corporate status, and schools may opt out of local education authority control, taking up grant-maintained status, and be funded directly by central government. The use of this mechanism is more limited within local government, though there is some use of internal companies, and a number of authorities have transferred housing and social services to independent trusts or companies. The creation of formal separation for the agencies that are responsible for the delivery of service may be seen as a logical development of the devolution of financial control, though, of course, the two can be combined, with the development of internal devolution within agencies and other independent forms. In the National Health Service, for example, the Resource Management Initiative has continued though it has been absorbed into the new system, based upon the purchaser–provider split, with attempts to devolve budgets to clinicians, for example, within hospitals. Many of the executive agencies in central government have programmes of devolving financial control.

Health service trusts

Trusts are seen by many as central to the development of the internal market in the National Health Service; Ham (1992a), for example argues:

> . . . NHS trusts . . . are needed to allow health authorities to take on a more independent role as purchasers . . . Only where real separation occurs are health authorities able to concentrate on the development of the purchasing function and establish themselves as the 'people's champions' that ministers have described (p. 8).

The limited effects of the various initiatives to decentralise financial control in government within existing organisational frameworks would suggest that Ham is correct. The producers are likely to dominate integrated organisations, given their greater numbers, particularly in a highly professional organisation such as the National Health Service. They will also have significant information advantages, although it is far from clear how the separation of purchaser and provider, and operation on the basis of contracts, will change that. In order for there to be fundamental change to the way that systems operate there must be fundamental changes in the organisational and institutional framework. In practice, as with many other aspects of public sector change, the information that is available to the purchasers is often too limited to allow them the necessary control. Certainly this is the case in the National Health Service.

National Health Service trusts are hospitals and other health service units, such as community health providers, that are established with their own boards of directors and independent management. Though they are not independent legal entities, they do have considerable freedom in practice. They have been given a considerable degree of independence in determining pay, staffing levels, and other aspects of the management of resources. As the government's advice on the establishment of trusts enthusiastically asserted:

> Trusts have the power to make their own decisions – right or wrong! – without being subject to bureaucratic procedures, processes or pressure from higher tiers of management.

Such a system obviously carries with it dangers of lack of accountability. Are trusts simply to be left alone if they do get it wrong? It is not surprising that the practice has been different from the theory.

Trusts do have considerable autonomy; they have the freedom to: acquire and dispose of assets; make capital expenditure requests direct to the centre rather than through the health authority; raise capital; independently determine their own organisational and staffing structures; and make their own decisions on pay and conditions. Trusts have been willing to make use of these powers especially in the way that they have gone about managing staff, for example the pay structures operated, though only to a limited degree. They have also been active in marketing the services that they provide, particularly to fundholding general practitioners. Trusts differ from traditional health units in having strong property rights; they can own land, buildings and other property, and are free to sell assets within certain limitations. The property rights are limited, in that the trust cannot choose to liquidate its assets and go into another business, but they do create a significantly different set of incentives for managers compared to those that operate in traditional health units.

National Health Service trusts operate with no direct funding, and are required to earn all their income from the services that they provide. They must fund capital as well as revenue expenditure from income, and make a rate of return on expenditure of 6 per cent. They are not required necessarily to break even every year, but rather 'taking one year with another', and may carry forward surpluses or deficits. Inevitably the operation of block contracts has made the budgeting of trusts relatively simple, but, as the pattern of contracts changes, and purchasers, particularly fundholding general practitioners, become more willing to change, they are having to move onto a more genuine trading basis. The change in the form of contracts, though, will not affect the degree of monopoly control that can in effect be exercised by many trusts, especially in rural areas.

Grant-maintained schools

If the establishment of trusts is the natural extension of the separation of purchaser and provider in the National Health

Service, the grant maintained school is the logical development of the local management of schools. Grant-maintained status involves schools becoming independent of the local education authority, and being funded directly by the Department for Education. Application for grant maintained status may be made following a favourable vote by parents. The number of grant-maintained schools has increased less quickly than the British Government hoped, but it is committed to the wholesale movement of schools out of local education authority control over the next ten years. Schools that have taken up grant-maintained status so far have been favourably treated, both in terms of revenue and capital expenditure, receiving a range of start-up and other grants. The money for funding grant-maintained schools has been deducted from the budgets of local education authorities. Finances previously held back by local authorities to provide for administrative costs, and to provide central services, are now directly allocated to the school.

Grant-maintained schools have strong property rights, being able to acquire and dispose of property, and enter into contracts with staff and other bodies. In the past the local authority has controlled the property in which the school operates, but now the grant-maintained school can use its resources to make profit. Many schools, for example, control leisure facilities and are willing to use them to make money. Grant-maintained schools let contracts for the services that they need, for example school meals or payroll services, often contracting with the local authority from which they have gained independence. They must cope with cash flow, but the favourable way in which they are paid, receiving funds well before they have to be paid out has allowed many of them to make favourable deals.

It is difficult to determine the extent to which the spending patterns of grant-maintained schools reflect the ability to make independent decisions, or the availability of more resources. There are examples of grant-maintained schools becoming more hierarchical in the way that they are managed, compared to more collegial patterns of administration, but, as Halpin and his (1992) colleagues argue, there is no tendency to favour one managerial style over another. They argue that the real management changes were the result of the development of the Local Management of Schools, rather than independent grant-maintained status. Grant-maintained schools have shown their desire for independence not only in financial matters, but also in attempts, in some cases, to change the basis of admission to introduce more selection. The independence of grant-maintained schools may be eroded by the influence of the Funding Agency for Schools. Much will also depend upon the nature of the common funding formula. The Funding Agency is intended to be significantly less influential than the local education authority has been, but the establishment of a new hierarchy illustrates the difficulty of establishing market processes.

Further education

Further education colleges were established as corporate bodies from April 1993, as the polytechnics – now universities – were in 1989. They will work in a world of contracts, with Training and Enterprise Councils, as principals, providing finance for specified courses, and contracting with the local authority for specific support, such as payroll management, should they so choose. The management of the further education world involves operating in a network of organisations, in which the local authority will have a part to play through the provision of information, and continuing responsibility for schools and youth services. There is a funding council to determine levels of financing, but its influence is relatively limited, compared with the control previously exercised by the local authority. College governing bodies and principals have strong powers, and well-entrenched property rights. Emphasis on management and administration has increased.

The move to independent status for colleges eliminates hierarchical control by the local authority, but enhances that within the colleges. As Rees (1992) says:

> As managerial and administrative tasks move from the Authority to the Colleges, the relative numbers and importance of support staff will increase, changing the traditional balance of power between teaching/support staff.

As well as employing more of their own support staff, as the schools have also tended to do, they are more likely to contract for services other than to the local authority, or to feel that they can provide services directly themselves. There are a number of cases of colleges contracting out payroll services, with the local authority bidding and losing. The move to corporate status for the colleges is less of a change than it is for schools. The same factors are at work, with increased property rights, and the ability to operate more flexibly, but colleges have always been much larger institutions and have had much greater autonomy, for example in employing more of their own support staff. The change is still welcomed by colleges generally, and particularly by the management.

Companies

The company form has been strongly used in delivering public services in some countries. In Canada, for example, many local services are provided through companies in some cities. In Germany public works organisations have a quasi-company form, and the local authority operates company-like mechanisms for the delivery of services such as electricity and heating. In Eastern Europe the delivery of many public services is carried out through company-like organisations. Companies of various forms, and with greater or lesser degrees of independence are increasingly being used in the public service in Britain. There has always been some use of companies, notably in local government in the provision of commercial or partly commercial services such as theatres, and for new projects, for example in environmental development. In some cases there have been joint ventures with the private sector, for example in housing or town centre development. Companies have also been a means of developing innovative services. Companies were also used by some local authorities in the 1980s as a means of avoiding financial controls.

The more extensive use of the company mechanism has been an explicit part of the development of the market based approach to the management of the public service. Legislation has required public transport to be operated through separate companies. Local authorities have formed companies in implementing the City Challenge Initiative. The Training and Enterprise Councils established as the key agencies in ensuring the development of a more effective pattern of training have the status of companies. The Environmental Protection Act 1990 required major changes in the way that refuse disposal was managed, involving the separation of direct service provision, regulation and purchase of the service. The approach requires a mixture of internal separation and competitive tendering, though the final result, in the long term, may be to increase the development of co-operative ventures with the private sector. The local authority is required to establish the operational elements of the waste disposal function as a separate organisation, with the status of a company. The company will own assets, which will be transferred from the local authority, as will the staff. The waste disposal company will be required to win work in a competitive tender process. The ability of the local authority waste disposal company to raise capital will be limited, and in the longer term it is unclear whether companies will be forced by commercial necessities to become fully independent of the local authority.

The use of the company form as part of the management of public services has been little developed, but it is significant in pointing to the way that the boundaries between the public and the private realms are being eroded. Some local authorities, concerned at the ability of their direct service and direct labour organisations to survive competition, are investigating various forms of company that might have an 'ethical' character. These approaches might involve employee ownership, already operated for some public transport, or the operation of intermediate trusts. Some residual influence would normally be retained by the public authority. Similar issues are being debated in other countries, particularly in Eastern Europe. When they are within the public service, companies have a stronger control of the property that they use than do traditional hierarchical departments. Managers also have more autonomy than is traditional, and greater claims on residual income. There is no obvious explanation as to why the government has chosen to use the company form in some cases rather than in others, but its use can be expected to increase.

Executive agencies

As grant maintained status was to the local management of schools, and trust status was to the resource management initiative in the National Health Service, so the move to executive agencies in UK central government can be seen as the fulfilment of the Financial

Management Initiative. The establishment of executive agencies was proposed in the Ibbs Report in 1988, which focussed on the policy orientation of the senior level of the civil service, the uniformity of approach to the organisation of government, and the difficulty of real decentralisation of decision making and resource management. The report proposed that the operational aspects of the work of central government departments should be separated from the process of policy advice, and established in separate agencies which would be headed by chief executives, who would have genuine autonomy in the way that they managed. The chief executives of agencies would have to work to targets, and the overall approach to be adopted was to be laid down in a framework agreement between the agency and the minister heading the department, which, in effect, formed a contract. The targets set would cover financial performance, efficiency, and quality of service. Framework agreements and targets would vary in form depending on the nature of the organisation involved, for example in the degree to which quantitative targets were set.

The recommendation was quickly acted upon, and the number of agencies has grown rapidly, so that they now cover the majority of the civil service in Britain. The size of agencies varies greatly, from the Benefits Agency, which employs more than 70 000 staff, to those such as the Queen Elizabeth II Conference Centre employing relatively few. If the establishment of agencies was relatively rapid, at least in terms of the pace at which government typically moves, the substantive change of management has been much slower. The Treasury has been slow to reduce the degree of central control and uniformity required in finance and staffing matters. Departments, too, have tended to retain control of their agencies, and been unwilling to grant chief executives the autonomy that is necessary to make genuine changes. Ministers have been unwilling to allow chief executives in agencies providing politically sensitive services to act autonomously. Most of the chief executives of agencies have been appointed from inside the civil service, and they have shown a limited willingness to confront traditional approaches, though the number appointed from outside has been increasing. Chief executives appointed from outside the civil service have been more critical of the lack of real freedom than those who had previously worked within the service. The assumption has been that the agency and its chief executive must justify changes, rather than having freedom to adopt the approaches that they think necessary. The controls exercised are still strong and agency managers must spend a good deal of their time trying to influence the department in which they operate. Central government has shown itself unwilling to allow agencies to operate as genuinely independent trading entities.

Change has been more rapid where the agencies have trading fund status, under which they earn income on a trading basis, rather than being funded according to the normal vote procedures of the civil service. The key issues are whether the agency has freedom from the requirement to operate on the basis of annuality, that is ensuring that its income and expenditure match each year, and whether they operate on a gross or net running cost basis, that is whether they must operate within a cash limit allocated at the beginning of the year, or can generate income. The typical agency, like the traditional civil service, operates on a gross running cost basis, with annuality of expenditure. Only a small number of agencies, typically those most removed from policy, such as Her Majesty's Stationery Office, have been granted freedom from the traditional controls, so that the target process is matched by a corresponding freedom of resource control. Core agencies, such as the Benefits Agency are subject to much stronger control. Departmental arrangements have not always changed to represent the quasi-contractual relationship between the minister and the head of the agency. Formal organisational change has not been matched by deeper change in the institutional character of the service. The use of full trading accounts, such as those which operate for direct service organisations in local government, or the freedoms granted to schools, has not been mirrored in the civil service.

The impact of the establishment of agencies has been reduced by the fact that they have limited independence in law. As Hood and Jones point out they compare unfavourably with the approach that has been adopted in New Zealand, where agencies are the employer, and the heads of agencies are responsible for specified output targets, with ministers retaining responsibility for outcomes. The performance targets of the heads of agencies in New Zealand are specified in contracts that have legal force. Agencies are also made independent of the policy departments, and, as Pallot (1991) shows, detailed attention has been given to the financial regime that is necessary for agencies to have an appropriate combination of freedom and incentive to deliver. New Zealand has given considerable attention to issues such as annuality, capital charges, and payment on the basis of market costs. The Swedish model of the separation of agencies responsible for the delivery of services from policy-making was cited in the Ibbs report as precedent for the development of the Next Steps agencies, but, as Harden argues, the legal limits on ministerial interference in the operation of agencies is not mirrored in Britain. The government has chosen not to give its agencies independent status, so that they are still subject to the direct exercise of ministerial authority. Compared to other countries the freedom of agencies, and the clarity of the system in which they operate, can be seen as limited, as indeed it is in comparison to some other areas of British government organisation.

The experience of agencies so far suggest that they are a very qualified success, but that they have not yet fundamentally challenged the ethos of the civil service. Heads of agencies do commonly feel that they have been able to make changes in the way that the services for which they are responsible are managed. There is much less difference in the standing of the agency itself within the service, compared with the traditional situation. Sir Robin Butler, the head of the British civil service in the mid-1990s, has stressed the need to retain the uniformity of the service, but there can be little doubt that this emphasis conflicts with the pursuit of the operational needs of different agencies, as has been clear in the clashes between some of the more independently minded agency chief executives and their parent departments or government more generally. The emphasis on the uniformity of the service is likely to mean an emphasis on hierarchical rather than market modes of organisation, and a limitation on local variation.

Early studies of the introduction of agencies shows that they have had limited internal effect. Common *et al.* in a study which included five agencies, found that 'Change is happening at all levels of the organisations we studied, yet seems to be felt least by those who are furthest down the hierarchy' (p. 75). Mellon (1993a) argues that the fact that the chief executive is held responsible for meeting targets tends to lead to centralisation in the organisation of agencies, a characteristic enhanced by the actions of ministers and the senior levels of departments. Common *et al.* conclude that the emphasis has been on the formation of agencies rather than making them work differently from the traditional civil service. This is perhaps to be expected in the early stages of the move to a radically new approach, and the speed with which the process has developed contrasts markedly with the pace of many previous changes.

More fundamental is the criticism by Mellon that the agencies were not necessary to many of the changes. She concludes that the delegations were minor and that agency status is not enough, alone, to generate major change. Executive agency status, she argues, was '. . . not really a structural attempt to bring a market or competitive model to bear in the public sector.' Elsewhere she (Mellon, 1993b) argues that:

> The key point about the agency initiative is that it seeks to decentralise the civil service, to take authority away from the centre and delegate more clearly to the service deliverers. What it does not do, except at the margin, is to increase the level of competition faced by the agency. It is emphatically not about rivalry, competition or privatisation. Yet agency-speak is not just about improved service delivery to customers, an entirely laudable aim, but also muddled with ideas of external enemies and beating the competition. This mismatch between rhetoric and reality is both confusing and demoralising for service deliverers who can detect little if any real difference between the jobs they do now and those they did prior to agency status, with the possible exception of a tighter focus on targets (p. 18).

Nor are these criticisms simply academic carping. The Efficiency Unit, in a review of progress in the development of agencies in 1991, found that:

> In a number of cases the personal responsibility and account-ability explicit in the direct relationship between the Minister and the Chief Executive was not matched by the departmental arrangements, where responsibility was dispersed and a number of different parts of the Department, at different levels, could be involved in detailed oversight of the agency.

More recently the Trosa report made similar findings.

It is not surprising, given this view that the government has added market testing to the market mix in the civil service, though that has been seen by some chief executives, in the way that it has been imposed, as being in contradiction to the notion of the independence of management of the chief executive.

The development of executive agencies in central government has, so far, had limited effect because it has not been accompanied by significant changes in the financial regime that operates within the civil service. The service is still dominated by an institutional framework that assumes central control, uniformity, and traditional concepts of financial control. This contrasts markedly, for example with the situation in schools and colleges. It is unlikely that organisational change on its own will be enough to bring about real change in the way that the service operates. It is early in the process of change, and many of those involved emphasise that there have already been significant developments, but the experience of other agencies and other countries suggests that without attention to fundamental institutional issues traditional approaches will tend to reassert themselves.

Conclusion

A review of the development of autonomous management within the public service suggested two broad conclusions. First that it is not enough to devolve budgets without real control of resources, based in the establishment of effective property rights at the local level, if the intention is to move from hierarchical to market forms of operation. Schools and trust hospitals have genuine independence from their parent authorities, based on control of the resources that they use. The emphasis is not so much on the downward delegation of financial control, as the establishment of operational independence for the organisations involved in service delivery. The focus is upon the independence of the point of delivery first and control second, well illustrated by the relatively loose arrangements for the audit of grant-maintained schools. Higher levels of organisations are seen as purchasers of outputs rather than controllers of the action of the providing agency. This approach, as we will argue in considering accountability in a market-oriented system, raises major political issues, but it does have the effect of assuring managerial autonomy. Central government itself has been less willing to operate such a bottom-up approach to the development of responsible management. The civil service has done more to establish formally independent agencies than to change the rules within which they work. The change to schools, which has certainly been as radical as any other, took place without any significant change in the structure of the education service. The successes and failures of devolved budgets suggest that process change must precede structural change, and that the latter on its own will have little effect.

The slow pace of change in the British civil service was justified by one senior civil servant as follows:

> . . . there's still a long way to go in terms of giving greater freedom and discretion to individual departments and, within departments, to individual line managers. We are working on it. We're working quite hard on it. But it will take time just as it takes time to set up the original systems for the Financial Management Initiative, then the delegated budgets.

> But, at the end of the day, there's a limit. And it's a different sort of limit from the sort you'll find in the private sector, when you can simply rely on the profit measure to determine what is and what is not acceptable for an organisation as a whole (Hennessy, 1989, p. 615).

Experience shows that it is harder to make change happen in the civil service than elsewhere in the public sector, which fits the traditional argument of the power of civil servants to avoid change. The civil service has tried to change by changing the pattern of organisation, whereas it is the underlying rules of the game that need to be confronted, if there is to be real change in behaviour.

The impact of the changes that have been made should not be underestimated, even if it is sometimes less than might have been intended. The challenge to traditional modes of operating is, potentially, fundamental. Should the development of relatively independent agencies take hold, then the result will be the provision of public service through a differentiated pattern of organisations rather than integrated hierarchies. Dispersion will in turn raise issues about the integration of the public services. The impact of changes, particularly in combination, can be difficult to predict, and different patterns are emerging. The focus of analysis is moving to the whole network of organisations rather than the focal organisation.

PART III
THE IMPACT OF MARKETISATION

8 Organisation and Accountability

I have so far considered the individual market mechanisms, pricing, contracts and so forth, that are being introduced into the management of government, but the impact of change is dependent on the combination of developments that are involved. One change tends to lead to another, for example, managers given responsibility for managing their own budgets are more likely to contract for services. The pattern of change has been the opposite of the incrementalism that has been argued to characterise the development of public policy in the post-war years. Major changes in the basic organisation of public services have been introduced, followed by more gradual adjustments to structures, systems and processes. Public service managers and politicians have had to learn how to make the new public management operate as they have gone along. Typically change involves a mixture of purchaser/provider splits, contracts, devolution of finance and competition. The particular pattern varies from service to service, with more emphasis on one mechanism rather than another.

The pattern of change can be considered at two levels, the public service as a whole and the organisation of individual services. There are common developments at each level, for example, the separation of politics and administration, and the proliferation of single-purpose appointed governmental bodies, replacing traditional elected organisations, and relating to each other through contracts and market processes. The structure of the public service is becoming more diverse and differentiated, as networks of organisations replace multi-purpose bodies. The main impact of the new approach to public service management has been to reduce the extent to which public service organisations have clear boundaries, as they overlap with each other and with private sector organisations, to create more or less integrated systems of service delivery.

The change in the structure of the public service is paralleled by a change in the culture of public service organisations, as commercial

Learning Resources
Centre

attitudes and practices challenge the traditional public service ethic, however ill-defined it may have been, and managerialism is emphasised over professionalism and politics. Organisational processes are changing. The development of market principles has led to change in the way that financial management operates, with incrementalism in budgeting becoming less tenable as many organisations are funded on the basis of formulae, or operate from a zero base, having to earn income in return for the services that they provide. Industrial relations and the way that staff are treated has been transformed, as it has become more difficult to maintain the relatively advantaged position that has characterised public employees and trade unions in the past, for example, in terms of job security or bargaining rights. The introduction of market mechanisms poses a profound challenge to traditional modes of public accountability and to the constitutional structure of the public service. I shall argue that, to some extent, management and markets are replacing traditional forms of political organisation and accountability, and creating changes in the relationships between politics and management in the public service.

Organisation

The twin foundations of the transformation of the organisation of public services are the breaking down of large organisations into smaller units, and the division between client and contractor or purchaser and provider. The new public service is characterised by networks of organisations rather than integrated bureaucratic hierarchies, with independent organisations or quasi-autonomous internal units, operating with devolved control, providing services on a contractual basis. The pattern is one of increasing differentiation, either between or within organisations. The coordination of the network tends to come from a mixture of planning, based upon authority, and mutual adjustment through unplanned market mechanisms. Planning tends to be retained, at least in the initial allocation of resources from the centre, with the market being allowed to operate for adjustment within the basic framework, as for example in the case of the National Health Service and education. Central planning is limited, focussing on the allocation of finance according to fairly simple criteria, such as population or pupil numbers, and setting the overall strategic framework, for example the national curriculum or broad health strategy. The centre sets constraints within which service providers must operate, rather than controlling directly, monitoring performance against stated targets. The pattern is most obvious in the case of the education system, with the growing power of the Secretary of State for Education, attempting to set a strong framework of constraint, the relative autonomy of the school to manage the externally defined budget, and the choice, however limited, available to the parent. The system that emerges is one of mutually limited discretion, in which each party in the system must adjust to each other. Order is emergent and negotiated rather than planned or imposed.

The new model of the public service is essentially conceived as comprising three elements: the corporate core responsible for strategy and policy making; the client side for services, responsible for setting and monitoring standards; and the service provider, who actually delivers services. This threefold distinction is being reflected both in the internal structuring of public organisations, and in the division of labour between them. In the extreme case organisations are becoming purely strategic clients, operating as linking pins between user and provider, and purchasing services in extensive organisational networks involving both public and private providers. Urban development corporations and Training and Enterprise Councils have a predominantly linking-pin role, providing little or no direct service. Radical proposals would remove government from the process of service delivery, privatising agencies, leaving it responsible for deciding what work should be done, purchasing it, and regulating the provision process.

The degree of coupling within service networks varies, some being tightly linked, for example, through formal contracts or service agreements, and others much looser conglomerations of organisations. Coupling is tightest between units within organisations, for example between purchasers and providers in the National Health Service, where authority and planning operate alongside markets. In other cases the relationships are much looser, for example between the various agencies involved in social care and education. Coupling is also tight between organisations when there are formal contracts and tightly defined services, as when local government contracts for environmental services such as refuse collection, and where the influence of traditional hierarchical relationships remain strong as in the case of the civil service in which the autonomy of agencies is continually threatened.

The nature of relationships within networks also varies, particularly in the degree of trust that is present. Trust takes time to develop, since it depends upon the development of confidence that comes from past experience, and the commitment to future relationships. In its early stages the development of contracts tends to erode trust, as existing relationships are broken down, and because the partners to exchanges are often unfamiliar with each other. The result tends to be a reliance on formal powers. The early stages of the introduction of market processes tends to be characterised by the development of conflict between organisations in networks, for example between purchaser and provider in the National Health Service or between client and contractor in local authority contracting-out. The introduction of market processes tends to drive out previous patterns of co-operation: in the case of community care, for example, the development of the mixed economy of care has tended to erode previous less formal relationships with voluntary organisations. The introduction of markets has created clearer differences of interest and incentives to pursue interests.

The types of organisation present in the public service are changing rapidly, with a proliferation of special purpose bodies, internal providers, external contractors, companies, trusts and free standing units within bureaucracies. Increasing differentiation is apparent as much within as between organisations, as service providers are separated from clients and the policy-making core. The development within organisations can be seen as analogous to the change identified by Chandler (1977), Williamson and others in the development of industrial enterprises from the U-form to the M-form of organisation. In the former there is an integrated hierarchy of control, with decision making concentrated at the centre; in the latter the centre acts as a holding company, exercising strategic rather than operational control (Goold and Campbell, 1991). The internal organisation is characterised by a network of relationships, just as much as is the interorganisational context. The mode of integration within the organisation is moving towards various forms of quasi-contract, and the evidence is that the establishment of contracts for one section of the organisation, for example direct service organisations in local government, tends to create pressure for others to operate on the same sorts of arrangements, since those operating on a market basis are concerned to ensure that they do not have to bear costs simply imposed by others not subject to comparable pressures. In the early stages of change there is a tendency for more formal to drive out less formal patterns of relationships; more diverse informal patterns only emerge as people learn what is possible within any given institutional framework.

There is a tendency for a new form of hierarchy to reassert itself within the market, as intermediate bodies are established to act as links between central government and the increasingly large number of local agencies actually providing services. This is most obvious in the education service, with the establishment of the various funding agencies, and in the National Health Service with the creation of the outposts of the Department of Health. The various agencies that are emerging to integrate the activities of individual service delivery units such as schools, constitute an intermediate tier of government, though one that is responsible, if at all, only to central government. This development of what has been called a new magistracy (Stewart, 1992) has implications for accountability which are considered below.

A crucial determinant of the operation of public service networks is the degree of monopoly that characterises the market mechanisms that have been established. In some cases there are a multitude of purchasers and a multitude of providers. In education schools and colleges operate as individual purchasers of such support services as building maintenance, and there are a large number of potential providers. In other cases, such as the National Health Service, there is a tendency to bilateral monopoly, with a single purchaser and a single provider. In between lie situations in which there are few providers and many purchasers, for example school inspection, or few purchasers and many providers, as in social care.

These patterns have obvious implications for power relationships, for example with the school having significant power against the local authority in the purchase of physical support services, since it can go elsewhere to purchase what it needs, and the social services department, as the monopsonist, able to exert substantial influence on the providers of residential care, or on voluntary organisations.

FIGURE 8.1

	Many providers	Few providers
Many purchasers	Free market	Monopoly/oligopoly
	e.g. school purchase of building maintenance	e.g. school inspection
Few purchasers	Monopsony/oligopsony	Bilateral monopoly/oligopoly
	e.g. social care	e.g. UK National Health Service

The nature of markets within networks may change, as the different parties seek to improve their position. Purchasers may come together in order to gain economies of scale or to increase their influence. Large commissioning organisations in the National Health Service will have strong purchasing power. Schools in Britain have come together to form consortia for purchasing support services in some cases, and various forms of co-operation are emerging in further education. Within organisations, integrated purchasing approaches are developing, with the client roles being integrated. Providers are also coming together in order to increase their ability to influence the purchaser. In the case of UK local government services subject to competition under the Local Government Act 1988 there is evidence of collusion between contractors. In social care private providers of residential care have formed organisations to represent their interests to the social services department as purchaser. The pattern of public service networks will also change through the operation of market processes, for example as successful contractors grow and the less successful decline or disappear.

The degree to which the market is managed varies between services. The National Health Service is a strongly managed market, and the British Government has been unwilling to let market processes operate. Agencies operating within the civil service are also subject to strong hierarchical control. In education, by contrast, there is much less management of the market, and schools and colleges may operate with a great deal of independence. In social care the pattern is varied, with some social services departments anxious to use their power to influence the nature of the market and others more willing to let patterns emerge as they will. In competitive tendering in local government some local authorities operate open bidding processes, while others operate more selective tendering procedures. Informal mechanisms are also used to limit the effects of the market, for example packaging work in contracts in such a way as to deter external bidders. New organisations whose job is to manage the market have been developed, such as funding agencies and training and enterprise councils. The general tendency is for central government to play an increasing part in the regulation of the emerging market system, involving an increase in ministerial power and the establishment of new regulatory and inspectorial bodies. Such developments are more likely the more difficult it is to state standards of service in an objective or observable form.

The development of a network-based approach to the provision of public services leads to increasing formalisation and complexity of management procedures. Whatever its faults, hierarchical authority as a basis for organisation has a degree of simplicity that is difficult to attain in highly differentiated systems. Communication between organisations is more difficult than within them, and informal relationships tend to be more difficult to create and maintain. Variation to the pattern of work is less easy to develop because the client cannot so easily give orders to the provider, but must operate through formal variation procedures. Contracts can be written with variation procedures, but it is likely that contractors will be able to make claims if the change is significant. The operation of contracts requires systems of works ordering and invoicing, detailed systems of work recording, procedures for letting and managing contracts, and arbitration mechanisms. Relationships that previously operated on a relatively informal basis are increasingly being formalised in explicit contracts and service level agreements, as, for example, with the funding of voluntary organisations moving from a grant to a contract basis.

Formalisation is just as great within organisations that operate on an internal market basis as it is between organisations in a network, with internal procedures for works ordering, invoicing, inspection and so forth. Service level agreements detailing the basis on which support services in local government are to be provided within the organisation, can lead to complexity and formalisation in relationships. The operation of organisations is also being formalised through business planning processes and performance measurement systems. Quality assurance systems, involving the detailing of organisational procedures, are increasingly being established. The increased clarity of roles and responsibilities that tends to follow from the division between purchaser and provider is often paralleled by increased bureaucracy. Formal systems need to be established to mediate and arbitrate on differences between the two sides of the organisation.

It is the new institutional framework of contracts and markets that constrains the pattern of relationships, leading to increased formalisation. Informality persists, as it must do in any organisational system, but the greater the extent of differentiation, the less likely informal relationships are to develop, particularly at the lower levels of the organisation where the purchaser/provider split is likely to operate more explicitly. In practice, at least in the early stages of the operation of market-based systems, formality drives out informality. Existing informal networks tend to break down under the pressures of working to a new set of rules. The new system leaves limited room for ambiguity and for informal adjustment. The need to account more precisely for the use of time leaves less space for informal relationships and for the gossip which March argues is so valuable to organisations. At the same time informal systems do tend to emerge to cope with areas in which the new market processes do not work especially well: there are cases, for example, where barter has emerged between clients and contractors in local authorities, when client budgets are fully spent, and contractors have covered their costs. Similar processes operate between hospital trusts.

The result of the development of market processes for the management of the public service is greater differentiation and complexity and problems of coordination. Processes of integration will take time to emerge, and, in the early stages it is to be expected that the formality of contracting and market mechanisms will dominate. There are clear management gains in terms of clarity of responsibility, and to a degree incentive, that follows from devolved budgets and more explicit personal responsibilities and targets. The main problems arise in ensuring that there is coherence in the new system of public service organisations. The move from an organisational to an interorganisational system, if it is to be effective, will involve the development of appropriate institutions which will take time to develop.

Centralisation and decentralisation

The new public service is subject to conflicting pressures for centralisation and decentralisation. Clearly the devolution of financial control closer to the point of delivery gives greater autonomy to service managers, but the need for coordination, allocation of resources, the establishment of strategic frameworks, and resolution of conflicts, can also lead to renewed centralisation. The result tends to be an erosion of the influence of intermediary tiers of government, notably the local authority. The need for redress and resolution of differences between purchaser and provider, and between provider and user requires a body beyond the immediate organisations and individuals involved. In the case of schools, for example, the aggrieved parent of a child in a city technology college or a grant maintained school can only have recourse to the courts or the Department for Education, rather than, as used to be the case, to the local authority. There has been a marked increase in the degree to which the courts have been called upon to make judgments on the adequacy of public service provision since the emergence of the market-based approach to public service management.

The erosion of the middle is apparent within public service organisations as well as in relations between local and central government, partly because of an attempt to reduce the role of middle managers and partly because of the nature of purchaser/provider splits and contracts. Differences between purchaser and provider can only be solved at crossover points in the organisation, and, as the integrated departmental hierarchy becomes less common, those points tend increasingly to be senior levels. It is common, for example, for chief executives in local authorities to become involved in resolving differences between internal purchasers and providers. The erosion of the middle reflects the assumption that market and performance based systems make it possible to manage at a distance. There is some evidence that the result is that issues that were previously resolved at a lower level are now tending to come to more senior staff. Headteachers for example have been heavily involved in issues over the management of contracts for cleaning and grounds maintenance.

Devolution of financial control leads those responsible for their own budgets to question the need for, and cost of, central services such as personnel, law and finance. Managers with devolved budgets are anxious to control their own costs and services, and tend to be unhappy with central rules about how they shall operate, for example over the recruitment of staff, or purchasing of supplies. Opted out schools, and the newly independent colleges, for example, have commonly chosen to provide for themselves or to let their own contracts. Central services are inevitably put under pressure in trading systems, because they are seen as creating costs and making it difficult to compete and meet targets. The result may be duplication, but local managers will often feel that is a price worth paying if they get the service that they want.

Decentralisation can itself create the need for greater centralisation, particularly in relation to the control of the resources. The issue is one of how autonomy can be maximised at the same time as ensuring that common interests are recognised. If finance is devolved then either one has to accept any misallocation of resources, or develop systems for ensuring that misallocations are dealt with as they emerge. The more finance is delegated the more likely it is that the allocations will not reflect need, simply because the law of large numbers ensures fewer mistakes the more aggregated the units to which resources are allocated. If, for example, an individual social care worker has been allocated finance on the basis that they will need to purchase services to meet a level of need which proves, in practice, to be an overestimate, the centre will want to be able to reallocate money during the course of the financial year. This will mean that the centre will need to have the ability to monitor, and the authority to reallocate resources during the financial year, otherwise inappropriate allocations are allowed to stand. The problems, if this is not done, are apparent in the underspending by a number of general practitioners who were fundholders and the inability of the UK Department of Health to redirect the money. The Audit Commission found that 40 fundholding general practitioners declared surpluses of more than £100 000 in 1991–1992, and five of more than £200 000. Organisational problems such as this require systems that allow strong residual central control, and effective information systems, if decentralisation is not to lead to misallocation of resources.

Budgeting and finance

The development of contracts and markets is contributing to changes in patterns of budgeting and financial control, making incremental systems of financial planning and management less tenable. This change is least apparent in central government, where the traditional vote-based approach to the setting of budgets persists, and more apparent in local government, where contracting and devolved finance have had most effect. The impact of markets is to create a separation between the process of supply and demand, which, in traditional systems, are sure to balance: they are, by definition, the same since productivity is largely defined in terms of inputs. Rationing, rather than the price mechanism, is the traditional method of ensuring balance. There is now less guarantee that the level of supply planned by providers will match the level of demand. The purpose of markets is to ensure balance over the long term, not the individual budgeting period. In a number of cases in British local authorities, competitive tendering led to prices being bid that were greater than had been allowed for in client-side budgets. In the National Health Service there have been cases of purchasers running out of money before the end of the year. In the extreme budgeting and market-based approaches simply do not fit together, and the process of making contracts in the market takes the place of traditional financial planning. Annuality of budgeting is particularly difficult to accommodate alongside markets.

Competitive tendering and contracting have a direct effect on the ability of the organisation to control its budget, and on the process of budget management. The traditional approach to financial management in hierarchical bureaucracies was to set a level of spending based on the availability of finance, the assessment of need, and the existing pattern of spending. Financial control was then concerned with ensuring that spending stayed within budgetary allocations, and that there was neither significant over- or under-spending. In the new system the concern of trading units is as much for income as for expenditure, since they are paid for work done in a given financial period, rather than allocated a budget. There is a need to be able to set prices for services within organisations and in trading between organisations. Given both the lack of experience and of information the prices will often be wrong, and therefore give inappropriate signals to clients and contractors. There are numerous examples of the prices that have been set in tenders being wrong, and adjustments having to be made during the year to ensure that the client side does not overspend, or of contingency budgets being used. The failures to develop adequate internal pricing and charging systems are most apparent in the National Health Service.

There is no guarantee that income and expenditure in a market-based trading system will match at the end of the year, and there are numerous examples of providers in local government and the National Health Service making significant deficits and surpluses on their trading accounts. Hospitals have spent up to the level of finance allocated by providers in the National Health Service before the end of the year. Direct service organisations in local government have found that they have under estimated the costs of providing services, winning contracts on inadequate bids, and making losses on their trading accounts. About ten per cent of direct service organisations operating under the Local Government Act 1988 have made losses in each trading year. GP fundholders have overspent in some cases (Glennerster *et al.*, 1994). There have as yet been few examples of schools making losses, but if the contract culture is allowed to develop it is almost inevitable that the numbers will increase. In the long term, trading organisations that make losses will go out of existence, but in the short term there is a need to be able to deal with trading failures, for example through contingency funds, and systems for ensuring the continuity of vital services.

The introduction of trading and contracting has led to total costs being more explicitly dealt with in public sector budgeting systems than was previously the case. Traditionally, capital costs were of little concern to direct service providers, being dealt with on a centralised basis, and capital and revenue costs were rigidly separated. Central overhead costs were dealt with 'below the line', that is they did not appear in operational budgets. In local government for example they were allocated to operational budgets as central establishment charges, but kept outside the operating budgets. In the market-based approach the full costs of providing services are increasingly being allocated to service delivery budgets, in order to ensure that opportunity costs are fully considered.

Capital costs are allocated, with a requirement to make a rate of return on capital employed. Capital budgeting is increasingly complex (Mayston, 1990), involving difficult issues of accounting for inflation and valuing assets, and the more capital costs are reflected directly in revenue budgets, the greater the impact of capital budgeting issues on the service delivered. These issues are particularly difficult in the National Health Service. If, for example the district, the purchasing unit, cóntrolled the distribution of capital, it would be able to influence the costs of providers, and consequently their prices. Paton (1992) argues that the regions will drive the process to a considerable degree:

> Regions will steer the process. They will advise on contracts and the location of services; provide capital on the supply side, financed from capital charges, now separated from purchasing through prices; and maybe even provide that capital via districts instead of direct to units (p. 92).

As regions disappear alternative mechanisms are necessary and may well involve increased centralisation.

The traditional separation between capital and revenue budgeting becomes less viable as capital costs are fully charged into revenue budgets. There are then theoretical issues about how property is owned. In practice the notional overall ownership of property is being centralised, with charges being made to provider budgets, and provider-side managers being given increased property rights, for example over the receipts from sale, or in the case of schools, control of payments by outside users.

In one sense the development of contracts tends to lead to simplification of the budget process. If there is a long term agreement to provide services on a contract at a specific price, then, in planning its future spending, the client has little ability to vary the price. The cost of the service is then fixed for the term of the contract. Contracts may of course be written in a way that allows the total cost to vary depending on the amount purchased, but unit costs are likely to be fixed in most cases. Certainty of costs is purchased at the expense of inflexibility. The result is that budgets may be less under the control of the purchaser than in a system that is organised on the basis of authority. One health authority found that when it wanted to cut a particular service regarded as of lower priority when making savings, it was not able to do so because it was committed to a contractual agreement. Local authorities have found difficulties in varying the amount of work done, and consequently the cost, under contracts let following the competitive tendering legislation. Management by contract increases long term flexibility, but, unless there is a highly developed spot market, may reduce the capacity for short term adaptation. Contracts have not, so far, proved to be very flexible mechanisms, though it is likely that more flexible systems will develop over time as is happening, though slowly, in the UK National Health Service.

Market mechanisms have been introduced for the allocation of resources from central government to local bodies in some cases, for example the competition for funds under the city challenge scheme. There has also been some development of the allocation of resources according to performance, for example in housing, which raises questions of the ability to maintain equity in market-based systems. The differential funding of grant maintained schools and city technology colleges raises similar issues. The ability for service providers to operate on an equitable basis is also raised by the limitation of discretion at the local level. Discretion in the allocation of resources is increasingly being controlled from the centre, with formula-based systems limiting discretion at lower levels particularly in relation to schools. The more centralised the system of allocation of finance, whether revenue or capital, and the greater the number of units to which finance must be allocated, the greater the difficulty in devising systems of resource allocation that are adequate to the demands of equity.

The move to markets within the public service means that traditional public sector budgeting and financial management procedures must be supplemented with management accounting regimes more akin to those used in the private sector. The traditional financial information systems of public organisations are seen as too slow for those who must operate in the market. There is a need for accrual and commitment systems, and more frequent management information. The result is a proliferation of financial information systems, often informal. It is common to find that those who manage trading accounts will keep their own parallel information systems because they do not find the formal system effective. The conflict within accounting systems expresses the conflicting purposes that the public sector must meet in the move to market principles, that is of public reporting for probity purposes and effective managerial control and decision making.

Industrial relations

Trade unions have traditionally been strong in the public services with high densities of membership both among manual and non-manual staff. Recognition of trade unions has been more or less universal, and employers have seen them as a natural part of the organisational landscape, encouraging membership through check-off facilities and, less frequently, closed shops. The aim of public service organisations as employers has traditionally been to be in the front rank of good employers, offering relatively good pay and conditions and security of employment. The pattern of bargaining has been highly centralised, both at the national level and within individual organisations. Change was only introduced after extensive bargaining. There has been strong emphasis on uniformity of pay and conditions not only in single systems, such as the civil service and the National Health Service, but also in local authorities. This pattern of strong centralisation in industrial relations is generally characteristic of the public sector internationally, and particularly of unitary states.

The new public sector management has undermined this traditional approach to the organisation of industrial relations in the public service. As Walsh (1991) argues for the case of New Zealand:

> The centralised control patterns are no longer appropriate in the new decentralised structures. The centre no long dictates. Managers want as much discretion as possible to achieve their targets, and do not want either themselves or their subordinates to be hamstrung by detailed work rules and instructions . . . Managers assume responsibility for the appointment and appraisal of staff and, consequently, their salary and promotion . . . (pp. 118–19).

There is more direct contact between managers and staff rather than negotiating through formal union representatives and structures. The pace of change has, in many cases, meant that traditional bargaining systems have come under strain because they are slow. The sorts of status quo agreements that were common in the early 1980s, for example for the introduction of new technology, no longer operate. The result has been the development of more informal negotiating processes that tend to bypass the formal bargaining systems. The extent of change has varied from one case to another. In the case of local government elected members are less involved in industrial relations than used to be the case, particularly in Conservative-controlled authorities. A small number of authorities, again predominantly Conservative controlled, have opted out of national bargaining systems. Delegation of financial control, on its own, is not sufficient to undermine centralised systems of bargaining, even where managers have been given formal freedom. In the Civil Service, for example, the Financial Management Initiative had little impact on the uniformity of pay and conditions and even the 'Next Steps' agencies have been slow to make basic changes in industrial relations, though changes, for example in grading systems, are beginning to emerge. Certainly there has been an increase in local bargaining, but it is still within a strong overall framework of centralisation.

Trusts within the National Health Service in Britain have also been slow to abandon national pay and conditions. There have been changes, and there is much more bargaining at the local level, but Trusts have not generally broken away from centralised systems. Seifert (1992) argues that, in the 1990s, there will be change, but within a framework of continuity:

> The national arrangements will bear witness to the continued relevance of a Whitley-type system and of the political convenience of the Pay Review Body solution. In both SGTs (self-governing trusts) and DMUs (directly managed units) the national elements of pay will continue to provide the minimum for most staff pay. Terms and conditions arrangements will be reached at national level through collective bargaining, although there will be an increase in the number of enabling agreements and ones with some local flexibility (p. 397).

Schools, equally, have made limited use of their ability to operate more independently, and a similar judgment would seem appropriate. While the pay and conditions of workers in health and education have stayed relatively similar across the country, bargaining structures at intermediate level, the health authority and the local education authority, have become increasingly irrelevant. In local government centralised bargaining structures remain at the national level, but the operation of central bargaining for the authority as a whole has been eroded, particularly for manual workers. Again there is the erosion of the middle levels of management systems, with the centre setting frameworks within which local adaptation takes place.

The move to markets has had most effect on manual workers in areas subject to compulsory competitive tendering or contracting out. Where work is contracted out to the private sector workers have either faced redundancy, or have had to move onto lower pay and inferior conditions of service, for example poorer provisions for sickness, holidays and superannuation. Even where work has been retained within the public service after market testing there are frequently changes in pay and conditions in order to ensure competitiveness compared with the private sector. The development of markets has also meant that the pace and organisation of work has changed; there is more use of technology, and the workers are required to work faster. The result has been significant reductions in the number of staff employed, typically by 20 per cent or more. Other developments include the development of cashless pay systems and greater flexibility in the way that staff are used, for example annual hours agreements. There is less uniformity in the pay of workers performing similar work as the market for service provision comes to have more influence.

The emphasis on performance and targets in the management of work is paralleled by performance related pay, typically at the top of organisations and for the front line workers. At senior levels performance related pay has gone along with fixed term contracts in UK local government and the National Health Service, though not in the civil service except for the heads of executive agencies. At lower levels traditional bonus systems, which were seen as involving little relationship between pay and productivity, have been giving way to simpler, and more tightly controlled systems. Attendance-based systems, which pay a bonus as long as a worker has an acceptable record of attendance at work, have tended to replace the work measured systems that emerged in the 1960s and 1970s. Overall there has been increase in the difference between what is paid at the upper and lower levels of organisations, as the segmentation of labour markets has grown.

The new public service involves the assertion of the right and responsibility of management to manage, and has led to tightening of systems of staff management. Absence levels, for example, have been seen as a major problem by public service organisations that are subject to competition, and strict regimes have been introduced in order to reduce them. There is evidence of significant reduction of absence levels in those organisations that are subject to strong competition, for example direct labour organisations in London (Audit Commission, 1990a). There is also evidence that absenteeism has declined in schools. There have been some changes in the flexibility with which workers are required to operate, for example in building maintenance direct labour organisations in local government. Professional workers have become more subject to the control of managers, and the degree of managerial control within institutions with devolved control, such as schools, has become greater.

The public service in the 1970s and 1980s gave greater attention to issues of equality in employment for ethnic minority groups, women and people with disabilities. It is increasingly difficult to maintain such policies in the face of competitive market forces. Managers faced with the need to be able to compete against private contractors, often operating with relatively poor employment conditions, do not feel that they can afford the costs of equal opportunities policies. There are pressures to return to traditional employment practices, such as depot gate recruitment, that can be seen as directly or indirectly discriminatory. The introduction of market mechanisms has, in its early stages, had a greater effect on women than on men workers. Part-time working has increased, and the average hours worked reduced in order to avoid national insurance payments. The sorts of jobs that are most subject to competitive tendering and market testing, for example cleaning and catering, are more likely to be he held by women than men. Women are more likely to be employed in work in which competition is fiercest, such as building cleaning. The extension of market mechanisms has also tended to increase the extent to which men have taken up managerial posts in areas of work, such as catering, where women might typically have hoped for advancement in the past.

In general terms the development of market principles in the management of the public service may be seen as having two main consequences for industrial relations. The first has been to shift the focus from the producers to the users of services. The second is to lead to the development of more flexible organisations, which are more able to vary the level of employment, the cost of labour and the nature of the work that is performed. What seems to be emerging, if only slowly, is an organisation that consists of a core of employees, seen as central to the organisation, and having relatively favourable conditions, and a range of more peripheral employees, with varying degrees of attachment to the organisation. Where there is a plentiful supply of labour then staff can be less directly attached to the organisation, operating on service contracts.

The changing pattern of industrial relations in the public service is partly the result of the recession and changes in the laws governing trade unions, but it is the change to market mechanisms that has had the greater effect. The private sector has been able to compete on the basis of low prices because of the recession, particularly in the construction industry, and the level of competition under competitive tendering might well have been less but for economic circumstances. The trade union laws have had much less effect on the operations of public service unions than on those in the private sector. It may be that the laws served to limit the opposition to such developments as competitive tendering, but there is little reason to think that they had a major effect. European legislation protecting the rights of workers may limit the change but it is unlikely to stop it.

Law, accountability and ethics

The development of the market-based approach to public service management calls into question traditional approaches to account-ability in government. Markets break the clear lines of hierarchical accountability that, at least in theory, characterise the traditional Weberian bureaucracy, with public servants reporting up the line to senior officials, who, in turn, report to politicians. Those at the peak of the organisation are responsible both for policy and for the delivery of service. The challenge to accountability in the public service has a number of strands. First, there is the separation of the political and the managerial levels within organisations, with politicians being seen as responsible for setting service policy and standards, and monitoring service delivery, rather than for the management of service delivery. Second there is the interaction of commercial and service motivations, and the challenge to the 'public service' ethic. Third there are the difficulties that arise in assigning responsibility in a more differentiated public service. Fourth, there is a growth of appointed bodies that operate without traditional controls and are not accountable through the electoral process. Finally, in the case of Britain, there is the decline of the role of intermediary political levels and the consequent concentration of power in the hands of central government politicians.

The proponents of the market argue that it is more democratic and accountable than traditional elected forms of government; as the Omega File (Levitas, 1982) argues:

> . . . it must be remembered that independent providers . . . are nearer to public demand than local authorities can ever be . . . their perpetual search for profitability . . . stimulates them to discover and produce what the consumer wants . . . In this sense the market sector is more genuinely democratic than the public sector, involving the decisions of far more individuals at far more frequent intervals.

The market is argued to maximise citizenship, defined as the possession of individual rights to the consumption of a specific set of services, but that is only one form of citizenship, and the collective communitarian aspect must also be considered (Walsh, 1994). The Omega File statement is, in any case, a utopian view of the market, and its failings cannot simply be wished away. There is a distinction between consumer wants and citizens needs and the collective or social good, and revealed preference is not likely to be particularly effective as a means of discovering what should be done in the health or social services, or in the maintenance of law and order. Unless we assume that some are not to have access to basic public services, then it will be necessary to make authoritative decisions at some level about the amount of resources that are to be allocated to public service. Certainly the public can have a voice in this process, but experiments have illustrated the difficulties that arise in trying to set spending levels for services such as health on the basis of public valuations, for example in health care in Oregon. This is not to say that market processes do not work, but that they are not enough, and must be supplemented by political decision.

In part the new public service management recognises the need for politics but sees it as purely strategic and totally separated from implementation. The separation of the political and the managerial is based upon a mechanical model of the relationship between policy-making and administration, which has been much criticised in studies of the implementation of public policy. It is impossible, even if it were desirable, to define a system of rules and standards so tightly that there is no discretion in implementation. Increasing distance can make it easier for policy-makers to avoid responsibility by blaming failures on those who implement policy. The Chief Ombudsman in New Zealand has commented that:

> In these cases the focus of attention may well be on outcomes, but more often the spotlight is on the ethical and moral impact on citizens of the outputs of government policies. Given the accountability structure for senior officials in relation to outputs, it becomes much easier to transfer the accountability justification to the shoulders of Chief Executives in the 'I am responsible but not to blame' syndrome. No matter how it is done, Ministers now have every opportunity if they wish to take it to transfer accountability for output to officials (Boston *et al.*, 1991, p. 372).

Similar difficulties are clearly likely in the case of central government agencies in Britain in their relationship with ministers and senior policy officials. The further danger is that accountability becomes reduced to the meeting of pre-stated performance targets, and that activity is manipulated to show that these have been met. A great deal of organisational work has shown that it is likely to be cheaper to manipulate organisational systems to meet targets than to pursue the outcomes that are desired. Indeed, this was, to a considerable degree, the failing of the discredited communist regimes of Eastern Europe and the Soviet Union. The very success of organisations in meeting targets, for example in central government agencies, makes one suspicious of the relevance of those targets. The separation of the spheres of operation of politicians and managers will clarify responsibility in some cases, but the more complex the public service the more there will be overlap between the two, as has been apparent in the cases of health and education.

The establishment of politicians in a strategic role, and purchasers in the role of specification and monitoring rather than delivery, raises issues about the way that public organisations learn. In the past there have been close relationships, particularly between local politicians and the service that they are responsible for, and senior officers have been responsible for the delivery service. The pattern of learning, embodied, for example, in career systems, depended upon contact with practice. The separation of the strategic and the operational that is embodied in the development of a market-based approach to the public service means that new means of learning must be found. In the case of competitive tendering there is increasing concern that clients find it difficult to develop service policy because the detailed understanding that is necessary lies with the provider. Similar concerns arise over the competence of the purchaser side in the British National Health Service. The separation of purchaser and provider alone will not undermine the power of the producer.

The introduction of market mechanisms to the management of the public service creates the possibility of conflict between the incentives facing managers. The simple argument is that there will be conflict of the commercial and public service ethic. In theory, as long as the client defines clearly the service that is to be provided, writes an appropriate contract, and monitors it effectively, the contractor will have a motivation to deliver the service because otherwise they will lose money. In practice the interaction between specification, contract and monitoring are complex, and contracts are unlikely to be self-enforcing. Providers will have an incentive to provide those services that generate the easiest return. This is true as much for internal as external providers. Direct service organisation managers in local authorities frequently comment on the way that commercial and service motivations can conflict. Headteachers may tend to exclude those pupils who are likely to do badly in tests and examinations to safeguard their place in league tables. Managers on performance related pay will tend to work to the target. There is evidence that hospitals may withdraw from the provision of certain services seen as not being commercially advantageous. Managers themselves are likely to see the incentives that they face as conflicting, and voluntary organisations have expressed concern about the impact of market mechanisms upon their traditional values.

Accountability is made difficult by the extension of lines of communication that result from contracting. Salamon (1981) has argued that, in the United States of America, contracts for public services:

> . . . continually place federal officials in the uncomfortable position of being responsible for the programmes they do not really control . . . Instead of a hierarchical relationship between the federal government and its agents, therefore, what exists in practice is a far more complex bargaining relationship in which the federal government has the weaker hand.

Kettl (1993, p. viii) argues that:

> . . . public reliance on private markets is far more complex than it appears on the surface. In these relationships the government inevitably finds itself sharing power, which requires it fundamentally to rethink not only how it manages, but how it governs.

The difficulty of control at a distance, through the monitoring of defined standards and targets, will be greater for complex services, such as care or health, than for simpler services such as refuse collection. The difficulties are not all on the side of the public service as purchaser, and there are instances of the clients taking advantage of their position to exploit the provider, for example claiming that what is, in fact, perfectly adequate work is substandard in order to avoid payment. The lengthening of lines of communication and control can also mean that what is theoretically political control will actually be exercised by officials, because of the concentration of responsibility at the centre. Ministers are likely to find themselves overloaded and the decision in practice will be made by officials.

Commercial secrecy, and the operation of commercial criteria for the provision of information, enhance the problem of accountability under market mechanisms. Private contractors, and public agencies that must compete, want to keep their costs and other commercially sensitive information secret. Tender bids are unlikely to be in the public domain. Trading organisations in the public service are unlikely to want to report openly to politicians, and committee meetings are generally held in private. In a number of cases the business plans of Next Steps agencies are not published on the grounds that they are commercially sensitive. Information is less willingly reported because it is seen as having commercial value.

The growth in the number of agencies that are involved in the provision of public services creates difficulties in being able precisely to allocate responsibilities. The danger is that blame for failure can be avoided by using the many hands arguments: outcomes are influenced by so many agencies that it is impossible to hold any one to blame. This difficulty has been apparent in New Zealand, for example in education, where the politically responsible minister, the head of the policy agency, and the head of the delivery agency have each tried to pass responsibility to the other. Separate organisations may act in ignorance of each other, with little acknowledgement of the common good. In New Zealand, following the State Sector reform legislation, the Government has argued that departments should not pursue a business-orientated approach by which they operate in isolation from each other. It sees it as important to re-establish formal and informal links that had been lost in the process of change, in order to prevent a loss of focus on the collective interest. The issue arises at its simplest in the purchaser/provider split, and the difficulty that can arise in deciding the extent to which poor service is the fault of the contractor or of the client for defining or monitoring the service inadequately. The likelihood of passing on the blame for failure is greater the more extensive the network of contracts, when contractors can blame each other.

The development of the new market-based approaches to the public in Britain has been strongly characterised by the use of appointed bodies, and the reduction of the powers of locally elected politicians. In some cases such bodies report to ministers, which, given their necessarily limited spans of attention, tends to mean responsibility to officials, or little accountability at all. In other cases appointed bodies become self-perpetuating and have little apparent accountability, as in the case of further education colleges. The normal criteria of clear requirements for declarations of interest, and strict audit processes, do not apply to such bodies as much as to traditionally elected political bodies. The 'new magistracy' as it has been called has come under strong criticism on grounds of lack of accountability, though ministers have countered that there is no 'democratic deficit', and that there is greater accountability within the new system. The minister responsible for the Citizen Charter, William Waldegrave (1993) argues that:

> ... far from presiding over a democratic deficit in the management of our public services, this Government has launched a public service reform programme that has helped create a democratic gain.

In large part this is a debate about the nature of accountability. The proponents of the market point to the emphasis on the consumer and the clarification of responsibilities. Critics tend to be concerned with issues of collective decision making, and the way that decision makers are appointed. The point is not the effectiveness of the system, but the political values that it embodies.

The move to markets and contracts within the public service in Britain does not sit easily with the British legal approach, with its tradition of applying private law in the public sector. There is no specific body of law that governs public sector contracts, and in the case of internal purchaser/provider splits there is no legal contract, since an organisation cannot have a contract with one of its constituent parts. Lawyers have argued that there is a need for recognition of the special character of contracts in the public service, and the creation of a public law contract (Harden, 1992). The character of new processes of service provision, monitoring and inspection arrangements, complaint handling and arbitration, and the establishment of enforceable rights for customers need to be regularised. Ministerial discretion, it is argued, cannot cope with those issues. Avoidable crises are arising in education, health, prisons. The need is for an explicit, public law contract to establish accountability for service providers, and to provide for crisis management when ministerial intervention in the arm's length arrangements does become necessary. The contracts that have been developed have typically been for large blocks of services, and tend to involve the formalisation of the existing pattern of provision; they do not create new rights for the public.

The market-based state is an evaluative state (Henkel, 1991). The specification of services and the standards to which they are to be delivered implies that the level of performance can be checked against the specified standards. The result has been that there has been a proliferation of inspection and audit bodies, and an increase in their powers. New inspection and audit bodies have been established, for example the Social Services Inspectorate and the Courts Inspectorate. The Audit Commission has played a major role in the overseeing of change in local government and now the National Health Service in Britain. The powers of inspection and audit bodies have been increased, particularly in ensuring that market changes are being effectively introduced. The Social Services Inspectorate, for example, played a central role in the introduction of the mixed economy of community care. Given the centrality of audit systems the question of how those who carry out audit are held to account becomes central. It also raises issues about who defines standards, and how they are to be defined.

Conclusion

The introduction of market principles into the public service, taken to its extreme, will lead to an enabling state, steering not rowing, setting the standards of the public services, which are checked by the various agencies of evaluation, and delivered by private or autonomous public organisations. In the case of failure there should be adequate means of redress for the service users. There would be a much more differentiated system of organisation, relating to each other through contract and market-based mechanisms, rather than through hierarchical authority. It is already apparent that the new public management is characterised by a series of tensions. There are organisational tensions, with contrasting pressures to decentralisation and autonomy, and to centralisation and control. There are tensions in the way that staff are treated and managed, with pressures for commitment to organisational culture and values combined with more differentiated personnel systems and harsher conditions for many. Increased transparency and clearer responsibilities go along with a decline in traditional political accountability.

These tensions and conflicts are, to some degree, the result of the early stage of development of the new public management. Organisational and operational systems have not had time to develop to give effective expression to broad institutional change. It is to be expected that many of the difficulties will be overcome as organisational systems develop, but other issues are more fundamental. Within organisations the tensions between the need for initiative and control are fundamental, and what the introduction of the mechanisms of the enabling state does is redefine the context within which it takes place. Traditional conflicts such as that between professionals and politicians over the control of services become redefined as a debate over quality, service standards and the rights of the user. The debate over testing in schools, and the trial of strength between the Secretary of State for Education and the teachers provides an obvious example. Similarly the conflict between labour and management now operate within a different institutional framework.

It is in the case of issues of accountability that the underlying tensions in the new public management are most apparent. Traditional arguments for democratic accountability have always been subject to the argument that it is, in practice, necessarily limited, and there is an inevitable tendency to oligarchy. The introduction of a new set of incentives has forced public officials and politicians to respond more effectively to service users in some cases. The introduction of the market is not in itself enough, and, in the new public management, relatively little has been done, as yet, to create the institutions that would make possible effective democratic control. The tension between individual and collective interests is not resolved by shifting the emphasis to the individual. It is notable that the reforms of the management of the public service have not been accompanied by significant levels of political reform. The approach of the reorganisation of the public service has been based very much upon the notion that 'it is the output that matters' (Waldegrave, 1993). Certainly we want services that work, but the operation of the public realm is about more than making sure that the trains arrive on time.

9 Efficiency and Quality

The fundamental argument for the introduction of market principles into the management of the public service is that it will improve the efficiency and the quality of service, and reduce costs. It is seen as improving allocative efficiency, X-efficiency and technical efficiency. The incentives to overproduction analysed by public choice theorists will, it is claimed, be eliminated by the introduction of internal competition and market pressures to public bureaucracies. The separation of the political and managerial levels of control, with the establishment of clear standards and performance measurement systems, will prevent the dominance of the official. The re-examination of methods of working will lead to improved technical efficiency in the public service, through the elimination of waste and restrictive practices, and through the introduction of modern methods. The introduction of user choice will ensure that the public are able to get what they want, and that the providers take note of their wishes, improving allocative efficiency. The development of such processes as competitive tendering reduces the power of the producers and ensures that X-efficiency is increased. The incentive to minimise costs ensures that the public service is organised along the most efficient lines, especially where managers are given more explicit property rights, for example through the elimination of annuality or the introduction of performance pay. The introduction of the market ensures that those parts of the public service that do not respond to public pressure will face decline.

There is much debate over the impact of market mechanisms on the quality of service, with proponents arguing that they are a means of ensuring better services, and opponents arguing that savings only result because services are worsened. A central purpose of the introduction of market mechanisms to the public service is to increase the level of choice that is available to the users of service, for example in schools or community care, and so to make services more accountable to those who use them. The requirement for clear standards is intended to ensure that the users of services are aware of the service that they are entitled to and can complain and obtain redress if they do not get what they are supposed to. User empowerment is seen as being attained through the enhancement of the role of the citizen as consumer. The concern for increased effectiveness of services in responding to the needs of users goes along with that for the efficiency of the public service. In this chapter I consider the extent to which the reform of the public service along market lines has actually increased efficiency, effectiveness and quality, and the impact that it has had on the pattern of user involvement.

The financial effects

The assessment of the impact of the introduction of market mechanisms on the efficiency and effectiveness of the public service is difficult both technically and because of the limitations of the available data. Even the most ardent advocates of the market accept the difficulty of making judgments; Savas (1987, p. 172) states that:

> Scientifically rigorous comparisons of the relative efficiency and effectiveness of alternative arrangements for service delivery require a large sample size and special-purpose, on-site date collection, using a standard framework to measure inputs and outputs. Such research is difficult, time-consuming and costly.

It is difficult to compare the costs of services before and after the changes because there are often reorganisations of the pattern of service management or changes in service standards at the same time as market mechanisms are introduced. Public sector accounting systems often make it difficult to identify costs in a comparable fashion. In some cases, for example, the costs of such support services as building cleaning were not separately identified before the introduction of market mechanisms, but were incorporated into the accounts of mainline services. Commercial confidentiality makes public services unwilling to provide information for purposes of evaluation. There are also difficulties in identifying ancillary and indirect costs, for example central support costs or capital costs, and, therefore, developing an understanding that involves a full analysis of the inputs involved in services. The certainties expressed by many of those who argue for the advantages of market mechanisms are weakly based, though, of course, many of the certainties of their opponents have no firmer a footing.

The costs of managing market-based systems are likely to be different from those of managing integrated bureaucracies because transaction costs vary. It is not immediately obvious whether the effects of market mechanisms will be to increase or decrease costs. The costs of preparation for an introduction of market mechanisms can be high. In letting contracts the work to be done must be measured and defined, and detailed specifications prepared. Management information systems must be overhauled. The separation of purchaser and provider may lead to costly overlap. There are also the social costs that may arise because of declining employment in the public service, for example the costs of increased unemployment and social security payment need to be considered. It is also difficult to determine the effects of competition through analysing the position at a single point in time. Long-term effects may be quite different from immediate results, for example, because of the impacts of monopoly.

A cynical view would be that what we know, given the narrow range of studies, is that the contracting out of refuse collection leads to a short term reduction in costs. While such a view would be overly narrow, it is certainly the case that broad conclusions about the value of market mechanisms may have been built on a limited base. Studies across the range of services have been few, there has been little analaysis of anything other than environmental services. The comparisons made have also, generally, been of cross-sectional rather than time series data, comparing organisations that have with those that have not engaged in the use of market mechanisms. Finally, the assessment of the financial impact of markets is limited by the fact that the data that is available refers largely to the use of competitive tendering and contracting out. The efficiency impacts of the use of other market mechanisms, such as internal markets, have received almost no consideration. That said, let us consider the data.

Service costs

Savas presents a summary of a very large number of studies, predominantly, but not solely, in the United States, that shows that the savings from contracting out for a wide range of services average 30 per cent and more. The data does not cover manual services alone, though the better data is for such services: savings of various levels are argued to follow from contracting for police, education, fire and care services (Poole, 1980). Substantial savings are claimed to have followed from the use of contracting in the United States federal government; the Congressional Budget Office estimates savings of $22 million per year, and $325 million on an accrual basis (Pack, 1991, p. 296). In Japan (Marlin, 1982, p. 14) the use of external contractors is seen as having led to higher efficiency, reduced costs, decreased staffing and improved quality of service. In Australia contracting has been used extensively in the Common-wealth Department of Defence, in a number of local authorities, and in hospitals with reports of savings of 20 per cent and more. (Domberger and Farago, 1994). A study of a range of services – waste collection, construction and maintenance, police services, animal control, pest control, administration, social and cultural services, transportation and other services – in Canada found savings of about 30 per cent (McDavid, 1987, quoted in Cornaghan and Bracewell-Milnes, 1993). There has been extensive study of the impact of the use of various forms of competition on health service costs particularly in the United States, which illustrate the impact of market structures. In many cases the pattern of market incentives has tended to produce results that are the opposite of those desired but appropriately designed approaches, such as prepayment on the basis of diagnosis related groups, have been found to result in savings.

Research in Britain has generally shown that savings follow from contracting out and competitive tendering. In central government considerable savings are reported. In the mid-1980s the government claimed savings of £100 million from contracting out, averaging perhaps 25 per cent of annual costs of the same services before competition. In its white paper in 1991 announcing the extension of market testing (Her Majesty's Treasury, 1991), the government made various claims for savings that had already been made as a result of contracting out. In the Department of Trade and Industry savings of £1.2 million were claimed in services that had previously cost £2.3 million, a reduction of 52 per cent. The Department of Transport was said to have saved £1.7 million on services that had previously cost £4.5 million, a reduction of 36 per cent. It is difficult to assess the validity of these claims since no details are reported on how they were calculated; it is not likely that they present an accurate picture of the full position before and after competition, given the poor knowledge of the costs of government services. Overall savings claimed from market testing of 24 per cent for 1989–90 and 31 per cent for 1990–91 for work in twenty-two government departments are equally difficult to assess (Her Majesty's Treasury, 1992). Improved efficiency is also seen as having followed from changes in purchasing procedures. The government claims that large savings followed from the extension of market testing to a wide range of services within the public service. Savings from the first major round of market-testing in 1993 are put at £135.6 million, an average of 22 per cent of the costs before competition (Prime Minister and Chancellor of the Duchy of Lancaster, 1994).

Large savings are claimed as a result of the competitive tendering of support functions such as cleaning and catering in the National Health Service, and the evidence is somewhat more soundly based than that for central government. In 1983–4 tendering was said to have resulted in savings of about 1 per cent, and in 1984–5 about 5.5 per cent. A National Audit Office study in 1986 reported savings of £73 million, about 20 per cent of the costs before competition. Domberger and his colleagues (1987), in a study of domestic costs in about 1500 hospitals, found that those that had contracted services out had reduced costs by 34 per cent, and, in those in hospitals in which the in-house provider had won the contract, costs were 22 per cent lower. The cost of cleaning and domestic services in hospitals is said to have fallen from £514 million to £482 million following competitive tendering, a real terms reduction of 29 per cent. The drive to market testing of support services in the National Health Service is said to have resulted in a saving of £625 million over seven years.

The most extensive and best controlled studies of the impact of competition on public service costs have been in local government. The Audit Commission (1987), in studies of voluntary competition, found that privatised refuse collection had lower than average costs, but that direct labour organisations did as well in many cases. The most competitive direct labour organisations were found to have lower costs than the average private sector company, but the average ones were more expensive. In its study of direct labour organisations carrying out building maintenance work (Audit

Commission, 1989b), the Commission found 'strong evidence that many DLOs' costs are far higher than they need to be', and that prices for similar jobs varied by plus or minus 20 per cent from one local authority to another. In a study of the tightening of the regulations governing competition by direct labour organisations for highways maintenance (Audit Commission, 1991), the Commission found that 'the price of work newly exposed to competition reduced on average by 14 per cent over the period 1986–7 to 1989–90'. A Local Government Chronicle (Local Government Chronicle, 1990), survey of competitive tendering following the first year of competition under the Local Government Act 1988 found that there were average savings of 5.6 per cent across a range of services, varying from 10.4 for refuse collection and 15 per cent for building cleaning to 0.2 per cent for catering. These studies all relate to manual services, and it cannot be assumed that similar savings would be made from the introduction of competitive tendering for non-manual and professional services. Authorities such as Berkshire, Hertfordshire and Oxfordshire claim to have made savings from contracting out such services as property management and payroll administration.

Academic studies have also found that savings follow from competitive tendering and contracting out in local government. Hartley and Huby (1985), in a survey of health and local authorities found average savings of 26 per cent, ranging from a decrease in costs of 68 per cent to an increase of 28 per cent. Domberger *et al.* (1986) and Cubbin *et al.* (1987) found significant savings of 22 per cent as a result of voluntary contracting out of refuse collection by local authorities. These figures have been confirmed in later studies, notably by Szymanski (1993) who argues that contracting has resulted in savings of at least 27 per cent in refuse collection. A study conducted for the UK Department of the Environment (Walsh and Davis, 1993), based on a panel of forty authorities found average savings of 6.5 per cent for services subject to competitive tendering under the Local Government Act 1988, ranging from an increase of 26.4 per cent to a reduction of 48.9 per cent. The results varied widely from service to service, with higher savings in refuse collection, building cleaning and grounds maintenance; in street cleaning, catering, vehicle maintenance and leisure management there were low savings or increases in costs. Studies of personal social services have shown that private provision may be cheaper by

15 to 25 per cent, though other evidence suggests that there are considerable efficiency improvements to be made in the private sector (Parry, 1990, p. 14).

The results of studies of the impact of contracting out and competitive tendering in Britain and other countries show that there are savings to be made on direct service costs. There is considerable variation in the results that have been found, and they lead to the conclusion that it is in simpler, repetitive services, where unskilled labour can be used, that the highest savings are likely to be found. There are few satisfactory studies of competition for more complex services such as legal or financial support. The public service does make extensive use of the private sector for certain aspects of professional services, where it is seen as more effective, for example in conveyancing, but it is difficult to judge the effects of contracting for core support services. A study of the impact of contracting on legal services in central government concluded that 'in the interests of effectiveness and economy, the bulk of these services should continue to be provided on an in-house basis' (Sparke, 1993, p. 119). The evidence to support this or an opposite conclusion is limited.

Charging

The limited introduction of charging for services makes it difficult to judge the effects. There is some evidence that it can lead to reduced usage of services such as museums. In health, charges for prescriptions result in reduced take-up by those who pay them. The study claims that voucher systems in the United States keep administrative costs low, minimise inefficiencies, and ensure that the money spent goes to those in need. Gormley (1991) concludes that voucher systems did work in the 1970s because they were adequately funded and were less successful in the 1980s.

Evidence about the impact of charges following the deregulation of public transport services is disputed. Foster (1992) concluded that:

Overall, it seems that fares are in fact higher, that subsidies are much lower, that in general frequencies are greater, but that use has not risen as had been expected. The bus user has not lost from the disappearance of either the National Bus Company or the conurbation monopolies. But whether consumers are better off is disputed (p. 122).

Impacts in public transport differ between rural and urban areas and from one part of the country to another. The main use of charging has been to raise income rather than to govern the way that services are produced and consumed. It may be that, if used more effectively, charges would have a beneficial effect, but, so far, the evidence is too limited to provide clear guidance.

Devolution and internal markets

Assessments of the impact in the UK of the Financial Management Initiative are generally favourable, though they argue that the effects have been limited and could easily be dissipated; continuous change is needed to ensure that gains are maintained over time (Metcalfe and Richards, 1987). The Initiative did have a strong initial impact on the identification and control of costs. The heads of Next Steps agencies generally argue that they have been able to achieve improved efficiency in internal management through better cost analysis and control (Fogden, 1993; Dopson, 1993). There has been a strong emphasis on cost cutting following the introduction of agencies (Common *et al.*, 1992, p. 41). The lack of accurate information on the position before the introduction of the new market mechanisms means that it is difficult to make any clear judgments about the overall impact of the changes. Certainly there is no obvious impact of agencies in overall figures for public expenditure, and it is not clear what happens to any savings that might be made.

The impact of the Resource Management Initiative in the National Health Service is also difficult to assess because of the lack of adequate accounting information.

. . . RM cannot yet be said to have produced a system that has demonstrated its ability to achieve significant measurable patient benefits. There are assertions of improvements in patient care and we have indicated examples of these where the link to the RM as a causal factor seems justifiable but, in a health service generally striving to make improvements, it is difficult to prove that they would not have happened without RM (Packwood *et al.*, 1991).

It is similarly difficult to isolate the financial effects of changes in the management of education and social services and the more recent reorganisation of the National Health Service to create an internal market. The attitudes of managers tends to suggest that the changes have improved the management of finances and the control of costs, for example the National Association of Health Authorities and Trusts' study (Appleby *et al.* 1992) of the National Health Service changes found that managers saw it as a stimulus to efficiency. It is difficult to have faith in these judgments. The Audit Commission, in its study of the internal market in health, argued that:

> Good comparison of prices between providers involves detailed analysis of such factors as case-mix, clinical practice, and asset utilisation. But prices are quoted on differing bases. For example, some providers quote prices for a total workload in surgical specialism, whereas others offer banded prices for minor, intermediate and major operations. It is also difficult to distinguish the impacts of the market and technological changes (Audit Commission, 1993d, p. 31).

It is early to assess the effects of the introduction of the mixed economy of care in the social services; initial indications are that the impact is likely to vary greatly, depending on the nature of the local market and the pattern of demand. Prices are higher, for example, in cities than in rural areas, because there is less supply. Devolved finance in education has generally been welcomed in schools and colleges as allowing more efficient use of resources through better targeting, though there are clearly difficulties in maintaining services that require economies of scale, such as school library services. Arnott *et al.* (1992) found that 83 per cent of headteachers managing their own devolved budgets felt that they were able to make better use of the resources available to them than when control had lain with the local education authority. The Audit Commission study (1993a) of the local management of schools found that they were generally managing their finances effectively, but that there were difficulties in a significant number of cases.

Discussion

It is well to be sceptical about the data on the efficiency impact of the introduction of market mechanisms. The information is difficult to gather, and, in many cases, studies rely either on assertion, or on surveys of managers' perceptions. Even in the United States of America, where there is much more experience, the evidence for financial savings following competition is limited. Van Horn (1991, p. 271) argues:

When pressed, few officials could supply any hard evidence to support their claim that private contracting was cheaper than government service delivery. If cost comparisons were ever made they were forgotten. Without any pressure to change, most local officials have long since decided that they would rely on private firms to perform a range of local, county and state government services.

Many of the claims either that the use of market mechanisms reduces costs or that they are costly are reliant on post hoc rationalisation. Ascher, in her summary of the experience of competition in the United States of America quotes a review by the Urban Institute:

The amount of independent, comprehensive evaluation of the effects of contracting . . . is quite small except for solid waste collection. Few trials of contracting, including the recent innovations, have been adequately evaluated to permit agencies nationally to learn under what conditions contracting works well.

For developments other than contracting the evidence is even more limited. The way that financial information has been collected by public agencies in the past means that it is difficult to make realistic comparisons across time.

There is some limited evidence that the initial savings that might result from market processes will be eroded over time. In the United States this has been found in a number of local jurisdictions (Rehfuss, 1989). Szymanski and Wilkins (1992) found that:

> . . . the cost savings associated with contracting fall significantly four years after the initial contract. This timing coincides with the renegotiation of initial contracts, and does indeed suggest that initial contracts were priced relatively low. It is possible that this effect was due to error (the winner's curse) or deliberate under-bidding (p. 3).

There were certainly examples of significant underbidding in the first round of competitive tendering in local government in Britain, whether by accident or design. Underbidding seems as likely to have occurred by internal public service providers as by the private sector (Walsh and Davis, 1993). In extreme cases contract prices have been renegotiated in the course of the contract. In some cases the long term impact of markets is likely to be different from the immediate results because of the growth of monopoly on the one hand or entry into the market on the other. It can simply be difficult to assess the long term impacts; Coopers and Lybrand and the National Foundation for Educational Research (1992) in their evaluation of the local management of schools argue that:

> It is difficult to say whether, in the long run, LMS by itself would lead to net savings or net costs; the position will vary considerably between LEAs. On balance, we would be surprised if there were net savings.

The initial savings may follow from the stimulating effects of change and may be dispersed over time. Savings may also be swallowed up in general service expenditure, reducing the pressure to make more general economies. Certainly there is little evidence that savings from competition serve to reduce overall public spending, rather than enabling politicians to make shifts in the pattern of expenditure.

The sources of changes in efficiency

There is dispute over the extent to which any savings that follow the introduction of market mechanism result from technical improvements in efficiency, for example replacing labour with capital or reorganising patterns of work, from the reduction of the pay and worsening of the conditions of public sector workers, or from increasing the pace of work. Cubbin and his colleagues found that the reduction in the costs of refuse collection services following competition resulted from technical improvement:

> . . . for those authorities with private contractors, the bulk of the savings can be attributed to improvements in technical efficiency – that is, physical productivity of both men and vehicles. Only a small residual remains that can be attributed to other, pecuniary factors.

In the case of compulsory competitive tendering in Scottish local government Kerley and Wynn (1991) argue that:

> . . . the best of private contractors seem able to bid for local authority services on the basis of high productivity, and yet pay wages at least comparable to those negotiated in the NJC [National Joint Council for wage bargaining].

This conclusion did not apply in cases where labour costs were a high proportion of total costs, notably in building cleaning, where there is exploitation of weak labour.

Walsh (1991) found that the main source of savings following competitive tendering was greater productivity resulting from improved working methods and organisation, and from investment in better equipment. There was an average increase in productivity of 24.8 per cent across a range of services. Discussions of other cases of the introduction of market mechanisms have also suggested that change has resulted in more effective patterns of organisation, for example as a result of devolution of finance. Headteachers, National Health Service managers, and the heads of executive agencies commonly argue that they have made improvements in work organisation and productivity. Despite the difficulties of measuring public sector productivity it seems likely that there have been improvements in some cases.

It is clear that there have been significant cuts in wages, particularly in labour intensive, unskilled services such as building cleaning, following the introduction of market mechanisms. In schools there are examples of more costly experienced teachers being made redundant, and the hiring of younger, less expensive staff.

Short-term contracts are more extensively used in the public service to give greater flexibility in staff costs. Studies such as those of Domberger, Cubbin and their colleagues have been argued to have neglected the wider social costs that result from poorer wages and reduced employment, for example the loss of taxes and the increase in benefit payment (Ganley and Grahl, 1988). Some see these costs and others as totally eroding any saving:

> Counterbalancing any gains have been the losses through redundancy, administrative burden, lower morale, industrial action, increased exploitation and unemployment and, for some districts at least, lower standards (Carnaghan and Bracewell-Milnes, 1993).

This is an overstatement, though a valuable corrective to the acceptance of the assertion that competition and contracting are always and everywhere valuable. The evidence suggests that saving comes from a mixture of new methods of working, reduced pay and conditions of workers, new methods of working and increased pace of work, with considerable variation from one type of service to another, for example with the nature of the labour market and the pattern of work.

It has been relatively easy to make changes in the pay and conditions of workers when unions were weak, labour markets loose, and when there was little regulation of the market. The experience of the 1960s and early 1970s, when difficulties in recruitment led to increased wages, and more direct provision as opposed to use of the market, shows that different economic and social circumstances will produce very different effects. Walsh and Davis found that the impact of competitive tendering in local government tended to increase over time as the market became more competitive, although the effect was not strong. Similar results have been found in the case of building and highways construction and maintenance. While the market for labour is likely to remain loose with relatively high unemployment in the near future, there will be different effects in particular local labour markets. Some local authorities, for example, have found that even building cleaning can be relatively expensive when there is high demand, as in certain parts of London and the south-east of England. The application of the European Commission regulations governing the transfer of staff is likely to make wage reduction more difficult in the future, which may heighten the search for savings through improved work methods, as well as making exploitation of weak workers more difficult, notably in the cleaning industry.

Transaction costs

The immediate results of market processes on the direct costs of services are not the only financial factors that must be considered in evaluating the impact of the introduction of market processes. There are considerable costs involved in introducing new organisational and managerial systems, even if they can be justified on the grounds that it is necessary to spend to save. The separation of purchaser and provider leads to increases in monitoring costs and the costs of communication. There are significant transaction costs involved in running organisations through the use of devolved budgets and trading accounts, for example the costs of information and financial management systems. Contracts can be expensive to prepare and let. Again it is difficult to assess these costs; the Comptroller and Auditor General of the National Audit Office, in his assessment of the Financial Management Initiative (National Audit Office, 1986), argued that:

> . . . I consider that the nature of the changes stemming from FMI is such that it would not be realistic to expect the improved financial management, particularly at the higher levels, to result in readily quantifiable savings. In the light of these considerations departments are clearly not in a position to measure the cost effectiveness of their FMI systems though this was clearly a desirable objective (p. 10).

Despite the difficulties in making a precise judgment of the costs of introducing market mechanisms it is clear that they are high. The introduction of the Financial Management Initiative is estimated to have cost £35 million in 1983–85. The costs of the introduction of the government's market testing process in the civil service has been criticised both by consultants and those directly involved in implementing the process. The initial report on market testing gives a cost of £26.4 million in implementing a programme of £1.1

billion, a preparation cost of 2.4 per cent. Central government has also made substantial investments in information technology over the last decade to make market mechanisms possible.

Criticism of the costs of the introduction of market mechanisms have been strongest in the National Health Service, with arguments that resources have been transferred from patient care to administration. Managers themselves express similar criticisms:

> When asked about the drawback of the Act, most DGMs cited administrative costs and bureaucracy mainly in relation to contracting (the requirement for more detailed information, more specificity, and for better invoicing and monitoring systems). The system of dealing with extra contractual referrals and the disproportionate amount of effort required for a small amount of total business was also criticised. There was also concern over increased management costs arising from the purchaser/provider split and the perception that money had been diverted away from patient care (Appleby *et al.*, 1992, pp. 19–20).

The costs of preparing for health units to become self-governing trusts has been estimated at more than £73 million between 1990 and 1993. In social services, although the government has provided resources for the implementation of the mixed economy of care under a specific grant, voluntary and private sector organisations, as well as local authorities, are concerned about the costs of the change. Similar reservations have been expressed by headteachers about the time taken up by administrative tasks. To some extent these transaction costs may decrease as the new systems become established and public service managers and politicians learn to operate them more effectively, but in some cases at least there is a permanent additional cost of running the public service on market principles.

There is rather more information available about the transaction costs associated with competitive tendering than other initiatives. Walsh and Davis (1993) found that the costs of preparation for compulsory competitive tendering in local government were 7.7 per cent of the annual contract value. These costs were largely associated with the preparation of specifications, for example the measurement of sites on which work is to be done, and the costs of letting contracts. It is also clear that the costs of preparation are specially high for small contracts, because of diseconomies of scale, which is particularly important given that so many small contracts are being let under the government's market testing initiative. Experience of contracting in the United States also shows that there are considerable costs of preparation. These costs are partly one-off, but managers suggest that about two thirds of the initial costs will be incurred every time a contract is let. The introduction of competitive tendering in the UK National Health Service also showed that there were considerable costs, managerial effort and time required for implementation. The National Audit Office estimated that up to five years of management effort would be needed at a total cost of £15 million. The costs to contractors of preparing tender bids must also be considered in each of these cases.

Walsh and Davis (1993) found that the client-side costs of managing contracts were about 30 per cent higher than comparable costs of managing the services before competition. The average costs of monitoring contracts was found to be 6.4 per cent of the total value of the contract, though some services such as vehicle maintenance and grounds maintenance were much more costly, about 10 per cent of the contract value. The Audit Commission (1993c) has found similar figures, varying from 1.4 per cent for education catering to 12.5 per cent for vehicle maintenance. Costs of monitoring are lowest for those services delivered directly to the public, such as refuse collection, where users can play a part in service monitoring. The Audit Commission (1993d) found that the costs of commissioning in the National Health Service varied from 0.5 to 2 per cent of total expenditure in different health authorities, averaging 1.3 per cent. In the United States of America the costs of managing contracts have been found to be rather higher, often up to 10 per cent of the value of the contract. Osborne and Gaebler argue that 'to do it right' cities often spend 20 per cent of the value of the service on monitoring. The costs of managing contracts for social care in Britain have been found to be high. The more complex the service the more costly it is likely to be to monitor the contract unless it can be made self-monitoring, or the provider can be trusted to act in the interests of the purchaser.

The transaction costs of the market-oriented public service are considerable. They may be justified on the grounds that they are offset by the gains that are made in the efficiency and effectiveness of the public service, but the immediate effect is likely to be seen by many as the growth of a new form of bureaucracy, established to manage the market. As Boston (Boston *et al.*, 1991, p. 255) says of the introduction of change in New Zealand:

> Whatever the merits of the new order, there are many areas of concern. One of these relates to the costs of changing organisational structures and departmental boundaries. These include the economic costs of reorganisation (including the costs of consultants' reports, departmental submissions, redundancy pay, redeployment and retraining, etc.), the costs of disruption to the ongoing business of government, and the social costs (including the stresses and strains caused by extra work pressures, job insecurity, the loss of morale, redundancy, etc.). To date, no comprehensive evaluation of the costs of Labour's machinery of government changes has been undertaken, although some figures have been published relating to the costs of redundancy pay and consultancy fees. For example, between September 1986 and July 1990 redundancy pay for state employees cost the government more than £310 million.

Costs in the United Kingdom are certainly much higher. New techniques such as the use of computer packages for monitoring contracts, or for managing the internal market in the National Health Service, may reduce costs in the long term, but will have high short-term costs. The costs of new computing systems in the British National Health Service have been estimated at £1749 million by 1999. The costs of management have risen both because the number of managers has increased and because they are paid more. A full cost-benefit analysis of the introduction of the new public service management, though it would necessarily be approximate, would be of value in the debate over the effectiveness of the change.

Effectiveness and quality

The second leg of the argument for the introduction of market mechanisms to the management of government services is that it will lead to the improvement of service to the public. It is about reinventing government as much as reducing public expenditure and increasing efficiency in the public service. As the government claims

for the Citizen's Charter, which largely depends upon the introduction of market mechanisms:

> These reforms have been about getting the internal organisation
> of the public service right. With the advent of the Citizen's
> Charter the focus of the Government's programme of reform has
> turned to looking at the external face of the public service: the
> relationship between public services and their users (Prime
> Minister and Chancellor of the Duchy of Lancaster, 1992, p. 10).

John Major has argued, for the specific case of central government
that:

> What we are seeing at the moment . . . is frankly, nothing less
> than a revolution in management of the Civil Service . . . an
> opportunity, I believe, to give managers and staff far more scope
> than ever before to achieve far greater effectiveness and greater
> value-for-money; . . . and above all perhaps, far greater scope for
> what we are there for in the first place – delivering a better service
> to the customer . . . Agencies are in no sense just another
> bureaucratic binge of reorganisation – that is not what Agencies
> are about. They are meant to provide a better service . . . (quoted
> by Common *et al.*, 1992, p. 120).

Standards and performance measurement have been a central part
of the initiatives for change, and there has been increasing emphasis
on the evaluation of public services and the right of the public to
complain and obtain redress if they do not receive an adequate
service.

Quality of service has become the overarching concept for the
discussion of change in public service management, but proponents
of change have, in some cases, recognised that market mechanisms
alone are not sufficient. The Audit Commission, in its study of the
role of the health authority, has argued that 'There is a need for
some element of supervision and regulation in the new market.'

Without institutional change the traditional forms of control will
tend to reassert themselves. The internal market introduced in
higher education failed because the changes gave no real power to
the user, and there was no possibility of increasing supply, making
collusion easy (Witzel, 1991). Partial change is unlikely to be

effective. Voucher systems, for example, have been argued to be ineffective without deregulation of supply. Both critics and proponents of the use of market mechanisms in the public service have been able to argue that the changes have been on the surface, rather than making fundamental changes to the nature of the services.

The strongest criticism of the government's chosen methods for improving the quality of service have come, as one might expect, from the trade unions, which have argued that the changes have been about controlling staff and cutting costs, and have been a disaster for quality. In the case of the British National Health Service, for example, they have argued that:

> . . . six years of competitive tendering in the health service has brought little more than cuts to already stretched services and a series of dramatic disasters by contractors – many of them very serious, some of them dangerous, and all of them distressing and costly to patients as well as budgets. Against this catalogue of complaints, the government has yet to produce real, convincing evidence of success – economic or otherwise – of their policy (Joint NHS Privatisation Research Unit, 1990, p. 4).

Similar claims are made for the effects of contracting and competitive tendering in the civil service and local government. The trade unions are not opposed to all changes: they have, for example, taken a more favourable attitude towards the introduction of executive agencies in central government, though they have been concerned about the impact of change on morale and the consequent implications for service standards.

It is certainly the case that contracts have failed, and that there have been quality problems in some cases. There have been a number of instances of termination of contracts in the National Health Service, and instances of contractors withdrawing from contracts because of difficulties in meeting the terms under which they were required to work. Local authorities have been left with the difficult problem of maintaining services after contractors have gone into liquidation, as happened with a number of leisure contracts in 1991. Training services privatised by means of a buy-out from central government have failed. In the National Health Service a major buy-out of computer services in the West Midlands failed.

The problem should not be exaggerated. The Local Government Management Board (1993) found that, of a total of 3468 contracts let under the Local Government Act 1988, only sixty-six (2 per cent) had been terminated because of failures to perform effectively. A much higher proportion had encountered difficulty without failing to a degree that would warrant contract termination, for example 28 per cent of refuse collection contracts, 21 per cent of street cleaning contracts, 16 per cent of contracts in grounds maintenance, and 17 per cent of those in building cleaning.

The private sector is more active in areas of work that are more prone to failure. Research for the UK Department of the Environment found that there were significant problems of failure to achieve the standards specified in the case of building cleaning and to a lesser extent other services. The most common problems were failure to meet the required standards and failure to complete work on time. There were problems, at least initially, with the contract for escorting prisoners awarded to Group 4, and in prison contracts. In many cases problems follow from the contractor, internal or external, putting in an excessively low price in order to win the contract.

Against these findings on contract failure and poor standards of performance in some cases, there are claimed to be significant gains from competitive tendering. First, public authorities have been forced to be specific and precise about the service standard that they want to have delivered, and to be clear about the relationship between cost and quality. Local government officers involved in competitive tendering commonly argue that the process has the advantage of forcing them to examine existing practice, and that they now know the cost of the services that they deliver. It is common, when working practices are examined, to find that the organisation has little real knowledge of present practices, and that unplanned variations from one place to another, for example from one school to another, are common. Much of the complaint about declining standards reflects standardisation, with some standards raised and others reduced. Complaint is then likely from those that have lost, even if the overall standard is improved. Overall, specific studies have found that, if anything, contracting leads to improved quality (Domberger *et al.*, 1993; Domberger *et al.*, 1994).

The introduction of the client-contractor split also means that standards are monitored in a way that was not previously the case.

As local authorities gain experience of competitive tendering they are developing more effective means of focussing on service performance and involving the public more in the development of and monitoring of standards, for example through the use of standing groups for monitoring. The Audit Commission (1993c) argues that:

> The first round of contracts tended to codify existing inputs or processes, possibly because authorities were basing their contracts on existing working methods and bonus schemes. Now the authorities are placing more emphasis on a quality service outcome for their consumers (p. 33).

Failings in quality are most likely at the beginning of contracts, partly because of changed processes and methods and partly because the contractors have to go through a learning period. The experience tends to be that services improve over time, and that initial failings are resolved. The time taken for learning varies with the complexity of the service.

The government makes strong claims for the effectiveness of the Next Steps initiative in improving standards:

> There have been significant improvements in services as a result of the Agency programme. For example: the waiting times for driving tests have been reduced from 13 weeks to less than six weeks, and the Passport Agency has improved its turn-round-time for processing applications from 24 to 7 days (Prime Minister and Chancellor of the Duchy of Lancaster, 1992, p. 5).

Framework documents are seen as forcing ministers and the heads of agencies to be clear about the standards that are to be delivered, and performance measurement as ensuring that they are attained.

Reviews of the Next Steps initiative have found that performance targets are attained in the majority of cases. There is always a tendency though, to focus on the measurable elements of performance, rather than on the effectiveness of what is provided. Mellon (1993a) quotes an official of the Council of Civil Service unions as stating that out of 200 agency targets only 20 were concerned with quality as opposed to cost cutting or quantity targets. Pollitt (1988) has argued that the majority of performance measurement systems are based upon targets defined by senior managers and politicians, rather than the users of services. Mellon cites this as a problem in the Next Steps initiative:

> . . . terms tend to be set by the centre and by Treasury and occasionally by the Minister: the chief executive faces new targets imposed often without consultation . . . While total quality management, an idea being adopted increasingly in the public sector, indicates that both cost reduction and quality improvement targets can be met simultaneously, usually some initial investment or outlay is needed, e.g. in new machinery, computers and so on. In contrast public sector managers are usually asked to do more with less (p. 23).

The proliferation of performance targets can conceal rather than enhance the ability to assess quality through making it difficult to focus, and make clear judgment of overall performance difficult. The development of Executive Agencies has led to a closer focus on the attitudes of customers, involving user attitude surveys, complaints systems and other mechanisms, such as internal service agreements with internal users, but the emphasis seems to have been on fairly straightforward performance targets (Pendlebury *et al.*, 1994).

User involvement and quality

The National Health Service reforms in Britain are seen by managers as having led to a greater emphasis on responsiveness to service users, though this had been achieved predominantly through relationships with general practitioners:

> The split was seen to have in turn facilitated a greater emphasis on consumers and GPs. DGMs reported improved relationships with GPs, and also a better understanding of, and responsiveness to, the needs of GPs. Although the cultural shift to a more consumer oriented NHS was cited as a benefit, the GP was frequently regarded as a proxy for the consumer . . . There was also a change noted by DGMs in the profile of quality, with a much greater

emphasis on all aspects of the way services are delivered to patients (Appleby *et al.*, 1992, pp. 16 and 19).

The reform of the National Health Service is theoretically based upon money following patients, but, in practice, little has been done to enhance the power of the user, and the standards embodied in the Patient's Charter are limited. There is evidence that fundholding general practitioners are effective in putting pressure on hospitals to be responsive. Glennerster argues that fundholders are able to persuade hospitals to improve efficiency and to be more innovative, but that many do not gain since they are not patients in fundholding practices. The National Health Service is treating increasing numbers of patients though it is not clear how much, if any, of this increase results from changes in organisation. There is little evidence that the changes have led to any increase in the voice of the users of health service, either directly, or indirectly, for example through the Community Health Councils, which seem if anything weaker. District Health Authorities, as purchasers, are searching for ways of investigating the views of local people more effectively. In developing the purchasing plans of health authorities do try to tap the views of the general public, through surveys, public meetings, group discussions and panels, though in most cases the methods used are not sophisticated. The development of means of closer involvement of the public is still at a very early stage.

The introduction of the mixed economy of care in social services is intended to be led by the needs of service users, but it is here that the conflict of consumerism and increasingly limited resources has become more obviously apparent. It is up to local authorities to determine the criteria of eligibility of the users of care services, and people have a right to have their needs assessed to determine whether they meet the criteria. Constraints in public expenditure have made it difficult to meet needs. User choice in social care contracts remains limited. Many in the voluntary sector would argue that market processes may damage the ethos they have developed, and pose a challenge to the ethic of volunteering. Anderson argues that:

In concentrating upon financial matters, there is an obvious danger of ignoring equally important issues: the problems of specifying quality in contracts for personal care, the need to work with the constraints of charity law, the failure of most contracts to offer voluntary organisations the security of funding which was held out as the great benefit of the new system. Above all, perhaps, there is the question of how to safeguard the rights of the actual service user, where the contract is between two other parties.

As in the case of contracting in local government more generally, the development of contracts for care has meant that social services departments have looked more closely at the service that they want to provide, and the quality standards that should be met. The development of the mixed economy of care has been accompanied by the development of a number of documents providing guidance on care service standards.

The impact of the changes in the management of the education service on the quality of education is, not surprisingly, difficult to assess. Studies of the determinants of educational quality have shown that the factors which impact upon it are various and difficult to quantify (Mortimore *et al.*, 1988; Rutter *et al.*, 1979). Bowe and Ball (1992) in their ethnographic study of the impact of the introduction of market principles in schools conclude that:

> The market is not value-free, and as a mechanism it is also driven by choices made by producers. The workings of a quasi-market in education present a whole set of difficult ethical issues which must be confronted by senior teachers in schools. Professional judgment would seem to have a central place here. Furthermore, the unproblematic relationships between market forces and educational standards seem, in practice, far from clear cut. The market encourages schools to compete for 'certain sorts of students'. And market activities in certain respects detract from educational ones. The insertion of quasi-market forces into education is a massive piece of social experimentation which is already generating a whole range of unanticipated consequences (p. 62).

There are arguments that more basic changes in the management of education have had an impact on educational standards in the United States. On the one hand performance measurement has been argued to produce hyper-rationalisation, with no improvement in the quality of service (Wise, 1979). Others argue that performance contracting in education produces beneficial results (Lieberman, 1989). The evidence to support either case is limited, and it is as well to be sceptical. The most sophisticated study is that of Chubb and Moe, which tends to find clear, though not very strong, statistical relationships between market-based reforms and educational outcomes. They argue that there cannot be real change without changing both the demand side, through parent empowerment, and the supply side, through making it easier to open up schools and change their character.

It can be argued that the market may undermine the quality of service by the creation of perverse incentives. There is clear evidence that poor suppliers have entered the market for some services, for example building cleaning, both in Britain and in the United States. In the case of more complex professional services, regulatory and inspection processes may give some general protection against quality failure but there is little evidence of what the long term effects will be. There is a danger of cream-skimming, with providers being unwilling to take on difficult and more costly cases in health, or schools imposing strong selection procedures.

There is clear evidence that the standard of many public services is being improved in some cases, as even such demanding critics as Pollitt (1990) are willing to acknowledge:

> Many public service organisations have vastly improved their complaints systems; information leaflets have multiplied and become more user friendly; reception staff have been initiated into the mysteries of 'customer care' and the opinions of NHS patients and residents about the service they receive have been relentlessly polled (p. 185).

Such developments clearly have value, but they can be criticised as being essentially surface changes. In a study of the quality of service in housing management, Walsh and Spencer (1989) found that there was a disjunction between what tenants thought local authorities did well and what they thought was most important. Tenants felt that housing departments were good at customer care, but that they were more concerned for effective problem solving, privacy in the way that their problems were dealt with and continuity in the people that they dealt with. Similarly, studies of care for elderly people have shown that the things that are done well in residential homes are not necessarily those that are of greatest concern. In hospitals much of the testing of patients' opinions has concerned the hotel aspects of the service that they receive, rather than more basic health-related aspects of care.

The evidence tends to show that market mechanisms are most able to improve quality in the case of relatively repetitive services, such as refuse collection or street cleaning. Such services can be closely specified, are relatively simple to monitor and are not subject to rapid or radical change. Difficulties arise when the service is more complex and needs to develop in response to changing circumstances. There are dangers of stagnation because the service is set down in a contract which it is difficult to change. There are problems that arise from the nature of the incentives in the market-based system. It is difficult to make judgments about the results of the market in the short term: the more complex the service the more likely it is that the full effects will only become apparent over a long period.

Conclusion

The arguments for the introduction of market mechanisms into the public service have gradually shifted from a concern with efficiency to a preoccupation with quality. Neither concept is simple, and the debate illustrates the deep conceptual issues involved. Efficiency is not easy to define, and it is necessary to distinguish between allocative efficiency, technical efficiency and X-efficiency. Most of the evidence on efficiency relates to the latter two, and there is little evidence about the impact on allocative efficiency. Experience so far would suggest that public organisations are likely to reproduce existing patterns of spending when they move to market mechanisms. It is likely that the evidence on these issues will only emerge in the long term, and it will be difficult to disentangle the effects of market changes from those that result from other factors. What are often presented as technical assessments of performance, such as the rates of return that are made on capital, involve implicit social values that are highly contestable.

The public service markets that have developed are essentially markets without customers, in which the normal price mechanisms and patterns of supply and demand do not operate. In the case of contracting out and competitive tendering there has been almost no involvement of the ultimate users of services in the writing of contracts. There does tend to be consultation of internal users, such as headteachers, but even that has been limited. The same is true in the case of health services, and obviously the changes in central government have been internally dominated. Markets are essentially internal to public organisations, and there has been real change, with internal users, in some cases, being allowed to opt out of the support services that are centrally provided, or with doctors having more choice over the hospitals to which they refer people. The extension of choice is so far limited. In the case of education the changes have had little impact on the real choice that is available to the majority of parents, with the schools that are available being determined largely by geography and wealth.

The evidence on efficiency shows that the gains are predominantly internal to organisations, rather than having any obvious impact on the person who receives the service. The nature of production technologies in the public sector is that it is often difficult to determine the relationship between inputs and outputs. It is rather easier to determine the nature of relationships within the organisation. In part the adoption of market-oriented mechanisms is the sign that the organisation is efficient. The practice is rather more difficult to evaluate. The emphasis on quality has often taken the form of bureaucratic procedures, with little relation to the actual service produced, and has served the interest of producers rather than users. As Pollitt (1987) argues for the case of health, where the emphasis on quality has been most marked:

> . . . while public service 'quality' is a popular theme in current political and managerial rhetoric, actual attempts to 'do anything about it' are both driven by conceptual inconsistencies and deeply contoured by bureaucratic and professional politics. As yet the final users of NHS service have played only a limited, and largely passive, role in the establishment of quality criteria and in the organisational arrangements by which such criteria are applied and monitored.

Quality is even more difficult to deal with conceptually than efficiency, and involves the possibility of conflict between the values held by different individuals more obviously. It is perfectly possible for one person to see a service as being of high quality and another to see it as of poor quality, with both citing precisely the same criteria in support of their argument. The market has always had difficulty dealing with the issue of quality, especially in the case of complex services. There is little evidence that the changes that have been introduced had either beneficial or deleterious impacts in the case of complex public services.

Conclusion

The search for more effective public services places the politics of everyday life at the centre of debate; low politics has become high politics. There is a tension in the attempt to present issues of schooling, health, income support, housing and so forth as matters that can most effectively be dealt with by good management, apparent in the way that management itself has become a matter of political debate. The management of public services continually forces itself back on the political agenda. There is constant political argument, for example, over how much management is needed, for example in the National Health Service. An approach which was intended to depoliticise public services is itself a central political issue. It may be that this is a short-term phenomenon, but that seems unlikely. Just as the debate over ownership and control in the private sector (Berle and Means, 1932) signalled a fundamental change in the nature of markets and their governance, so the debate over management in the public service is a sign of profound changes. This change may be considered in terms of the relationship between the public and private realms, and between the market of the state.

The argument for markets in the public realm is based on the assumption that the delivery of services is essentially a private issue for the individual user. If this is so then the role of politicians can be limited to the setting of the broad framework within which services operate. The role of the state is small and that of the private, management-oriented market realm is to be extensive. Management, in turn, is controlled by audit and inspection procedures. Politics is replaced by management, which, in turn, is replaced by audit. As Armstrong (1989) has argued, we must in the end trust somebody and, in the evaluative state, trust has increasingly come to lie with the auditor and inspector.

In the argument in Britain over the Citizen's Charter, democracy is evaluated on the basis of the ability of consumers of public services to make choices, and their right to receive efficient and effective services. Legitimacy is a matter of efficiency. This perspective is at odds with a view of effective government as a matter of mutual commitment, rather than efficient services. As Dunn (1990) puts it:

> What modern state agency legitimately consists in is the collective agency of its own citizenry; and any contempory state which cannot plausibly present its agency in those terms, or which chooses not to do so, faces persisting and acute difficulty in representing its agency as legitimate at all. In addition, every modern state also claims a wide and peremptory authority over many aspects of its subjects' lives and an entitlement to determine in the last instance, by some legal process or other, just how widely that entitlement may reach.

The remnants of such an active, and obligatory, relationship between the state and the citizen are apparent in the subsidiary emphasis in the new public management upon the active citizen, a rather different concept from that of the citizen-consumer.

The contractual exchange between consumer and producer lies at the basis of the market exchange in the private sector. The contractarian perspective on politics uses the notion of exchange in explaining the role of the state. It is difficult, as Gray argues, for the notion of contract to create a value base for the public service:

> . . . .contractarian theory can no more give us a criterion of political choice for our contemporary dilemmas of liberty and distribution than it can deliver universal prescriptive principles of political justice.

The development of market-based approaches to the management of public services may generate financial or quality gains, though the evidence is not yet present; it cannot tell us what government ought to do. The market is a mechanism, which does not embody any particular political philosophy.

The danger of defining the public realm as the arena in which we exchange taxes for public service is that we reduce politics to service consumption, rather than authoritive decision based upon collective commitment. The concepts which we use to understand the public realm are different from those of the market, emphasising need rather than demand, citizenship rather than consumption, and 'voice' rather than 'exit'. The liberal concept of the state is described by Pangle (1992) as follows:

> Government is best understood as the rationally constructed artifice by which individuals contract with one another to create a collective police power that will limit everyone's pursuit of the objects of his or her passions so as to make such pursuit more secure for all.

This impoverished view provides justification for a very thin state, concerned with procedural rather than substantive justices.

The market-based approach to the organisation and management of government involves a double process of distancing of the political. First, government has little to say about the substantive content of the good life which individuals may pursue. The government withdraws from decisions about what ends should be pursued. It is about how we do things rather than what we do. The second distancing is then from the way that government is conducted, though the introduction of market procedures, distancing government from its own actions. The process of introducing markets into the operation of the state is a process of withdrawal of government from the substantive operations of the state. At the same time, the need for regulation of markets is becoming more apparent. It is difficult to see how government can withdraw from responsibility for its own services. The initial conditions, for example basic funding, are decided by government, and market mechanisms, such as choice, only exist within these initial conditions. The problems of government attempting to withdraw from responsibility for its own services are apparent in debates over education and health, where government is continually forced back in, because management and political issues interact.

Changes in organisations have a rhetorical as well as a substantive component. Change is partly effected through changing the way that people talk about and think about what they do. The rhetoric of the market has developed very strongly in the public service. Talk of 'customers', 'business plans', 'competition' and 'marketing' is common. The danger of the translation of political issues and relationships into the language of the market is that we become separated from our responsibilities, and political debate becomes more difficult. Even those responsible for introducing market processes have shown awareness of the issues. William Waldegrave (1990), then UK Secretary of State for Health, argued that:

Our 'customers' do not come because the price of beans is less . . . they come because they are ill, not seldom frightened, and they want help and expect care . . . without remitting for one moment the pressure to get a better management system, borrowing what is useful from business, let us watch our language a bit.

It just bears saying straight out: the NHS is not a business; it is a public service and a great one.

The danger is that the hard-edged clarity of the market may drive out the more ambiguous and diffuse language of politics, which necessarily involves conflicting values, and multi-valued choice.

The introduction of market principles into the management of public services has certainly had benefits in clarifying the nature and purposes of services and yielding efficiency and quality gains in some cases. But, as the change proceeds, we are driven back to larger questions. Alvesson (1993) has argued that changes in the nature of the economy have made ideas increasingly important:

The important trend away from mass production to service and information in the economy makes ideational aspects – the regulation of beliefs and images, more important, for example in service management. Associated with this is a change in emphasis from control of behaviour and measurement of outputs to control of employees' attitudes and commitments, the latter being crucial for employee service-mindedness which in turn determines the level of customer satisfaction.

The move from concern for control to working through motivation is apparent in the changing nature of public service management in the last twenty years. What is now emerging is a renewed interest in the nature of the public realm, apparent, for example, in the recent work of Handy (1994) and Etzioni (1993).

The specific nature of the public realm requires a balance between the anonymous mechanisms of the market, and political decision between contrasting values and between coordinated and uncoordinated action. The issue is how we can accommodate the use of market mechanisms within the management of the public service, without undermining what is specific to it. The need for a wider concept of the nature of the public realm is clear in the limitations of the notion of the citizen/customer, in which citizenship is a set of separate consumer identities, patient, parent and so forth.

The idea of the citizen as customer is based upon a concept of rights that is difficult to sustain. Even if we accept a wide-ranging notion of rights there will be problems of conflicting rights, differences between individual and collective rights, and differences of the long and the short-term impact of the exercise of rights. The 'non-negotiable' nature of 'rights talk' as Beiner (1992) argues, means that it is impossible to resolve these differences within 'rights talk' itself. Other political methods and conventions are needed. The absolutist character of rights leaves us with major difficulties where they conflict, as they will inevitably do.

The market is the realm of choice, but we not only want to choose, if we do, but also to get what we want. The process of choice is of limited value if it does not lead to greater want satisfaction, except to the degree to which choice is valued for itself. In the public realm the pattern of service that is inherited, for example the distribution of schools, will set limits to choice. It is difficult to argue that individuals are not generally more aware of their preferences than are producers, but there are clearly cases in which individuals have little ability to make choices in practice. It is also difficult to see how effective choices can be made in many public services, which are essentially experience goods, the value of which we can only assess in use, or even credence goods, where we must rely on trust in the producer, because any external objective evaluation is difficult or impossible. The possibilities and nature of choice depends upon the character of the goods and services involved.

The requirement for precise standards, which is a key emphasis of the new public management, raises the issue of whether we can state standards in complex circumstances, and, if we can, who should do so (Stewart and Walsh, 1994). There is little doubt that professionals have been over-dominant in the development of the welfare state. The development of professionalism, though, is necessary if we are to be able to respond to difficult and unforeseen circumstances. The difficulties for contract, then, are how it can deal with unforeseen circumstances, and the likelihood of the contractor taking advantage of uncertainty. It is difficult to write contracts for medical or social care, where there are significant problems of moral hazard and adverse selection, that is of systematically misleading those letting contracts about competence and performance. The development of trust is central to the maintenance of social systems, and the danger of contract is that it undermines trust, through basing contracts on punishment for failure. If we undermine trust then we may find that the making of agreements, and ensuring that they are kept, will become very costly. The value of trust is that it is cheaper to trust people, and to develop institutions that will ensure trust, rather than to watch them. Control and influence over producers may go along with trust and the development of distrust make efficient public service impossible to attain.

The purchaser/provider split is at the core of the development of the new public management, and it is accepted surprisingly widely, both on the Right and the Left, with little questioning either of its theoretical basis or examination of the empirical evidence on its effects. It is often justified on the analogy with Marks and Spencer's purchasing procedures, based on tight and continuing relationships with a limited number of suppliers. The analogy is difficult to make. The dependence of the suppliers and the nature of power relationships is fundamentally different. The products to be supplied to Marks and Spencer are simple, easy to specify and their quality can easily be checked. Public services do not have this character. If we adopt the purchaser/provider split, then it may be difficult to avoid the problems of duplication, bureaucracy, and the complexity that result from billing and other systems.

At a deeper level there are issues about the ability of a system based on the purchaser/provider split to cope with change and to learn from experience. The professional who is no longer involved in actually providing a service may find it difficult to learn from experience, and, indeed, to gain relevant experience. It can be argued that the role of the purchaser is to operate at a strategic level. The danger is that the concept of strategy can be so broad and vague as to mean little. The divorce between strategy and practice may make strategic decisions difficult, because of lack of adequate knowledge of services. There is a danger that the introduction of market mechanisms for the management of the public service will make it difficult to adjust to changed circumstances and make policy change.

The issue is not so much one of whether or not we should use market mechanisms in the public realm, but how to make them work given its distinctive character. The public realm is one where values must be balanced one against the other. In order to do so we need to develop the power of judgment, which involves the ability to weigh values one against the other in order to reach acceptable conclusions. Judgment is difficult, but the public realm deals with the sort of services that can not be managed without discretion at the point of implementation and delivery, and choice at the political level, both of which demand good judgment. The public realm is constituted by conflicting values, and there is no overriding purpose against which we can measure. It is the existence of conflicting purposes and values that makes the political level necessary to public service management. The reaching of decisions through balanced judgments is the determination of what is the public interest. There does not exist something separate against which we can justify our choices. This is not to retreat to collectivism, for the public realm must balance the collective interest against the interests of the individual in making political judgments. The market will have a much wider role in this process in future and we might be much more radical in our experimentation with such market mechanisms as vouchers in the social services, or allowing individuals genuine choices in Britain within the National Health Service. The mix of market adjustment and authoritative decision will vary.

The use of market mechanisms for the management of government is at an early stage, and it is not surprising that the evidence on their effectiveness is limited. It is clear that there are gains and losses, for example for public sector employees. It is also clear that there is a need to develop a more effective organisational infrastructure, for example of information and accounting, if the changes are to succeed. At a more fundamental level, the introduction of market mechanism raises issues about the nature of government and of the public realm. We inherit a relatively undeveloped and unsophisticated concept of the public service. The introduction of market mechanisms has highlighted our limited understanding of the nature of government, and how market processes might contribute to it. The next stage of development of the organisation of public services needs to create an approach that recognises the limits both of markets and bureaucracy, and the need for government as well as management.

References

Ahmed, M. N., and R. W. Scapens (1991) 'Cost Allocation Theory and Practice: The Continuing Debate', in D. Ashton, T. Hopper and R. W. Scapens, *Issues in Management Accounting*, pp. 29–60 (Hemel Hempstead: Prentice-Hall).

Akerlof, G. A. (1970) 'The Market for Lemons: Quality Uncertainty and the Market Mechanism', *Quarterly Journal of Economics*, 84, pp. 488–500.

Alford, R. (1975) *Health Care Politics: Ideological and Interest Group Barriers to Reform* (Chicago: University of Chicago Press).

Alvesson, M. (1993) *Cultural Perspectives on Organisations* (Cambridge: Cambridge University Press).

Anderson, B. (n.d.) 'Care Contracts', typescript.

Aoki, M., Gustafsson, B., and O.E. Williamson (1990) *The Firm as a Nexus of Treaties* (London: Sage).

Appleby, J., Little, V., Ranade, W., Robinson, R., and P. Smith (1992) *Implementing the Reforms: A Second National Survey of District General Managers* (Birmingham: National Association of Health Authorities and Trusts).

Appleby, J., Smith, P., Ranade, W., Little, V., and R. Robinson (1994) 'Monitoring Managed Competition', in R. Robinson and J. Le Grand, *Evaluating the NHS Reforms* (Newbury: Policy Journals).

Armstrong, P. (1989) 'Management, Labour Process and Agency', *Work, Employment and Society*, 3, 3, pp. 307–32.

Arnott, M., Bullock, A., and H. Thomas (1992) *The Impact of Local Management in Schools* (Birmingham: School of Education, University of Birmingham).

Arrow, K. (1974) *The Limits of Organization* (New York: Norton).

Ascher, K. (1987) *The Politics of Privatisation: Contracting Out Public Services* (London: Macmillan).

Atiyah, P. (1979) *The Rise and Fall of Freedom of Contract* (Oxford: Clarendon Press).

Audit Commission (1986a) *Improving Cash Flow Management in Local Government* (London: Her Majesty's Stationery Office).

Audit Commission (1986b) *Making a Reality of Community Care* (London: Her Majesty's Stationery Office).

Audit Commission (1987) *Competitiveness and the Contracting Out of Local Authority Services* (London: Her Majesty's Stationery Office).

Audit Commission (1989a) *Better Financial Management* (London: Her Majesty's Stationery Office).

Audit Commission (1989b) *Building Maintenance Direct Labour Organisations: A Management Handbook* (London: Her Majesty's Stationery Office).

Audit Commission (1989c) *Building Maintenance DLOs in London* (London: Her Majesty's Stationery Office).

Audit Commission (1989d) *Preparing for Compulsory Competition* (London: Her Majesty's Stationery Office).

Audit Commission (1990a) *Managing Sickness Absence in London* (London: Her Majesty's Stationery Office).

Audit Commission (1990b) *We Can't Go On Meeting Like This: The Changing Role of Local Authority Members* (London: Her Majesty's Stationery Office).

Audit Commission (1991) *The Impact of Competitive Tendering on Highways Maintenance* (London: Her Majesty's Stationery Office).

Audit Commission (1993a) *Adding Up the Sums: Schools' Management of Their Finances* (London: Her Majesty's Stationery Office).

Audit Commission (1993b) *Practices Make Perfect: The Role of the Family Health Services Authority* (London: Her Majesty's Stationery Office).

Audit Commission (1993c) *Realising the Benefits of Competition: The Client Role for Contracted Services* (London: Her Majesty's Stationery Office).

Audit Commission (1993d) *Their Health, Your Business: The New Role of the District Health Authority* (London: Her Majesty's Stationery Office).

Audit Commission (1994) *Behind Closed Doors: The Revolution in Central Support Services* (London: Her Majesty's Stationery Office).

Axelrod, R. (1984) *The Evolution of Cooperation* (New York: Basic Books).

Bacon, R. W., and W. A. Eltis (1976) *Britain's Economic Problem: Too Few Producers* (London: Macmillan).

Bahl, R. (1984) 'The Fiscal Health of State and Local Governments; 1982 and Beyond', in J. H. Carr (ed.), *Crisis and Constraint in a Period of Uncertainty* (New Jersey: Centre for Urban Policy Research).

Barber, J. (1989) 'Risk Method of Construction' in J. Uff and P. Capper (eds), *Construction Contract Policy, Improved Procedures and Practice* (London: Centre of Construction Law and Management, King's College).

Bartlett, W., and J. Le Grand (1994) 'The Performance of Trusts', in R. Robinson and J. Le Grand (eds), *Evaluating the NHS Reforms* (Newbury: King's Fund Institute).

Barzel, Y. (1989) *Economic Analysis and Property Rights* (Cambridge: Cambridge University Press).

Baumol, W.J. (1967) 'The Macroeconomics of Unbalanced Growth: Anatomy of Urban Crisis', *American Economic Review*, 57, pp. 415–26.

Baumol, W.J., Panzer, J.C., and R.D. Willis (1982) *Contestable Markets and the Theory of Industry Structure* (New York: Harcourt Brace Jovanovich).

Beale, H., and T. Dugdale (1975) 'Contracts between Businessmen', *British Journal of Law and Society*, 2.

Beardsworth, A. D., Keil, E. T., Bresnen, M., and A. Bryman (1988) 'Management Transcience and Sub-Contracting: The Case of the Construction Site', *Journal of Management Studies*, 25, 6, November, pp. 603–25.

Beiner, R. (1992) *What's the Matter with Liberalism?* (Berkeley: University of California Press).

Berle, A. A., and G. C. Means (1982) *The Modern Corporation and Private Property* (New York: Macmillan).

Best, M. (1990) *The New Competition: Institutions of Industrial Restructuring* (Cambridge: Polity Press).

Birch, A. (1988) 'Extracting the Logic of Increased Charges', *Health Services Journal*, 21, April, p. 445.

Blore, I., and N. Devas (1992) *Policy Determinants of Municipal Credit in Hungary* (Birmingham: Development Administration Group, University of Birmingham).

Bormeo, N. (1990) 'The Politics of Public Enterprise in Portugal, Spain and Greece', in E. N. Suleiman and J. Waterbury (eds), *The Political Economy of Public Sector Reform and Privatization* (Oxford: Westview Press).

Boston, J. (1987) 'Thatcherism and Rogernomics: Changing the Rules of the Game, Comparisons and Contrasts', *Political Science*, 39, 2, pp. 129–52.

Boston, J., and K. Jackson (1988) 'The New Zealand General Election of 1987', *Electoral Studies*, 7,1, pp. 70–5.

Boston, J., Martin, J., Pallot, J., and P. Walsh (eds) (1991) *Reshaping the State: New Zealand's Bureaucratic Revolution* (Auckland: Oxford University Press).

Bovaird, A.G. (1981) *Review of Charging Policy in Dudley MBC* (Birmingham: Joint Unit for Research in the Urban Environment).

Bovaird, A. G., Tricker, M. J., and R. Stoakes (1994) *Recreation Management and Pricing* (London: Gower).

Bowe, R., and S. J. Ball (1992) *Reforming Education and Changing Schools: Case Studies in Policy Sociology* (London: Routledge).

Bramley, J., and J. Le Grand (1992) *Who Uses Local Services? Striving for Equity* (Luton: Local Government Management Board).

Brennan, G., and J.M. Buchanan (1980) *The Power to Tax: Analytical Foundations of a Fiscal Constitution* (Cambridge: Cambridge University Press).

Brennan, G., and J. M. Buchanan (1985) *The Reason of Rules: Constitutional Political Economy* (Cambridge: Cambridge University Press).

Breton, A., and R. Wintrobe (1982) *The Logic of Bureaucratic Conduct* (Cambridge: Cambridge University Press).

Brittan, S. (1983) *The Role and Limits of Government: Essays in Political Economy* (London: Temple Smith).

Brunsson, N., and J. P. Olsen (1993) *The Reforming Organisation* (London: Routledge).

Buchanan, J. (1986) *Liberty, Market and State* (Brighton: Wheatsheaf).

Buchanan, J. M., and G. Tullock (1962) *The Calculus of Consent* (Ann Arbor: University of Michigan Press).

Burnheim, J. (1988) *Is Democracy Possible? The Alternative to Democratic Politics* (Cambridge: Polity Press).

Campbell, D., and D. Harris (1993) 'Flexibility in Long-Term Contractual Relationships: The Role of Cooperation', *British Journal of Law and Society*, 20, 2, pp. 166–91.

Carnaghan, R., and B. Bracewell-Milnes (1993) *Testing the Market: The Role of Competitive Tendering for Government Services in Britain and Abroad* (London: Institute of Economic Affairs).

Carter, N., Klein, R., and P. Day (1992) *How Organisations Measure Success: The Use of Performance Indicators in Government* (London: Routledge).

Chandhry, K. A. (1992) 'Economic Liberalism and Oil-Exporting Countries: Iraq and Saudi Arabia', in I. Harik and D. J. Sullivan (eds), *Privatization and Liberalization in the Middle East* (Bloomington and Indianapolis: Indiana University Press).

Chandler, A. D. (1977) *The Visible Hand: The Managerial Role in American Business* (Cambridge, MA: Harvard University Press).

Chapman, C. B., Ward, S. C., and B. Curtis (1989) 'Risk Theory for Contracting', in J. Uff and P. Capper (eds), *Construction Contract Policy: Improved Procedures and Practice*, pp. 74–109 (London: Centre of Construction Law and Management, King's College London).

Chapman, L. (1979) *Your Disobedient Servant* (Harmondsworth: Penguin).

Chapman R. (1989) 'Core Public Sector Reform in New Zealand and the United Kingdom', *Public Money and Management*, 9, 1, pp. 44–8.

Child, J. (1987) 'Information Technology, Organisation and the Response to Strategic Challenges', *California Management Review*, Fall, 33–50.

Chubb, J., and T. Moe (1990) *Politics, Markets and America's Schools* (Washington: Brookings Institution).

Clarke, T., and C. Pitelis (eds) (1993) *The Political Economy of Privatisation* (London: Routledge).

Clegg, S. R. (1990) *Modern Organisations: Organisation Studies in the Post-Modern World* (London: Sage).

Cleveland, L. (1986) 'New Zealand Political Culture: A Historical Note', *Political Science*, 88, 1, July, pp. 61–9.

Colson, E. (1975) *Tradition and Contract: The Problems of Order* (London: Heinemann).

Common, R., Flynn, N., and E. Mellon (1992) *Managing Public Services: Competition and Decentralisation* (Oxford: Butterworth-Heinemann).

Considine, M. (1990) 'Administrative Reform Down-Under: Recent Public Sector Change in Australia and New Zealand', *International Review of Administrative Sciences*, 56, 1, pp. 171–84.

Cook, P., and C. Kirkpatrick (1988) *Privatisation in Less Developed Countries* (Brighton: Wheatsheaf Books).

Coopers and Lybrand (1981) *Service Provision and Pricing in Local Government Studies in Local Environmental Services* (London: Her Majesty's Stationery Office).

Coopers and Lybrand (1988) *The Local Management of Schools: A Report to the DES* (London: Coopers and Lybrand).

Coopers and Lybrand and National Foundation for Educational Research (1992) *Local Management in Schools: A Study into Formula Funding and Management Issues* (London: Chartered Institute of Public Finance and Accountancy).

Crasswell, R. (1988) 'Contract Remedies, Renegotiation and the Theory of Efficient Breach', *Southern California Law Review*, 61, p. 629.

Crompton, R., and G. Jones (1984) *White-Collar Proletariat: Deskilling and Gender in Clerical Work* (London: Macmillan).

Cubbin, J., Domberger, S., and S. Meadowcroft (1987) 'Competitive Tendering and Refuse Collection: Identifying the Sources of Efficiency Gains', *Fiscal Studies*, 8, 3, pp. 49–58.

Davies, B. (1978) *Universality, Selectivity and Effectiveness in Social Policy* (London: Heinemann).

Davis, J. (1992) *Exchange* (Buckingham: Open University Press).

De Alessi, L. (1989) 'Implications of Property Rights for Government Investment Choices', *American Economic Review*, March.

Dearlove, J. (1979) *The Reorganisation of British Local Government: Old Orthodoxies and a Political Perspective* (Cambridge: Cambridge University Press).

Dente, B. (1991) 'Italian Local Services: The Difficult Road Towards Privatisation', in R. Batley and G. Stoker (eds), *Local Government in Europe: Trends and Developments* (London: Macmillan).

Department of the Environment (1986) *Paying for Local Government* (London: Her Majesty's Stationery Office).

Department of the Environment (1991) *Competing for Quality – Competitiveness in the Provision of Local Services; A Consultation Paper* (London: Department of the Environment).

Department of the Environment (1991) *A New Tax for Local Government: Consultation Document* (London: Department of the Environment).

Department of Health (1989) *Working for Patients* (London: Her Majesty's Stationery Office).

Department of Health (1990a) *Community Care in the Next Decade and Beyond: Policy Guidance* (London: Her Majesty's Stationery Office).

Department of Health (1990b) *NHS Trusts: A Working Guide* (London: Her Majesty's Stationery Office).

Di Maggio, P. J., and W. W. Powell (1983) 'The Iron Cage Revisited: Institutional Isomorphism and Collective Rationality in Organizational Fields', *American Sociological Review*, 48, pp. 147–60.

Dingwall, R., and P. Fenn (1987) ' "A Responsible Profession"? Sociological and Economic Perspectives in the Regulation of Professional Services', *International Review of Law and Economics*, 7, pp. 51–64.

Domberger, S., Meadowcroft, S., and D. Thompson (1986) 'Competitive Tendering and Efficiency: The Case of Refuse Collection', *Fiscal Studies*, 7, 4, pp. 69–87.

Domberger, S., Meadowcroft, S., and D. Thompson (1987) 'The Impact of Competitive Tendering in the Costs of Hospital Domestic Services', *Fiscal Studies*, 8, 4, pp. 39–54.

Domberger, S., Meadowcroft, S., and D. Thompson (1988) 'Competition and Efficiency in Refuse Collection; A Reply', *Fiscal Studies*, 9, 1, pp. 86–90.

Domberger, S., and D. Hensher (1993) 'On the Performance of Competitively Tendered, Public Sector Cleaning Contracts', *Public Administration*, 71, 3, pp. 441–54.

Domberger, S., and S. Faiago (1994) *Competitive Tendering and the Performance of Government Trading Enterprises in NSW* (Sydney:

Graduate School of Business, Management Research Centre, University of Sydney).

Domberger, S., Hall, C., and E. A. L. Li (1994) *The Determinants of Price and Quality in Competitively Tendered Contracts* (Sydney: Graduate School of Business, Management Research Centre, Univeristy of Sydney).

Donahue, J. D. (1989) *The Privatization Decision* (New York: Basic Books).

Donaldson, C., and K. Gerard (1993) *Economics of Health Care: The Visible Hand* (London: Macmillan).

Dopson, S. (1993) 'Are Agencies an Act of Faith? The Experience of HMSO', *Public Money and Management*, 13, 2, pp. 17–23.

Dunleavy, P. (1986) 'Explaining the Privatization Boom: Public Choice and Radical Approaches', *Public Administration*, 64, 2, pp. 13–34.

Dunleavy, P. (1991) *Democracy, Bureaucracy and Public Choice: Economic Explanations in Political Science* (Brighton: Wheatsheaf).

Dunn, J. (1990) *Interpreting Political Responsibility: Essays 1981–1989* (Cambridge, Polity Press).

Dunsire, A., Hartley, K., Parker, D., and B. Dimitrios (1988) 'Organisational Status and Performance: A Conceptual Framework for Testing Public Choice Theories', *Public Administration*, 66, 4, pp. 363–88.

Easton, B. (1990) 'Government Management: A Review of its Political Content', *Political Science*, 42, 2, pp. 34–42.

Eccles, R.G. (1981) 'The Quasi-Firm in the Construction Industry', *Journal of Economic Behaviour and Organisation*, 2, pp. 335–51.

Eccles, R.G. (1985) *The Transfer Pricing Problem: A Theory for Practice* (Lexington, MA: Lexington Books).

Edgell, J., and V. Duke (1991) *A Measure of Thatcherism: A Sociology of Britain* (London: HarperCollins).

Efficiency Unit (1991) *Making the Most of Next Steps: The Management of Ministers' Departments and their Executive Agencies: Report to the Prime Minister* (London: Her Majesty' Stationery Office).

Eggertsson, A. (1990) *Economic Behaviour and Institutions* (Cambridge: Cambridge University Press).

Enthoven, A. (1985) *Reflections on the Management of the National Health Service* (London: Nuffield Hospital Trust).

Esping-Anderson, G. (1990) *The Three Worlds of Welfare Capitalism* (Cambridge: Polity Press).

Etzioni, A. (1993) *The Spirit of Community Rights: Responsibilities and the Communitarian Agenda* (New York: Crown).

Farago, S., and J. Domberger (1994) *Competitive Tendering and Contracting in NSW Government Trading Enterprises: A Survey* (Sydney, Graduate School of Business, Management Research Centre, University of Sydney).

Flynn, R. (1992) *Structures of Control in Health Management* (London: Routledge).

Fogden, M. E. G. (1993) 'Managing Change in the Employment Service', *Public Money and Management*, 13, 2, pp. 9–16.

Foster, C. D. (1992) *Privatization, Public Ownership and Natural Monopoly* (Oxford: Blackwell).

Foster, C. D., Jackson, R. A., and M. Perlman (1980) *Local Government Finance in a Unitary State* (London: George Allen and Unwin).

Fox, A. (1974) *Beyond Contract: Work, Power and Trust Relations* (London: Faber and Faber).

Francome, C. (1991) *NHS Reforms: The First Six Months: A Survey of Directors of Public Health Medicine* (Hatfield: Middlesex Polytechnic, Health Research Centre).

Friedman, D. (1973) *The Machinery of Freedom* (New York: Harper and Row).

Fudge, C., and L. Gustafsson (1989) 'Administrative Reform and Public Management in Sweden and the United Kingdom', *Public Money and Management*, 9,2, pp. 29–34.

Ganley, J., and J. Grahl (1988) 'Competitive and Efficiency in Refuse Collective: A Critical Comment', *Fiscal Studies*, 9, 1, pp. 80–5.

George, B., and M. Stenhouse (1988) 'The Turkish General Election of 29 November 1987', *Electoral Studies*, 7, 2, pp. 173–8.

Glennerster, H., Matsaganis, M., Owens, P., and S. Hancock (1994) 'GP Fundholding: Wild Card or Winning Hand?' in R. Robinson and J. Le Grand (eds), *Evaluating the NHS Reforms* (Newbury: King's Fund Institute).

Goodsell, C. T. (1984) 'The Grace Commission: Seeking Efficiency for the Whole People', *Public Administration Review*, 44, pp. 196–204.

Goold, M., and A. Campbell (1987) *Strategies and Styles: The Role of the Centre in Managing Diversified Corporations* (Oxford: Blackwell).

Gordon, R. (1985) 'Macauley, Macneil, and the Discovery of Solidarity and Power in Contract Law', *Wisconsin Law Review*.

Gormley, W. T. (ed) (1991) *Privatization and its Alternatives* (Madison: University of Wisconsin Press).

Gray, A., Jenkins, B., Flynn, A., and B. Rutherford (1991) 'The Management of Change in Whitehall: The Experience of the FMI', *Public Administration*, 69, 1, pp. 41–59.

Gray, J. (1989) *Liberalisms: Essays in Political Philosophy* (London: Routledge).

Griffiths, R. (1988) *Community Care: Agenda for Change* (London: Her Majesty's Stationery Office).

Gustafsson, L. (1987) 'Renewal in the Public Sector in Sweden', *Public Administration*, 65, pp. 179–91.

Gutch, R. (1992) *Contracting Lessons from the US* (London: National Council for Voluntary Organisations).

Haggard, S. (1988) 'The Philippines: Picking up after Marcos', in R. Vernon (ed.), *The Promise of Privatization: A Challenge to US Policy*, pp. 91–121 (New York: Council for Foreign Relations).

Hahn, F. (1991) 'Benevolence', in T. G. T. Meeks (ed.), *Thoughtful Economic Men: Essays in Rationality, Moral Rules and Benevolence* (Cambridge, Cambridge University Press).

Hallgren, T. (n.d.) 'Changes in Municipal Service Delivery and Management: The Trends in Sweden', typescript.

Halpin, D., Power, S., and J. Fitz (1992) 'Opting for Self-Governance and Continuity in Grant-Maintained Schools' in T. Simkins, L. Ellison, V. Garrett (eds), *Implementing Educational Reform: The Early Lessons* (Harlow: Longman).

Ham C. (1992a) *Locality Purchasing* (Birmingham: Health Services Management Centre, University of Birmingham).

Ham C. (1992b) *Managed Competition in the NHS: Progress and Prospect* (Manchester: Manchester Statistical Society).

Ham C., and P. Spurgeon (1992) *Effective Purchasing* (Birmingham: Health Services Management Centre, University of Birmingham).

Handy, C. (1989) *The Age of Unreason* (London: Business Books).

Handy, C. (1994) *The Empty Raincoat: Making Sense of the Future* (London: Hutchinson).

Hansen, P. (1993) *Hannah Arendt: History, Politics and Citizens* (Cambridge: Polity Press).

Harden I. (1992) *The Contracting State* (Buckingham: Open University Press).

Harrison, M.L. (1991) 'Citizenship, Consumption and Rights: A Comment', *Sociology*, 25, 2, pp. 209–13.

Harrison, S., Hunter, D.J., Marnock, G., and C. Pollitt (1992) *Just Managing: Power and Culture in the National Health Service* (London: Macmillan).

Hartley, K., and M. Huby (1985) 'Contracting Out in Health and Local Authorities; Prospects and Pitfalls', *Public Money*, pp. 23–6.

Hayek, F. (1944) *The Road to Serfdom* (London: Routledge and Kegan Paul).

Heald, D. (1990) 'Charging for British Government: Evidence from the Public Expenditure Survey', *Financial Accountability and Management*, 6, 4, pp. 229–61.

Heimer, C. (1985) *Reactive Risk and Rational Action* (Los Angeles: University of California Press).

Heimer, C. (1985) 'Allocating Information Costs in a Negotiated Information Order: Interorganizational Constraints on Decisionmaking in Norwegian Oil Insurance', *Administrative Science Quarterly*, 39, 3, pp. 395–417.

Henkel, M. (1991) *Government, Evaluation and Change* (London: Jessica Kingsley).

Hennessy, P. (1989) *Whitehall* (London: Secker and Warburg).

Her Majesty's Treasury (1991) *Competing for Quality: Buying Better Public Services* (London: Her Majesty's Stationery Office).

Her Majesty's Treasury (1992) *Government Purchasing: Progress Report to the Prime Minister, 1991* (London: Her Majesty's Stationery Office).

Hinings, C.R., and R. Greenwood (1988) *The Dynamics of Strategic Change* (Oxford: Blackwell).

Hirsch, F. (1977) *The Social Limits to Growth* (London: Routledge and Kegan Paul).

Hirschman, A.O. (1970) *Exit, Voice and Loyalty: Responses to Decline in Firms, Organizations and States* (Harvard: Harvard University Press).

Hirst, P. (1993) *Associative Democracy: New Forms of Economic and Social Governance* (Cambridge: Polity Press).

Hodgson, G. M. 1988, *Economics and Institutions: A Manifesto for a Modern Institutional Economics* (Cambridge: Polity Press).

Hood, C. (1976) *The Limits of Administration* (London: Wiley).

Hood, C. (1991) 'A Public Management for All Seasons?', *Public Administration*, 69, 1, pp. 3–19.

ICM Research (1993) *Citizens Charter Customer Survey: A Research Report* (London: ICM Research).

Ikenberry, G. J. (1990) 'The International Spread of Privatization Policies: Inducements, Learning and Policy Bandwaggoning' in E. N. Suleiman and J. Waterbury (eds), *The Political Economy of Public Service Reform and Privatization* (Oxford: Westview Press).

Institute of Economic Affairs (1973) *The Economics of Charity* (London: Institute of Economic Affairs).

International City Managers Association (1989) *Service Delivery in the '90s: Alternative Approaches for Local Government* (Washington: International City Managers Association).

Jensen, M. E., and W. H. Meckling (1973) 'Theory of the Firm: Management Behaviour, Agency Costs and Ownership Structure', *Journal of Financial Economics*, 3, pp. 305–60.

Jensen, M.E., and W.H. Meckling (1992) 'Specific and General Knowledge and Organizational Structure', in L. Werin and H. Wijkander (eds), *Contract Economics* (Oxford: Blackwell).

Johnson, H. T. (1992) *Relevance Regained: From Top-Down Control to Bottom-Up Empowerment* (New York: Free Press).

Johnson, H. T., and K. S. Kaplan (1987) *Relevance Lost: The Rise and Fall of Management Accounting* (Boston, MA: Harvard Business School Press).

Johnston, L. (1992) *The Rebirth of Private Policing* (London: Routledge).

Joint NHS Privatisation Research Unit (1990) *The Privatisation Experience: Competitive Tendering for NHS Services* (London: Joint Privatisation Unit).

Judge, K. (1978) *Rationing Social Services: A Study of Resource Allocation and the Personal Social Services* (London: Heinemann).

Kalt, J. P. (1981) *The Economics and Politics of Oil Price Regulation* (Cambridge, MA: MIT Press).

Kay, J. (1993) *Foundations of Corporate Success: How Business Strategies Add Value* (Oxford: Oxford University Press).

Kenney, R. W., and B. Klein (1983) 'The Economics of Block Booking', *Journal of Law and Economics*, XXVI, pp. 497–540.

Kerley, R., and D. Wynn (1991) 'Competitive Tendering: Transition to Contracted Services in Scottish Local Authorities', *Local Government Studies*, 17, 5, pp. 33–51.

Kettl, D. F. (1988) 'Government by Proxy and the Public Service', *International Review of Administrative Scienes*, 54,4, pp. 501–16.

Kettl, D. F. (1993) *Sharing Power: Public Governance and Private Markets* (Washington: The Brookings Institution).

King, A. (1975) 'Overload: Problems of Governing in the 1970s', *Political Studies*, 23.

King, D. S., and J. Waldron (1988) 'Citizenship, Social Citizenship and the Defence of Welfare Provision', *British Journal of Political Science*, 18, pp. 415–45.

Klein, B. (1980) 'Transaction Cost Determinants of Unfair Contract Arrangements', *American Economic Review*, 70, pp. 356–62.

Klein, B. (1992) 'Contracts and Initiatives: The Role of Contract Terms in Assuring Performance', in L. Werin and H. Wijkander, (eds) *Contract Economics* (Oxford: Blackwell).

Kolderie, T. (1986) 'Two Different Concepts of Privatization', *Public Administration Review*, 46, pp. 285–91.

Konig, K. (1988) 'Developments in Privatization in the Federal Republic of Germany: Problems, Status, Outlook', *International Review of Administrative Sciences*, 54, 4, pp. 517–32.

Kreps, D. M. (1990) *Game Theory and Economic Modelling* (Oxford: Oxford University Press).

Kreps, D. M., and R. Wilson (1982) 'Reputation and Imperfect Information, *Journal of Economic Theory*, 27, pp. 253–79.

Krieger, J. (1986) *Reagan, Thatcher and the Politics of Decline* (Cambridge: Polity Press).

Lalonde, M. (1990) 'Privatizing Government', *Montreal Mirror*, April 4–11, p. 7.

Le Grand, J. (1991) 'The Theory of Government Failure', *British Journal of Political Science*, 21, pp. 423–42.

Le Grand, J., and W. Bartlett (1993) (eds), *Quasi-Markets and Social Policy* (London: Macmillan).

Le Grand, J. (1991) 'Quasi-Markets and Social Policy', *Economic Journal*, 101, pp. 1256–67.

Leibenstein, H., 1966, 'Allocative Efficiency vs X-Efficiency', *American Economic Review*, 56, pp. 392–415.

Leibenstein, H. (1987) *Inside the Firm: The Inefficiencies of Hierarchy* (Cambridge: Harvard University Press).

Levitas, R. (1982) 'Competition and Compliance: The Utopias of the New Right', in R. Levitas (ed.), *The Ideology of the New Right* (Cambridge: Polity Press).

Lewin, L. (1991) *Self-Interest and Public Interest in Western Politics* (Oxford: Oxford University Press).

Lieberman, M. (1989) *Privatization and Educational Choice* (Basingstoke: Macmillan).

Lindblom, C. (1959) 'The Science of Muddling Through', *Public Administration Review*, 9, pp. 70–88.

Lipsky, M. (1980) *Street Level Bureaucracy* (New York: Russell Sage Foundation).

Local Government Chronicle (1990) *Supplement*, 6 July.

Local Government Management Board (1993) *CCT Information Service: Survey Report No. 7* (London: Local Government Management Board).

Lorange, P., and J. Roos (1992) *Strategic Alliances: Formation, Implementation and Evolution* (Oxford: Blackwell).

Lorrain, D. (1991) 'Public Goods and Private Operators in France', in R. Batley and G. Stoker (eds), *Government in Europe: Trends and Developments* (London: Macmillan).

McAfee, R. P., and J. McMillan (1988) *Incentives in Government Contracting* (Toronto: Toronto University Press).

McAllister, H., and D. J. Studlar (1989) 'Popular versus Elite Views of Privatisation: The Case of Britain', *Journal of Public Policy*, 9, 2, pp. 157–78.

Macauley, S. 1963 'Non-Contractual Relations in Business', *American Sociological Review*, 28, pp. 55–70.

Macauley, S. (1985) 'An Empirical View of Contract', *Wisconsin Law Review*, pp. 465–82.

McChesney, E.S. (1991) 'Excises, Earmarked Taxes and Government Use of Changes in a Rent-Seeking model', in R. E. Wagner (ed.), *Charging for Government: User Charges and Earmarked Taxes in Principle and Practice* (London: Routledge).

McDavid, J. (1987) 'Privatizing Local Government Services in Canada', in *Privatization, Tactics and Techniques*, Proceedings of a Symposium held 22–24 July (1987) Vancouver, BC: Fraser Institute.

Macneil, I. R. (1980) *The Social Contract* (London: Yale University Press).

Macneil, I. R. (1981) 'Economic Analysis of Contract Relations' in P. Burrows and C.G. Veljanovski (eds), *The Economic Approach to Law* (London: Butterworths).

Major, J. (1989) *Public Service Management: The Revolution in Progress* (London: Her Majesty's Treasury).

Malkin, J., and A. Wildavsky (1991) 'Why the Traditional Distinction between Public and Private Goods Should be Abandoned', *Journal of Theoretical Politics*, 3, 4, pp. 355–78.

March, J.G., and J.P. Olsen (1989) *Rediscovering Institutions: The Organizational Basis of Politics* (New York: Free Press).

Marlin, J.T. (1982) *Privatization of Local Government Activities: Lessons from Japan* (New York: Council for Municipal Performance).

Marshall, T.H. (1963) 'Citizenship and Social Class', in T.H. Marshall, *Sociology at the Crossroads* (London: Heinemann).

Marshall, J., and F. Moutt (1988) 'Privatization in Chile', in P. Cook and C. Kirkpatrick (eds), *Privatisation in Less Developed Countries* (Brighton: Wheatsheaf).

Marven, E., and R. Levačić (1992) 'Implementing and Local Management of Schools: First Year Spending Decisions', in T. Simkins, L. Ellison and V. Garrett (eds), *Implementing Educational Reform: The Early Lessons* (Harlow: Longman).

Mather, G. (1989) 'Thatcherism and Local Government: An Evaluation', in J.D. Stewart and G. Stoker (eds), *The Future of Local Government* (London: Macmillan).

Maynard, A. (1988) 'From an Ivory Tower', *Health Services Journal*, 28 January, p. 123.

Mayston, D. (1990) 'Managing Capital Resources in the NHS', in A. J. Culyer, A. Maynard and J. Posnett (eds), *Competition in Health Care: Reforming the NHS* (London: Macmillan).

Mellon, E. (1993a) Executive Agencies in Central Government', in A. Harrison (ed.), *From Hierarchy to Market* (Oxford: Transaction Books).

Mellon, E. (1993b) 'Executive Agencies: Leading Change from the Outside In', *Public Money and Management*, 13, 2, pp. 25–31.

Metcalfe, L., and S. Richards (1987) *Improving Public Management* (London: Sage).

Meyer, J. W., and B. Rowan (1977) 'Institutionalised Organizations: Formal Structure as Myth and Ceremony', *American Journal of Sociology*, 83, pp. 340–63.

Milgrom, P., and J. Roberts (1988) 'An Economic Approach to Influence Activities in Organizations', *American Journal of Sociology*, 94, Supplement, pp. 154–79.

Miller, D., and P. Friesen (1984) *Organizations: A Quantum View* (New York: Prentice-Hall).

Milne, R. G. (1987) 'Competitive Tendering in the National Health Service: An Economic Analysis of Early Implementation of HC(83)18', *Public Administration*, 65, 2, pp. 145–60.

Milne, R. G., and M. A. McGee (1992) 'Compulsory Competitive Tendering in the NHS: A New Look at Some Old Estimates', *Fiscal Studies*, 13, 3, pp. 96–111.

Mortimore, P., Sammons, P., Stoll, L., Lewis, D., and R. Ecob (1988) *School Matters: The Junior Years* (Wells: Open Books).

Mueller, D. C. (1979) *Public Choice* (Cambridge: Cambridge University Press).

Mullen, P. (1990) Which Internal Market? The NHS White Paper and Internal Markets', *Financial Accountability and Management*, 6, 1, pp. 33–50.

National Audit Office (1986) *The Financial Management Initiative*, London: Her Majesty's Stationery Office

National Audit Office (1987) *Competitive Tendering for Support Services in the National Health Service* (London: Her Majesty's Stationery Office).

National Health Service Management Executive (1993) *Review of Contracting: 1993–1994* (London: Department of Health).

Nelson, P. (1970) 'Information and Consumer Behaviour', *Journal of Political Economy*, 78, pp. 729–54.

Nesbitt, M. B. (1976) *Labor Relations in the Federal Government Service* (Washington: The Bureau of International Affairs).

Niskanen, W. A. (1971) *Bureaucracy and Representative Government* (Chicago: Aldine Atherton).

North, D. C. (1990) *Institutions, Institutional Change and Economic Performance* (Cambridge: Cambridge University Press).

Nove, A. (1983) *The Economics of Feasible Socialism* (London: George Allen and Unwin).

Nozick, R. (1974) *Anarchy, State and Utopia* (Oxford: Blackwell).

O'Connor, J. (1973) *The Fiscal Crisis of the State* (New York: St Martin's Press).

Offe, C. (1984) *Contradictions of the Welfare State*, J. Keane (ed.) (London: Hutchinson).

Olson, M. (1982) *The Rise and Decline of Nations: Economic Growth, Stagflation, and Social Rigidities* (New Haven: Yale University Press).

Onis, Z. (1991) 'Privatization and the Logic of Coalition Building: A Comparative Study of State Divestiture in Turkey and the United Kingdom', *Comparative Political Studies*, 24, 2, pp. 231–53.

Organisation for Economic Cooperation and Development (1990) *Public Management Developments, Survey, 1990* (Paris: Organisation for Economic Co-operation and Development).

Organisation for Economic Co-operation and Development (1992) *Public Management Developments, Update 1992* (Paris: Organisation for Economic Co-operation and Development).

Orzechowski, W. (1977) 'Economic Models of Bureaucracy: Survey, Extensions and Evidence', in T. E. Borcherding (ed.), *Budgets and Bureaucrats: The Sources of Government Growth*, pp. 229–59 (Durham: Duke University Press).

Osborne, D, and T. Gaebler (1992) *Reinventing Government: How the Entrepreneurial Spirit is Transforming the Public Sector* (Reading, MA: Addison-Wesley).

Ostrom, E. (1990) *Governing the Commons: The Evolution of Institutions of Collective Action* (Cambridge: Cambridge University Press).

Owens, P., and H. Glennerster (1990) *Nursing in Conflict* (London: Macmillan).

Pack, J. A. (1990) 'The Opportunities and Constraints of Privatization' in W. T. Gormley (ed.), *Privatization and Its Alternatives* (Madison: Wisconsin University Press).

Packwood, T., Keen, J., and M. Buxton (1991) *Hospitals in Transition: The Resource Management Experiment* (Buckingham: Open University Press).

Pallot, J. (1991) 'Financial Management Reform', in J. Boston, J. Martin, J. Pallot and P. Walsh (eds), *Reshaping the State: New Zealand's Bureaucratic Revolution* (Auckland: Oxford University Press).

Pangle, T. L. (1992) *The Enabling of Democracy: The Challenge of the Postmodern Age* (Baltimore: The Johns Hopkins University Press).

Parker, R. A. (1976) 'Charging for Social Services', *Journal of Social Policy*, 5, 4.

Parry, R. (1990) 'The Private Challenge for Practitioners' in R. Parry (ed.), *Privatisation* (London: Jessica Kingsley).

Paton, C. (1992) *Competition and Planning in the National Health Service: The Danger of Unplanned Markets* (London: Chapman and Hall).

Peacock, A. T. (1983) 'Public-inefficiency: Informational and Institutional Constraints', in H. Hamisch (ed.), *Anatomy of Government Deficiencies* (Heidelberg: Springer Verlag).

Pendlebury, M., Jones, R., and Y. Karbhari (1994) 'Developments in the Accountability and Financial Reporting Practices of Executive Agencies', *Financial Accountability and Management*, 10, 1, pp. 33–46.

Perrin, J. (1988) *Resource Management in the NHS* (London: Chapman and Hall).

Peters, T., and R. Waterman (1982) *In Search of Excellence* (New York: Harper and Row).

Pitelis, C. (ed.) (1993) *Transaction Costs, Markets and Hierarchies* (Oxford: Blackwell).

Pollert, A. (1988) 'The Flexible Firm: Fixation or Fact?', *Work, Organisation and Society*, 2, 3, pp. 281–316.

Pollitt, C. (1987) 'Capturing Quality? The Quality Issue in British and American Health Politics', *Journal of Social Policy*, 7, 1, pp. 71–92.

Pollitt, C. (1988) 'Bringing Consumers into Performance Measurement: Concepts, Consequences and Constraints', *Policy and Politics*, 10, 2, pp. 1–11.

Pollitt, C. (1990) *Managerialism and the Public Service: The Anglo-American Experience* (Oxford: Blackwell, Second Edition, 1993).

Poole, R. W. (1980) *Cutting Back City Hall* (New York: Universe Books).

Powell, W. W., and P. J. Di Maggio (eds) (1991) *The New Institutionalism in Organizational Analysis* (Chicago: Chicago University Press).

Premfors, R. (1991) 'The "Swedish Model" and Public Sector Reform', *West European Politics*, 14, 3, pp. 83–95.

Prime Minister (1991) *The Citizen's Charter* (London: Her Majesty's Stationery Office).

Prime Minister and Chancellor of the Duchy of Lancaster (1992) *The Citizen's Charter: First Report* (London: Her Majesty's Stationery Office).

Prime Minister and Chancellor of the Duchy of Lancaster (1994) *The Citizen's Charter: Second Report 1994* (London: Her Majesty's Stationery Office).

Propper, C. (1992) *Quasi-Markets, Contracts and Quality* (Bristol: School of Advanced Urban Studies, Studies in Decentralisation and Quasi-Markets, University of Bristol).

Rees, J. (1992) 'New Directions for Schools and Colleges', mimeo.

Rehfuss, J. A. (1989) *Contracting in Government: A Guide to Working with Outside Contractors to Supply Public Services* (London: Jossey-Bass).

Reiter, B. (1981) 'The Control of Contract Power', *Oxford Journal of Legal Studies*, 1, pp. 347–74.

Rhodes, R. A. W., and D. Marsh (1992) 'New Directions on the Study of Policy Networks', *European Journal of Political Research*, 21, pp. 181–205.

Richards, S., and J. Rodrigues (1993) 'Strategies for Management in the Civil Service', *Public Money and Management*, 13, 2, pp. 33–8.

Richardson, J. (1993) *Reinventing Contracts: Transatlantic Perspectives on the Future of Contracting* (London: National Council for Voluntary Organisations).

Ricketts, M. (1987) *The Economics of Business Enterprise: New Approaches to the Firm* (Brighton: Wheatsheaf).

Ridley, N. (1988) *The Local Right: Enabling Not Providing* (London: Centre for Policy Studies).

Rose, R. (1989) 'Charges as Contested Signals', *Journal of Social Policy*, 9, 3, pp. 261–80.

Rose, R. (1990) 'Charging for Public Services', *Public Administration*, 68, 3, pp. 297–313.

Rose, R. (1988) *The Postmodern Presidency: The White House Meets the World* (Chatham, NJ: Chatham House).

Rose, R., and P. Falconer (1992) 'Individual Taste or Collective Decision? Public Policy on School Meals', *Journal of Social Policy*, 21, 3, pp. 349–73.

Rose, R., and G. Peters (1978) *Can Government Go Bankrupt?* (London: Macmillan).

Ross, S. (1973) 'The Economic Theory of Agency: The Principal's Problem', *American Economic Review*, 63, pp. 134–9.

Rothbard, M. (1973) *For a New Liberty* (New York: Macmillan).

Rowley, C., and R. Elgin (1988) 'Government and Its Bureaucracy: A Bilateral Bargaining versus a Principal-Agent Approach', in C. K. Rowley, R. D. Tollison and G. Tullock (eds), *The Political Economy of Rent-Seeking* (Boston: Kluwer Academic Publishing).

Rutter, M., Maughan, B. Mortimore, P., and J. Ouston (1979) *Fifteen Thousand Hours: Secondary Schools and Their Effects on Children* (London: Open Books).

Ryan, M. and T. Ward (1989) *Privatisation and the Penal System: The American Experience and the Debate in Britain* (Milton Keynes: Open University Press).

Sako, M. (1992) *Prices, Quality and Trust: Inter-Firm Relations in Britain and Japan* (Cambridge: Cambridge University Press).

Salamon, L. (1981) 'Rethinking Public Management', *Public Policy*, 29, pp. 255–60.

Saltman, R. B., and C. Von Otter (1992) *Planned Markets and Public Competition: Strategic Reform in Northern European Health Systems* (Buckingham: Open University Press).

Saunders, P. (1993) 'Citizenship in a Liberal Society', in B. S. Turner (ed.), *Citizenship and Social Theory*, pp. 57–90 (London: Sage).

Saunders, P. and C. Harris (1989) *Popular Attitudes to State Welfare Services: A Growing Demand for Alternatives?* (London: Social Affairs Unit).

Savas, E. S. (1987) *Privatization: The Key to Better Government* (Chatham, NJ: Chatham House).

Scott, G., and P. Gorringe (1989) 'Reform of the Core Public Sector: The New Zealand Experience', *Australian Journal of Public Administration*, 48, 1, pp. 81–92 .

Seifert, R. (1992) *Industrial Relations in the NHS* (London: Chapman and Hall).

Seldon, A. (1977) *Charge* (London: Temple Smith).

Self, P. (1993) *Government by the Market? The Politics of Public Choice* (London: Macmillan).

Sheaff, M. (1990) 'The Leningrad Experience' in H. Cook (ed.), *The NHS – Private Sector Interface* (Harlow: Longman).

Smith, D. G. (1992) *Paying for Medicine: The Politics of Reform* (New York: Aldine de Gruyter).

Smith, S. R., and M. Lipsky (1993) *Non-Profits for Hire: The Welfare State in the Age of Contracting* (Cambridge, MA: Harvard University Press).

Sparke, A. (1993) *The Compulsory Competitive Tendering Guide* (London: Butterworth).

Spence, M. (1972) *Market Signalling: The Informal Structure of Job Markets and Related Phenomena* (Cambridge: Harvard University Press).

Spicer, M., and R. D. Bingham (1991) 'Public Finance and Budgetting' in R. D. Bingham *et al.*, *Managing Local Government* (London: Sage).

Stewart, J. D. (1992) *Accountability to the Public* (London: European Policy Forum).

Stewart, J., and K. Walsh (1992) 'Change in Public Sector Management', *Public Administration*, 70,4.

Stewart, J., and K. Walsh (1994) 'Performance Measurement When Performance Can Never Be Finally Defined', *Public Money and Management*.

Stinchcombe, A. (1990) 'Organizing Information Outside the Firm: Contracts as Hierarchical Documents', in A. Stinchcombe, *Information and Organizations*, pp. 194–239 (London: University of California Press).

Stinchcombe, A., and C. A. Heimer (1985) *Organisation Theory and Project Management: Administering Uncertainty in Norweigan Offshore Oil* (Oslo: Norwegian University Press).

Stockman, D. (1986) *The Triumph of Politics* (New York: Harper and Row).

Stoker, G. (1989) 'Creating a Local Government for a Post-Fordist Society: The Thatcherite Project', in J. Stewart and G. Stoker (eds), *The Future of Local Government* (London: Macmillan).

Stoker, G., and D. Wilson (1986) 'Intra-Organisational Politics in Local Authorities; Towards a New Approach', *Public Administration*, 64, pp. 285–302.

Suleiman, E. N. (1990) 'The Politics of Privatization in Britain and France', in E. N. Suleiman and J. Waterbury (eds), *The Political Economy of Public Sector Reform and Privatization* (Oxford: Westview Press).

Sullivan, D. J. (1992) 'Extra-State Actors and Privatization in Egypt', in I. Harik and D. J. Sullivan (eds), *Privatization and Liberalization in the Middle East* (Bloomington and Indianapolis: Indiana State University).

Szymanski, S. (1993) 'Cheap Rubbish? Competitive Tendering and Contracting Out Refuse Collection', *Fiscal Studies*, 14, 3, pp. 109–30.

Szymanski, S., and T. Jones (1993) *The Cost Savings from Compulsory Competitive Tendering of Refuse Collection: A Statistical Analysis* (London: CDC Research).

Szymanski, S., and S. Wilkins (1992) *Cheap Rubbish? Competitive Tendering and Contracting Out in Refuse Collection – 1981–1988* (London: London Business School, Centre for Business Strategy).

Taylor-Gooby, P. (1986) *Public Opinion, Ideology and State Welfare* (London: Routledge).

Thomas, H. (1988) 'Pupils-as-vouchers', *Times Educational Supplement*, 2 December, p. 23.

Thomas, H., and A. Bullock (1992) 'Local Management Funding Forumulae and LEA Discretion', in T. Simkins, L. Ellison, and V. Garrett (eds), *Implementing Educational Reform: The Early Years* (Harlow: Longman).

Titmuss, R. M. (1969) *The Gift Relationship* (Harmondsworth: Penguin).

Townsend, P. (1979) *Poverty in the United Kingdom* (Harmondsworth: Penguin).

Tushman, M., and E. Romanelli (1985) 'Organizational Evolution: A Metamorphosis Model of Convergence and Reorientation', in L. Cummings and B. Staw (eds), *Research in Organizational Behaviour*, 7, pp. 333–65.

Van Horn, C. (1991) 'The Myths and Reality of Privatization' in W.T. Gormley (ed.), *Privatization and Its Alternatives* (Madison: University of Wisconsin Press).

Vining, A. R., and D. L. Weimer (1990) 'Government Supply and Government Production Failures: A Framework Based on Contestability', *Journal of Public Policy*, 10, 1, pp. 1–22.

Vincent-Jones, P. (1989) 'Contracts and Business Transactions: A Socio-Legal Analysis', *Journal of Law and Society*, 16, 2, pp. 166–86.

Von Otter, C., and R. B. Saltman (1991) 'Towards a Swedish Health Policy for the 1990s: Planned Markets and Public Firms', *Social Medicine Review*, 32, 4, pp. 473–81.

Voytek, K. P. (1991) 'Privatizing Government Service Delivery: Theory, Evidence and Implications', *Environment and Planning*, 9, pp. 155–71.

Waldegrave, W. (1990) 'Trafford Memorial Lecture', typescript.

Waldegrave, W. (1993) *The Reality of Reform and Accountability in Today's Public Service* (London: Public Finance Foundation, BDO Consulting, Chartered Institute of Public Finance and Accountancy).

Walker, B. (1993) *Competing for Building Maintenance: Direct Labour Organisations and Compulsory Competitive Tendering* (London: Her Majesty's Stationery Office).

Walsh, K. (1991) 'Quality and Public Services', *Public Administration*, 69, pp. 503–14.

Walsh, K. (1991) *Competition for Local Authority Services: Initial Experiences* (London: Her Majesty's Stationery Office).

Walsh, K. (1994) 'Citizens, Charters and Contracts' in R. Keat, N. Whitely and N. Abercrombie (eds), *The Authority of the Consumer* (London: Routledge).

Walsh, K., and H. Davis (1993) *Competition and Service: The Impact of the Local Government Act (1988)* (London: Her Majesty's Stationery Office).

Walsh, K., and K. Spencer (1989) *The Quality of Service in Housing Management* (Birmingham: INLOGOV, University of Birmingham).

Walsh, P. (1991) 'Industrial Relations and Personnel Policies under the State Sector Act', in J. Boston, J. Martin, J. Pallot and P. Walsh (eds), *Reshaping the State, New Zealand's Bureaucratic Revolution*, pp. 52–80 (Auckland: Oxford University Press).

Walzer, M. (1983) *Spheres of Justice: A Defence of Pluralism and Equality* (New York: Basic Books).

Wildavsky, A. (1964) *The Politics of the Budgetary Process* (Boston, MA: Little, Brown).

Williamson, O. E. (1975) *Markets and Hierarchies: Analysis and Anti-Trust Implications* (New York: Free Press).

Williamson, O. E. (1985) *The Economic Institutions of Capitalism* (New York: Free Press).

Wills, G. (1988) *Reagan's America: Innocents at Home* (London: Heinemann).

Wilson, J. A. (1980) 'Adaptation to Uncertainty and Small Numbers Exchange: The New England Fresh Fish Market', *Bell Journal of Economics*, 11, 2, pp. 491–504.

Wise, A. E. (1979) *Legislated Learning: The Bureaucratization of the American Classroom* (Berkeley: University of California Press).

Wistrich, E. (1992) 'Restructuring Government New Zealand Style', *Public Administration*, 70, pp. 119–35.

Wistow, G., Knapp, M., Hardy, B., and C. Allen (1992) 'From Providing to Enabling: Local Authorities and the Mixed Economy of Social Care', *Public Administration*, 70,1, pp. 25–45.

Witzel, M. L. (1991) 'The Failure of the Internal Market: The Universities Funding Council Bid System', *Public Money and Management*, 11, 2.

Wolf, M. (1988) *Markets or Government: Choosing Between Imperfect Alternatives* (Cambridge: MIT Press).

Wolfe, A. (1977) *The Limits of Legitimacy: Political Contradictions of Contemporary Capitalism* (New York: Free Press).

Young, K., and L. Mills (1993) *A Portrait of Change* (Luton: Local Government Management Board).

Index

277